Here's what parents and professionals are saying about Kelly DuMar's book, *Before You Forget*, and her *Through the Diary Door* workshops:

"Recommended reading for all parents who want to enrich their relationships and build permanent bonds with their children."

— Charles E. Fiero, Co-Chairman
Family Business Magazine

"This book is a wonderful addition to any parent's library."

— Lois Halzel Freedman, M.Ed.
Author of *Birth as a Healing Experience*

"This is such a beautiful book on so many levels! Kelly models the very best parenting in her courageous entries that show her acknowledging difficulties and dispensing true wisdom. Her book gives encouragement and guidance to parents while simultaneously offering healing to those who have not received the parenting they needed. The poetry of her entries is inspirational and her therapeutic teachings are expertly given. The world must read Kelly DuMar's book!"

— Tonya Quillen, M.A., L.M.H.C., C.P.
Tampa, FL

"Your excellent workshop gave me an opportunity to write a story for my son that reminded me of how much I've learned about life from him. I also learned much about parenting from you that I will use to help my clients."

— Don Caroli, M.A., Ed.S.
Freehold, New Jersey

"Kelly DuMar has written an intriguing and provocative book for parents and lovers of children. Kelly invites us through the Diary Door, into a realm of story writing to and for the children in our lives. Not only does she explain the many benefits of this process – touching our own higher wisdom as well as connecting in profound and fun ways with our children - but she gives us tools to get there.

"Reading this book made me feel like Alice in Wonderland, experiencing the shapes, sizes, and sensations of everyday life in new and entrancing ways. Kelly brings her parenting, writing, and psychodramatic skills to the page in a warm, down-to-earth style. Her conviction about the importance of the diary process comes from her own experience with her three children. Throughout the book, she offers humorous, loving and poetic examples of diary entries she has written to them."

— Lisa Friedlander, M.A., M.S.W., L.I.C.S.W.
Tewksbury, MA

"Kelly DuMar lives what she teaches. In her diaries, she paints images of moments with her children and family. Her writings give accounts of everyday life, as well as her insights as a woman and mother. Kelly is a gifted teacher. She has the skills and strategies to draw out the timid writer and she is an inspiring coach for the more seasoned writer. She combines writing, psychodrama, and poetry for a wonderful experience."

> — Trudy Duffy, L.I.C.S.W., T.E.P.,
> Co-chair, Clinical Faculty
> Boston University School of Social Work

"I had given up – I had too many empty spaces in my diaries and thought that I was doomed. *Before You Forget* gave me permission to pick up my diary again and be creative with my memories. The author's magical view of her children's world is contagious. It puts me in a place where I am happiest, back in my own children's world and creating a picture-book of our lives to share, reminisce, and discover each other and ourselves."

> — Joanna Sherblom, mother of three
> West Boylston, MA

"[Kelly's workshop is] a truly meaningful experience for any parent (or adult child). Kelly is a wonderfully sensitive and respectful facilitator. I was able to discover a very touching memory, write it and later share it with my daughter. It helped deepen our relationship in a new way."

> — Herb Propper, Ph.D, P.A.T.
> Montpelier, VT

"As a parent, group leader and creative artist, I assure you that Kelly DuMar in her Parenting Through the Diary Door workshops will lead you to the door of your most creative parenting abilities. Kelly's wisdom and truth combined with her sophisticated group leadership skills meld into a truly stunning experience. With her, parenting is elevated to the art we all wish it to be."

> — Lorri Boone Naylor, M.M., R.M.T, T.E.P.,
> Music Teacher
> Tampa, FL

"Here is a successful woman who is in love with her work. She is the teacher we remember fondly years after graduation, because she changed our lives. Kelly's leading skills and the camaraderie and safe haven she creates bring forth the talents and resources you never thought you had."

> — Nivart Chatalbash
> Sherborn, MA

Before You Forget

To Webb & Burrie,

Two incredibly talented

actors ~ Blessings

Keir Dullea

Before You Forget

The Wisdom of Writing Diaries for Your Children

Kelly DuMar, M.Ed.

Red Pail Press

SHERBORN, MA

Published by:
Red Pail Press, Inc.
P.O. Box 297
Sherborn, MA 01770
Email: Redpailpress@aol.com

Excerpt from "Letting Go," Copyright © 1996 by Alice B. Fogel,
from *I Love This Dark World*, Zoland Books, Cambridge, MA,
reprinted by permission of the publisher.
Excerpt from "The Morning Baking," Copyright © 1976 by Carolyn Forché,
from *Gathering the Tribes*, Yale University Press, New Haven,
reprinted by permission of the publisher.
Excerpt from *Falling Through Space*, Copyright © 1987 by Ellen Gilchrist,
Don Congdon Assoc., Inc., NY, reprinted by permission of the publisher.
Excerpt from *The Little Prince*, Copyright © 1943 by Antoine de Saint-Exupéry,
and renewed 1971 by Harcourt, Inc., reprinted by permission of the publisher.
Excerpts adapted and reproduced from *The American Heritage Dictionary of the
English Language, Fourth Edition*, Copyright © 2000 by Houghton Mifflin Company,
reprinted by permission of the publisher.

Edited by: Grace Sheldrick/Wordsworth Associates, Wellesley, MA

Cover Design and Illustration by: Leane R. Waddington, website: www.visualrose.com
Cover Illustration Copyright © 2001 by Red Pail Press, Inc.

Book Design, Typography & Composition by: Arrow Graphics, Inc.

Author Photo by: Heath Photography © 2001

ISBN 0-9708401-0-1
Library of Congress Control Number: 2001116703

To

—

Landon, Perri, Franci
&
Frank

Acknowledgments

I am grateful to many people who have influenced me, directly and indirectly, in writing this book. First of all, this book has a fairy godmother. My friend Tonya Quillen has played the role to perfection, waving the magic wand of her encouragement at this book in every stage of its development, helping to transform scribbled notes into cohesive chapters, and a final book. Her patience, grace, find mind and healing heart have nurtured me through every phase of this project for three years.

Barbara Casasa, Ph.D., mentor and friend, has for many years provided me with a sanctuary, (very much like a secret garden) where truth and fiction, memory and enchantment grow from the same roots, blossom in their own season, and bear exquisite fruit.

Margo Culley, professor of English at the University of Massachusetts at Amherst, insightful teacher and diary scholar, whose class on the history of diary literature of American women inspired me to take diary writing seriously, and to find my own voice and use it.

Nina Garcia, my brilliant psychodrama trainer, created a psychodrama learning space that allowed me to give birth to my passion for storytelling, paving the way for me to combine storytelling with my love of diary writing. My co-trainees, particularly Debbie, Tony, Dolores, Lorri, Bob, Christina, Byron, Bryan, and Tonya have been some of the best playmates I have ever found. Their courageous stories live in my heart and have helped me tell my own.

Supporters, colleagues and friends who read and commented on the manuscript include Lorri Boone Naylor, Lisa Friedlander, Bob Stiepock, and Chuck Fiero who gave generously of their limited time, reviewing drafts of this book and offering insightful feedback. My coach, Maggie Klee Lichtenberg, came into my life at the perfect time, kept the project on track, offered practical advice, and provided me with a map to guide me into unknown territory. I'm grateful to Leane Waddington, whose cover design captured the spirit of the book, and for her cover illustration based on my husband's photograph. Grace Sheldrick's editing taught me a great deal. Alvart Badalian skillfully guided every phase of production. My friend Deb has been a wonderful cheerleader.

I'm particularly grateful to my sister, Joanna, who has been an enormous source of encouragement, reading and commenting on drafts, and sharing the pleasure and value of family storytelling. I am also grateful to my brothers, Dusty, and Bob, and sister, Karen, as well as my many cousins, particularly Debbie, who made childhood an enchanting experience that I have wanted to re-experience, again and again, in my memory, in my heart, and in writing. I thank my nieces and nephews for bringing me joy and laughter and for appearing from time to time in stories in this book.

A muse visits a writer in mysterious ways, and the forever-young spirit of Kelly James Chandler has nurtured this book from its infancy.

My parents have supported this book in countless ways. My father knew he was raising a writer and has always urged me to overcome obstacles, write, and publish. My mother raised enchanting children and continues to inspire me by her commitment to the value of home and family life, and whose help with childcare and errands has sustained me through hectic times. I'm also grateful to my mother-in-law and her husband who have gone to extraordinary efforts to entertain and care for my children, often enabling me to travel without stress when needed.

My children have blessed this book since the beginning with their curiosity, enchanting improvisation, and zest for storytelling. They make me laugh, make me cry, open my heart and stretch my mind, nourish my imagination and spirit, and provide me with that supreme satisfaction of a perfect audience. Their profound influence is captured in every story of this book.

My husband Frank is this book's Wizard of Oz. His whimsically spiritual approach to problem-solving, combined with his often clumsily acquired wisdom, have helped me find the powers within that I've needed to begin, continue, and follow this project wherever it leads. His energy and vitality blow through my imagination like a Kansas tornado, stirring up all kinds of scary quests and fun adventures, before landing me in an entirely new landscape that is always home, when he's there to share it with me.

Contents

Notes on the Text

Throughout the book, I quote from the diaries of my three children. These quotes are identifiable in the text by indentation. They also have an introductory line of text that includes the name of the child from whose diary the entry was taken, the child's age at the time that I wrote the entry to him or her, and the date the entry was written. For example:

To Perrin (age 5), May 28, 1997

My children, who appear throughout the book as the protagonists of chosen stories, are, in order of their birth:

My son, Landon, born 12/02/87

My daughter, Perrin, born 3/14/92

My daughter, Frances, born 4/10/97

Any diarist who chooses to publish excerpts must make a decision about how to edit the diaries. I have chosen to respect the integrity of the original diary, and I have not corrected diary entries for grammar, punctuation, or spelling. I have used ellipses to indicate a sentence or a paragraph or more that has been omitted. I have changed many last names to initials, and I have edited certain stories according to my children's wishes—any changes and clarifications to the original diary entry are noted in brackets or with the use of ellipses.

Introduction

Daily Rites and Diary Writing

A friend gave me a blank notebook at my first baby shower and, with both a diarist's and a mother's instincts, I began writing to my unborn child as if writing letters to a loved one in a remote place. Beginning the diary during pregnancy allowed me to do two things at once—bond with my baby as well as with the grown child who existed in my imagination who would appreciate, I hoped, opening the book when he or she became a parent some day.

Of course, I kept writing in my own individual diary, just as I had since the age of thirteen, about my own personal reflections to myself. The child's diary was for all the things I felt compelled to tell him as they happened, preserving as much of his early life for him as I could. I realized that by writing about the pregnancy to him I could record memories for him before he could make any of his own. The pleasure of the process has kept me writing for him regularly since his birth thirteen years ago and has inspired me to keep diaries in the same way for the two daughters who were born later on.

But more than simply enjoying it, I keep writing to my children because the process makes me feel that I am doing something significant and meaningful, not only as a writer, but also as a mother, that my children will value long after I am gone. Every diarist seems to be, at least in part, motivated by a desire for immortality. My personal diaries may or may not ever interest anyone else. But how will my children be able to resist reading daily or periodic accounts of their own lives from birth?

After about eight years of keeping these diaries, I had a dream in which the primary motivation behind my impulse may have been made clear, and I saved it in this entry from my daughter's diary:

To Perrin (age 3), November 29, 1995

...In this recent dream I discovered that I was dying of skin cancer—I had a "butterfly" shaped patch of it on my left forearm. The rest of the dream consisted of my grieving process about leaving you two and Daddy. I told Daddy he must find love

and marry again. I clung to you with great grief about not being there to see you grow up.

And then, in Robert B's childhood bedroom that looks out over Grammy's field toward the house, I set yours and Landon's journals down beside each other in front of the closet, each stack tied and held together by a ribbon, and I asked my friend Lorri to save them and give them to you and Landon.

Then, standing at the window which now looked out on Tampa Bay, from the Radisson hotel where we stayed overnight when we closed the offices, and leaning out the window I dropped the single, white delicate flower, and cried out to the workmen standing below:

"But that was for me! That was for me!"

And before I knew it, somehow the workmen, I think, replaced my single flower w/a huge bouquet which I held, overflowing, in my arms, and squeezed them tight to me, crushing their beauty into me, feeling,

*"This is **life**. This is life. Catching the moments of beauty and really feeling them, really embracing them in all their beauty and significance for the moment."*

The diaries feed the illusion that I never have to leave my children—the books will nurture them long after I am gone.

Diary writing allows me to speak to my growing and grown children about the process of parenting them, particularly to have a place to record things they say and do that I want never to forget.

So often, diary entries that begin with the desire to record one precious phrase or expression evolve into classic family stories or entries about important lessons in life. My son, cuddling beside me in bed one school morning as we were both waking up, said:

> "The next two days are going to be the most exciting two days of my life, because, I'm playing the trumpet for the school today, tonight is Joey's rollerblading party, and tomorrow I try out for the hockey league with all my new equipment!"

A diary entry I made for him later that morning began with that joyful quote, but took a sharp turn into anxiety just as the blissful morning had. As I wrote spontaneously, what unfolded in the diary was the whole story of how he suddenly and unexpectedly encountered stage fright after he had an impromptu trumpet practice in his bedroom before school. The plot developed around how I coached him through his fears and helped him to get on the bus after he ran to back into his room declaring that he *"wasn't going to go to school!"* The diary entry ended, just as the drama did, in the school auditorium where I left him horsing around with his friends after his successful performance.

Will it mean anything to him later on that his mother captured this slice of life, making a record of his joy, his fear of failure, his follow-through, and his success? Perhaps it's the psychotherapist in me that is convinced it matters *now* as much as it will later. I keep the diaries and save the stories to show my children that their feelings are worth listening to, and also to show them that with support and guidance they can learn healthy ways of handling the difficult ones. I keep the diaries and tell the stories because they help me cope with my own feelings about what it means to be a parent. I keep the diaries because writing them leads me to connect with inner resources that spring from my wisest self.

As I began giving birth to my own children, I was counseling adults who were trying to make sense of painful childhoods often involving periods of complete or partial memory loss. These were clients whose unresolved issues from childhood were interfering with their ability to create meaningful and rewarding relationships with other people. Many of my clients, both men and women, were trying to build a healthy foundation of self-esteem that they never had because of growing up in a dysfunctional, physically or sexually abusive, or emotionally neglectful family. For many of my courageous clients, even lost painful memories were worth the painstaking process of reclaiming, because memories of childhood are fundamentally important to our sense of identity and to our capacity to feel whole and complete as adults. I began the diaries for each of my children realizing how desperately we each need a sense of our own personal history from conception. I wanted my children to have a concrete picture—the story—of how they were wanted, and of how they were welcomed into the world.

So many of my clients who had children or who wanted to have children have said to me—"But I have no idea how to parent. I don't want to make my parents' mistakes with my children!" Friends, colleagues, and most of the parents I meet say this. I think we all want to parent better than our own parents did—to do it well, do it right, maybe even do it perfectly. And we think we don't know how. I began keeping the diaries for my children because I didn't know everything I needed to know to be a good parent, but I knew how to use diary writing for personal growth. For more than twenty-five years, diary writing has always led me to my inner thoughts, my inner feelings, my conscience, my values, my intuition, and my inner wisdom. It has comforted, guided, and supported me through painful times, and kept a record of my bliss. It has never failed to provide me with a creative solution to a problem. The diary doesn't judge my writing or me. It saves the best and worst of my feelings and my writing as if it all had equal value. Intuitively, I realized that my children could teach me how to parent them if I wrote to them in the diaries.

They have. They do. They've taught me more than how to parent, they keep teaching me more about how to live my life meaningfully.

When my first child was less than a year old, I began my eight-year process of training as a psychodramatist. Psychodrama is a method of group psychotherapy in which participants enact spontaneous, unrehearsed scenes from their lives, performing in plays made of their conflicts, dreams, and wishes so that they can explore and practice creative solutions to problems, as well as discover and fulfill their dreams. My experience with acting in and directing psychodramas has profoundly influenced my parenting, my diary writing, and my ability to find *and tell* the meaningful stories of daily life with my own children. The most fundamental tool of psychodrama—*role reversal*—is the most fundamental tool of parenting—the ability to stand in the shoes of another person and see the world through his or her eyes, and to be willing to grow and change from the encounter. Diary writing for my children is a vehicle for looking at the world—and thus for evaluating my parenting—through their eyes.

A couple of years into my psychodrama training, I made a disturbing discovery about myself as a storyteller. As a group of twenty of us sat around in a circle, we were invited to tell a brief story about ourselves as a child and to choose other members of the group to perform it for us. But trying to pull up stories from my own childhood felt like dropping a bucket into an empty well. For what seemed like hours, I sat watching the funny, tender, intriguing stories of my friends performed with gales of laughter or tears. My mind was blank; I felt numb. I couldn't think of a single story to tell about myself as the protagonist, myself as the "heroic" child. All that came to mind were embarrassing stories about me making a mistake, or creating stress for authority figures, or stories of me being fearful or shy. I did not yet know how to shape a story about my childhood that celebrated myself as a child. So, I told a story about someone else.

Even though I eventually went on to perform many psychodramas about my own childhood and to reclaim my stories, the loss I recognized in that moment led to an awakening for me as a parent. I needed to tell my children wonderful, funny, interesting, creative stories about themselves, to teach them to see themselves as the story makers of their lives, and to make those stories from the simple stuff of our everyday lives together. I put the stories into the diaries, where my children will have them now and later.

Storytelling may have thrived during some distant period of my family history, but for at least the past few generations of family history, for a variety of reasons, it had become a lost art. I want to be part of the generation that reclaims the gift of family storytelling. I want stories of my parents' childhood for my children, so I began asking my parents, and writing the stories down. Recognizing that my son enjoyed hearing stories about me getting in trouble as a child as a way of healing from his own mistakes, one day I asked my father to tell Landon a story about when he got in trouble as a kid. My father's face turned bright red and he confessed to me, sheepishly, "I don't think I ever did!" That was okay. My mother, it turned out, was a great source of many mischief stories that we now treasure.

For more than twelve years, I have taught diary-writing workshops for personal growth and creativity, and I encourage my students who are parents to keep diaries for their children or grandchildren. Most of the men and women who have attended my diary-writing classes over the years do not consider themselves writers or even diarists. I do not think it is necessary to love writing or even to be a talented writer to begin keeping diaries for your children. When you write about what you love, you tend to write well. The beauty and clarity of their own prose often astonish participants in diary-writing workshops. The writing that is shared in a diary workshop is often creative, inspirational, and touching, because that's the kind of writing that happens when you are encouraged to write about what is real and true in your heart, your mind, and your experience. Your children, more than anyone ever may, want to read your words. My hope is to engage and inspire the writer within every parent.

Even though the excerpts I use in this book speak with a mother's voice, I have tried to reach both mothers and fathers throughout this book. This book is for parents. I hope fathers, as well as mothers, will be inspired to write to their children, to leave the legacy, and to build the bond. Fathers have often been short-changed in our culture and inhibited from expressing the full capacity of their nurturing instincts. The nurturing that fathers can provide through the diary door is essential to the healthy development of their sons and daughters.

The information in this book is specifically addressed to parents, but it is also appropriate for grandparents, godparents, stepparents, foster and adoptive parents, and other people who play a special role in nurturing children.

The teacher in me wants to share what I have learned about diary writing to my children with other parents. The storyteller in me who performs stories for children wants to inspire you with the stories themselves. The psychodramatist in me wants to show you how to do this *in action* with real players on the stage of daily, family life. I know the parent in me wants to learn about parenting from other parents—from their successes, their vulnerabilities, and their journeys of discovery. I suspect you do, too. My children have allowed me to invite you through our own diary door. The book is organized around topics and themes that we have encountered over the years using excerpts from the diaries of my three children begun before birth through the time that my eldest son, Landon, is twelve, my older daughter, Perrin, is eight, and my younger daughter, Frances, is three.

I hope you will find, as I have, that if you open the diary door you will be opening the door to your inner wisdom as a parent and to your intuitive ability to parent well. After many years of keeping the diaries, this was made clear to me in a writing class I was taking with a group of women. An older woman had written, according to the assignment that week, a history of her hair. The moment in the story that captured my attention as she read it was her reminiscence about when, as a child, her mother would without fail every morning painstakingly curl her luxuriously long and thick hair into two layers of banana curls. When she finished reading, I said wistfully, "It's too bad that so much of that kind of tender, daily contact and attention to detail has faded with the informality of appearances now. My daughter doesn't even usually comb her hair before leaving the house, and I couldn't imagine if she *did* have long hair that I could make curling it for her daily a high priority."

The teacher jumped in, surprised, and said, "But of course *you* do. This is what you do with your children's diaries, isn't it?"

Everyone in class agreed with her. Most of them had already raised their children and expressed regret that they had never thought of keeping diaries for them. One of the participants asked if I would stop once they were able to keep diaries for themselves. My daughter Perrin, at age eight, now does. But it certainly hasn't diminished my own desire to observe, appreciate, and seek to understand her—to weave together the separate strands of the long day—to tell and save stories of her childhood that will help make the story of her life complete.

Chapter 1

The Door to Parenting Wisdom
Writing a Living History of Childhood

Seek the wise parent within.
Embrace the beauty, magic, and meaning
of everyday life with your children.
Tell them stories, save their stories.
Create a living legacy before you forget.

Are you listening? If you listen, you can hear them. Your children are inviting you through the diary door. *Come in.* They want to take you to a magical place where memories thrive. They want to go there with you, now, and again and again. Whether they are age three or five or eight, or waiting to be born in seven months, they want you to keep a diary for them. They want you to write to them. They want you to tell them stories about how they came into this world. They want you to tell them what they were like before *they* can remember. They want you to tell them what they did when they were in the womb. They want you to tell them stories about what they did to make you shriek with laughter, and they want you to tell them the stories that made you pulse with pride. They want you to tell them about where they lived, whom they played with, and what they said before they can remember.

Children Trust You to Remember, but You *Will* Forget

Your children want you to keep writing, even after they begin to form their memories, because *they* will forget. Yet, they will expect *you* to remember, and they will ask you to tell them everything you remember about what they were like when they were little, and you, to your horror, will have forgotten so much. You will not want to say you don't remember. They want you to preserve this fascinating period of their personal history *before you forget*. This book will be your guide.

Buy a Blank Book Instead of a Baby Book

Every baby receives at least one baby book. But what every baby needs is a *blank* book. Your children want to know so much more about their lives than what you can record in their baby books. There is only so much space in those pre-arranged lines. Baby books are pretty and organized, and if you don't leave them blank they may preserve some useful information. You can write how old your child was when she said "Da-Da," or how much your son weighed on his three-month check-up, and whether or not he liked peas. Baby books are fun to save and to look at, perhaps, but not so much fun in which to write, because you have to write what they tell you to write on the dates or mile-markers they have chosen, not necessarily the ones that suit you and your child. It's easy to forget to keep them up-to-date, and then it's easy for them to become a burden that you avoid and plan to catch up on later.

The following pre birth entry in my second daughter's diary points out the powerful need that each child has to have a parent keep a book of memories of which she is the *star* preserved as she grows, not after the fact, retrospectively, from memory. It describes a baby shower gift given to me by a friend in anticipation of my daughter's arrival:

To Frances (a month before birth), March 10, 1997

> . . . One very nice gift was a baby book w/bunnies on the cover from my friend R. She told me the story of her three daughters and Baby Books. It seems that she kept Baby Books for her first two daughters assiduously, but, as often happens, she failed to do so for the third. This, of course, was a source of hurt for the third daughter for many years. So R tried to make it up to her, and on her 16th birthday she put together a Baby Book w/her memories as best she could, and gave it to her daughter. "Mother," she said. "I'm sorry, but this just isn't good enough. I **still** wish you had kept one for me when I was a baby!"
>
> Well, I need you to know, Franny, that I have never been a Baby Book keeper. I have managed to pull together a photo album each for your brother and sister, but I'm afraid I will probably fail you miserably w/your "Baby Book," because I am a diarist, and I so much prefer writing to you like this, just as I have w/each of my children starting before birth. I want to give you the **stories**, as well as the facts, fantasies and foibles. To me, **this** is the only place to do that.

Diaries are different than baby books, because they are as blank as a baby's future. Baby books provide fill-in-the-boxes, but diaries open doors. Writing diaries opens the door to your imagination, your insight, and your highest parenting wisdom. They aren't just records of statistics and brief sentences about babyhood. Diaries for kids aren't like baby books that sit safely on shelves waiting for grown children to look at them someday, because diaries for kids contain stories that can be read aloud, again and again, by parents to eager listeners. Diaries record life histories written as they are unfolding in the moment, day by day.

These diaries may be read and reread throughout the years just as all classic childhood storybooks are mined again and again for meaning and pleasure. And diaries, because they offer parents the opportunity for the insight and reflection that storytelling always provides, nurture parents profoundly in the process of writing them. Diary stories may be a better investment of time and energy than baby books, because they allow you to bring your child to life on the page and to explore your relationship in depth.

Parents and Children Are Natural Storytellers

As a parent you have had, or will have, the experience of hearing your child say something so charming that you rush off to share the gem with anyone who will listen. We are dying to tell stories that celebrate the humor, the delight, and the challenge of raising our children. Why not tell these stories directly to those people who *most* want to hear them—our own children? Diaries are the perfect container for the stories of our daily lives together. Your children will, of course, treasure the photo albums you keep for them. They will peruse them for hours, and they will pass them down to their children. And the videos you make will be watched and treasured, time after time, for years to come.

But children also want your stories. They want all the stories you can write and save for them and more. They will grow up wanting to feel connected to the child they once were. They want the flesh on the skeleton of their childhood years filled out in tales that will preserve and reconnect them to the ordinary things that happened as they grew up with you. Whether we're experienced writers or novices with spelling phobias, we can trust that our children have insatiable appetites for reading the diary stories we write about their adventures each day. Especially when the entries immortalize their imaginative point of view.

One early morning many years ago, my daughter Perri, at age two, told me this story, and because I knew it held more truth and beauty than I could possibly grasp in that one, stunning moment of delight, I wrote it down and saved it in her diary. It is only a simple, one-sentence story. But, to me as a parent, it speaks volumes. Every time I recall it, every time I read it to her, every time I share it with someone else, I smile, I remember, and I learn something new about being her parent:

To Perrin (age 2 ½), November 6, 1994

. . . A week or so ago, in the early morning, just after taking Landon to school, we were walking up to the house from the car when you saw the bit of moon over the house. You said:

"When Daddy gets home he'll get it for me, and I'll hold it in my hands and I won't break it."

Our children can teach us everything we need to know to parent them well, if we are willing to watch, listen, and learn. They speak in metaphor, poetry, and story, always inviting us to see both the world we live in and our role as parent through their eyes. This story about discovering the moon isn't just my daughter's story. All children discover the beautiful, awesome moon and seek a heroic parent who will claim it for them. This childlike wish to grasp the mystery of the moon captures the approach to parenting that diary writing encourages. Through the diary door, we reach for and try to grasp the awesome mystery and beauty of our children, and we promise to handle them with care.

The Extraordinary Power of Ordinary Stories

Parents can never underestimate the power that stories of ordinary life have to bring pleasure, satisfaction, and much more to their children and themselves. If you go through the diary door with your children, you will be writing about what you are passionate about; and because the diaries are all about them and their world, you will hold their interest, attention, and fascination. You do not need to worry about boring your audience. It didn't occur to me, at first, to read aloud from the diaries to my children until a friend asked me if I did so. When I did, I got all the validation I needed about how much pleasure the process provided them, as the following entry shows:

To Landon (age 7), May 24, 1995

It is just by chance at dinner that I discover how much you enjoy me reading your diaries to you. When someone asked me, nine weeks ago when I started the writing class w/ Mopsy, if I read to you & Perri from your diaries I said no, I had not yet tried that.

Until tonight. I had some of them handy . . . [and] as we sat talking at dinner, the three of us, I grabbed the one from the Spring of '91 when Daddy says he's ready to try for a second child. I begin reading and you don't want me to stop, and you laugh hysterically at the conversations and antics I recorded. I am so satisfied that this pleases you, that all the hours spent writing are worth it if they bring you pleasure in yourself, which is of course, what I had hoped, trusting you would be entranced by yourself as protagonist. We would have perhaps continued all night if we hadn't been interrupted by a long call from Grammy B.L. . . .

There is something worth writing about every day to your children that rises from the rhythm of daily ritual, daily play, daily work, and daily struggles. It could be as simple as a story about your child's first taste of food. Children don't just want to know that they took their first mouthful of peas at age seven months. They want to know *the story* about their first taste of food filled in with all the details that make ordinary life memorable. Children want to see *how* they grew in the prose and poetry of your story making about their lives in the diaries. My third daughter's first taste of food was by no means a momentous event, but it was an important family event:

To Frances (age 4 months), August 23, 1997

It was a family event, a family effort. The Sunday after the First Annual Bean Hole Bake, it was time to start you on your first food. For a couple of weeks I had been warming up to it, just waiting for the right moment, and on this lazy, sunny day we had—for once! no other commitments.

Daddy, Land & Perri were outside on the swings at lunch time, and I brought you out and announced that it was time to try your rice cereal. We came in to put you in your high chair—the one we bought for Landon nine years ago, and put your bib on. I mixed the cereal and gave it to Dad for the first bites. You opened your mouth greedily, and let him shovel it in as if you'd been waiting for "real" food your whole four months of life! . . .

Diaries Are Gifts That Keep on Giving

All we ever really have is this moment, this day. And yet, it is so easy to take the moments and the days for granted, letting the days of childhood fly by without really noticing and appreciating the beauty, wisdom, pleasure, and potential meaning of daily life with our children. Diary writing offers us the gift of conscious awareness and appreciation of the moment. When you keep diaries for your children, you pay attention to things in their world that they may never notice. And in the process, they teach you to pay attention to things *you* might never notice. You learn to sift and to save what really matters in the long run. Diary writing helps you to live day by day, experiencing the rich flavor and meaning of each moment, and to appreciate the moment for all it is worth.

What Is Diary Writing for Your Children?

Diary writing for your children grows out of the fertile process of personal diary writing, embracing all of its purposes and possibilities and more. It is a kind of storyteller's personal growth process in which you embrace the highest parenting skills within.

Even though it is not necessary to be a writer or a diarist to begin keeping diaries for your children, a basic understanding of the value and purpose of diary writing may help you to begin. You may be unfamiliar with the rich process of diary/journal writing that has evolved out of centuries of personal and periodic diary writing by women and men to the contemporary practice that today is often referred to as journal writing or "journaling." As diary and journal writing have evolved for centuries in our own American culture, the purpose and nature of keeping diaries and journals have changed and are always changing. Anyone may keep a diary or a journal at some period of their lives, either as a habitual practice of record keeping, a creative warm-up to other projects, or as a process of personal exploration. The reasons are as varied as the people who open blank notebooks and begin writing in them.

Journal writing and diary writing for children have some important similarities and differences. There is much of value for parents to borrow from the practice of personal diary writing in writing diaries for children.

If you are new to the practice of diary or journal writing, you may wonder—what does it mean to be a diarist? To be a diarist is to develop a practice of attending to the interior and exterior landscape of one's daily life the way a painter might imagine a frame around a vista and attempt to capture it on an easel. Diarists wander through their minds and hearts and draw the landscape on the dated but otherwise blank page. Diarists gaze and write—without planning—what the world looks like, feels like, sounds like, smells like, tastes like, in this moment, from this day's perspective. Diarists write about how the past and future look in the context of the present scene.

Diarists and journal writers may write in order to remember significant experiences in their lives, because remembering the past can be pleasant, fun, and comforting—and because the past is a teacher. Diaries keep an eye on you—they watch you grow. But diaries do more than keep an eye on you, they open your eyes. Diaries are mirrors for self-contemplation, opening doors to self-discovery. Diary writing is a way to think, a way to feel, a way to center and quiet or purge and pole vault oneself into the unfamiliar, unknown landscape of the imaginative self. Diaries and journals can take the role of friend, therapist, healer, or a higher power and help you through a tough time. Diary and journal writing are a way to seek and grasp an understanding of the purpose or meaning in your life.

Defining the Terms—Diary versus Journal

Is diary writing different from journal writing or journaling? No. What you call this process is a matter of your personal preference. Both *diary* and *journal* have their roots in the word *day*. Some people keep diaries. Some people keep journals. Some people make the noun, *journal*, into a verb and call the writing process *journaling*. They all refer to a process of regular or sporadic personal, spontaneous writing kept for a variety of reasons in a myriad of styles. Mostly they are written in the first person, "I"—and the audience, or the primary reader, is the self. For consistency, and simply because I prefer the word *diary*, I call the process *diary writing* from now on, except where the word *journal* was used within a diary entry.

Distinct Aspects of a New Genre

Diaries for your children blend diary writing, memoir, autobiography, and biography into a new and distinct genre with unique features. Unlike personal diaries, in which your audience is yourself and you are writing in the first person, the children's diaries are written directly to each child as if writing letters to their future selves. Your audience (or rather, your reader) is your child, so you are writing in the second person, as in, "you played in the yard after lunch." But this "you" is a multidimensional audience. You are writing to your present child and your growing child and your grown child all at the same time, as I do in the following entry to my daughter Perrin at age three months. Writing to my infant daughter allows me to project into the future and to imagine what my relationship with my adult daughter will be like later on. These reflections allow me to make a conscious plan for my wishes to come true:

To Perri (age 3 months), June 12, 1992

> ... I know some day that you will read this book and probably will feel the endearments, like "plumpkin," are silly, but I can't resist. You are a huggable, loveable, squishable infant right now. Maybe you will feel that other parts of this journal are silly. I look at you and wonder who you will be. It's hard to imagine, looking at you now, at 3 months, that you will ever reject anything at all about me—so incredibly loving and **happy** you always are toward me—everyone, really. But I know some day you will have lots of opinions about me: surely some unfavorable ones!
>
> But I do hope you like this journal, and all the others I hope will follow ...
>
> I would have loved having a journal from my mother....
>
> A few years ago—**quite a few**—I was sunning myself at Farm Pond on a crowded beach day. Must have been in my mid-20's, I guess. I happened to notice two women, lying prone, facing each other, elbows supporting their heads, perhaps, lean-

ing towards each other in eager, soft conversation. I realized that I recognized them as Hunting Lane neighbors I knew very little: M.E., a year behind me in school, and her mother. . . .

*As I watched them, I felt a huge, sad sense of incredible longing, **and** surprise. Here was a mother/daughter relationship—with intimacy. Here was a daughter who seemed to be eagerly sharing secrets with her mother, and, stranger yet, here was a mother listening! Listening with pleasure, respect, and gentleness. . . .*

. . . I'll share a blanket on the beach with you any day, any time, and I'll listen. I promise you, I'll listen. . . .

Diaries for your children are written *as they are happening*, in the moment while your child is growing day to day. Diaries are about the present even though they may contain recollections from the past and they project through an open door into the future. Whereas memoir, autobiography, and biography look backwards from the other side of the door, diaries for kids begin a life story and imagine where it might go.

No Experience Is Necessary

You may have kept a diary for yourself or done some periodic life writing but never kept a diary for your children. If you have found your way through the diary door for your children already, this guide may lead you into unexplored territory.

If you've never gone through the diary door, this book will show you how to begin keeping diaries for your children. *It is not necessary to have any particular writing experience to go through the diary door with your children. Anyone can.* This is not a book for a specific group of parents who happen to like to write. It is not a book for a specific group of parents who write *well*. It is a book for the writer, the storyteller, in *every* parent.

Is it Ever Too Late to Begin?

You may be an experienced parent who did not begin the diary writing process from birth and who wonders whether you can begin now even though your children are older, in school, or adolescents even. Certainly you can. Chapter Two covers when and how to begin, and all the chapters throughout the book offer you inspiration, permission, encouragement, and guidance for how to begin this process any time as your children grow. The diary-door-writing process may sound so appealing to you that you regret not having started sooner. You can always write retrospectively about certain stories, like your child's birth story, if you like. But don't let regret stand in your way of beginning the process now by writing a story about what your child is like *today*. As you continue writing, many opportunities for reflection on previous stories from your child's life history will float up to the surface of your mind for you to gather and save.

The Personal Growth Journey of Parenting

This writing space beyond the diary door leads and follows you on the personal growth journey of raising children. When you go through the diary door, the daily act of observing and describing your children provides a path to greater consciousness of your choices, values, decisions, and behavior. When you write to your children, you can reflect on your own gifts, shortcomings, and conflicts as you grow into the parenting role.

For most parents, there is no greater intellectual, emotional, physical, and spiritual challenge and opportunity for growth than parenting. You may strive to be as good or better parents than your own were; but no one can parent ideally, only humanly. You want to help your children develop cognitively, emotionally, and spiritually; yet only when you're smack into the process of parenting do you realize how much that will depend on *your* own parallel process of struggle, growth, and change.

Diary writing for your children does not offer a perfect path to parenting, but it gives you access to a process that will call out the best parenting you can find within yourself, engaging you in a process of communicating with your child that strengthens skills you already possess. The bond you create with your children through the diaries will flow into all aspects of your life with them.

Reaching for the Wise Parent Within

Parenting is the role you may be least prepared for in life, and yet the one that you wish you could perform perfectly. Mistakes and insecurities haunt you because you feel that it is the lives of those you love most that are riding on your success or failure. Though you may start by looking outside yourself to the so-called "experts" for your parenting answers and choices, you learn that you must, if you are to parent authentically, encounter your deepest self. Diary writing for children helps you learn to develop and use your intuition and to more fully understand who your children are as unique individuals and where they are in the developmental process. Diary writing for your children connects you with your inner wisdom as a parent. It can help you to understand and overcome your own internal stumbling blocks in your parenting style and skills.

Diary writing for your children helps you cope with the reality that you are the real rather than the ideal parent. In addition to observing, describing, and reflecting on your parenting, diary writing offers possibilities for resolving problems with your children. In the diaries you can make amends for your mistakes, rewrite or revise your bad days, pay attention in moments of quiet reflection to the best parts of parenting, or the best parts of the day. On bad days, writing a diary entry may allow you to feed you and your children the nourishing meal you may have failed to prepare or share with them that day.

This writing process is a way of giving your children attention now that will offer them a deeper understanding of themselves, both now and later. Diary writing for your children provides the perfect vehicle for expressing your highest intentions as parents if you pick up the pen, open the notebook, open the door.

Embrace the Enchantment of Daily Life

Your children want you to spin straw into gold. You have a Rumpelstiltskin within who knows exactly how to do this, effortlessly. They will be spellbound when you capture them in the everyday act of doing or saying something funny, unusual, or unexpected—particularly when you capture them in the midst of their own enchanted exploration, as I did my son in the following exchange he had with the Tooth Fairy:

To Landon (age 7), September 23, 1995

…Wednesday evening, Dad's first one home last week, he headed into your room to kiss you goodnight because he got in so late. He found your tooth pillow [for the tooth fairy] with a note in it:

"tack this toth ples."

It seems that the last time she visited she left you money for your tooth but then she forgot to take the tooth! You told me about it the next day, and then I forgot about it. So, after waiting patiently a couple of days for her to claim her prize, you decided to make yourself perfectly clear.

And it worked! The next morning the tooth was gone and you had another dollar!

Look at the World through Their Eyes

Diary writing for your children teaches you through the role of the writer/observer to slow down and be more attentive to and aware of the present moment and all there is to learn and appreciate about parenting. When you write daily or periodically to your children you begin to understand and validate their point of view. Our children invite us to play, and through playing with them we have the opportunity to enrich our adult lives. Play keeps our attitudes young and gives us a needed break from our adult concerns and responsibilities. Writing the following entry also helped me appreciate the significance of my daughter's imaginative play with her dolls and to validate her desire to experiment with the nurturing role:

To Perrin (age 5), May 28, 1997

…After your recital rehearsal last night, on the way home you promised to jump right into bed. But that must have reminded you of your responsibilities, first:

"Oh no! What about Addie?" you cried. It seems that, in the late morning when you had time to yourself in the backyard, you had brought Addie [American Girl Doll] out to the tree house (which you are modelling after the Babysitters Club) and left her out there. We agreed that it would not be a good idea to leave her out there.

*So, I took a flashlight out into the dark yard and scared Mrs. Bunny who was snacking on the fresh spring clover as I found my way to the Treehouse. There, sitting facing me in the crook of the tree sat Addie, the Bookworm, w/ a book propped in her hands, reading in the **very** dim light.*

"Addie," I scolded, "You'll ruin your eyes trying to read in this light!" I made her take her book, her basket of books, plus her two boxes of crackers and come inside out of the moist night air. Then you tucked her in and both of you went right to sleep…

Let Your Wise Child Be the Teacher

Over and over again through the diary door you will discover and learn from the natural wisdom your children possess and are eager to share when you listen and respond to their suggestions and advice. You can write and save stories in the diaries that validate your children when they really do know what's best *for you*, as my daughter Frances did in this story of her providing me with a calming close to a long, hectic day:

To Frances (age 2), July 3, 1999

You took me for a walk tonight after dark, before bed. Now you drink your milk quietly in your crib while I sit on the deck outside your window.

The walk was exquisite, and I didn't want to go. We had, as usual, a very busy, active 4th of July, (although it's really only the third). Field events this morning. Parade. Deb, Mike and kids for backyard cookout. Then, Daddy and boy and P [Landon and Perri] off to airport to pick up Amanda & Josh and Grampy and Cindy who are flying in for a surprise weekend.

You and me alone in the backyard, cheerfully alone, cleaning up. You, sensing bedtime was somewhere in your very near future, asked for a walk.

Without realizing how tired I felt, and the dishes still undone, I agreed. Then I was too tired. But you were not. I offered to sit w/ you in the dark back yard instead, and you agreed. . . .

*Until you saw that it meant **instead** of a walk.*

"Walk!" you cried, insisting.

"A short one," I agreed.

How gorgeous an evening. My exhaustion lifting in the warm, moist air, rising to the stars. Decided to walk to Grammy's driveway—she's at Laurel Lake.

Sound of fireworks.

Fireflies in the road. Flash. Flash. Boom!

Still, still, heavy air. Night birds last calls. Our silence. No cars. You falling into your trance of enjoyment, sitting up straight, just looking. No fidgets.

And I'm so glad you insisted. One should always have a loved one to take on a walk, or to be coaxed into one. . . .

Grasp Your Child's Developmental Concerns

Diary writing for your children allows you to embrace the poetic, artistic, or spiritual moment to learn what it has to teach you about your child's developmental concerns. Besides, what else is there to do when your child says something she or he may never say again, that is so funny, unique, tender, wise, beautiful, or unexpected that just telling your husband, your child's grandmother, or your friends simply isn't enough? You want to make it concrete, to set it within the context in which it was made, to save it as a story for your child to enjoy later on:

To Perrin (age 5), October 17, 1997

A sunny, October day one week ago as we drove to Carson's birthday, just you, me and the baby on the way to Chuck E Cheese.

"I know what I want to be when I grow up," you said.

"Oh?"

"A doctor, or a policeman . . ."

"Oh"

"I want to be a policeman 'cause they're like in charge of the world."

"Oh"

"Aren't they? What's the world mean? Is it the same as the universe? Landon says it isn't . . ."

"Ummm . . ."

"No, I know what I want. I want to grow up to be God!" . . .

Make the Laughs Last

Children are fun, and one of the most gratifying experiences as a parent is sharing a laugh with our children. They possess an innocent charm that regularly brings us surprises and delight. They love to laugh, and they delight in their own power to make us laugh. This is often not difficult for them to do. Writing diaries for your kids is a way of making the laughs last. We always laugh together when we reread this entry from my son's diary:

> ### To Landon (age 9), November 13, 1996
>
> . . . *Anyway, you know we are having this new baby. Well, a few weeks ago, you and I were riding in the car, and I told you that Dad and I had decided to let you . . . take part in the delivery.*
>
> *"Oh wow . . . now I'll die a happy man because I'll have seen at least one baby born in case I never get married!"*

Speak to an Ideal Listener

You learn quickly as a parent that your children often relax and talk most openly to you at a particular time of day, or during a particular activity—such as while you are riding in the car or just before bedtime. As a parent, you also develop your own rhythm for when you feel like opening up and communicating with your children. You may find that you are warmed up to writing in the diaries in those quiet moments just after you put them to sleep or before going to bed yourself. Or perhaps you feel most like writing during your child's naps or while you're waiting at sporting activities or doctor's offices. If you take the time to write in your child's diary when you have an opportunity, you will find that the process offers relaxation and the chance to "speak" about what's really on your mind that you might not otherwise get a chance to tell your children. Diary writing doesn't take the place of directly spoken, honest communication with your kids. But, realistically, just as you are not always available when your kids have something important to say, neither can *they* always be available for your moments of disclosure. The diary *is* always available, however, with its blank, white pages a constant, open invitation to listen to your words, your feelings, your thoughts, your stories.

Before my children were born, there were things I was feeling that I wanted to be able to communicate to them. Through the diary door, it seemed as if my future child was listening to me as I wrote:

To Frances (four months before birth), December 7, 1996, 4:45 a.m.

... Do you know I took communion w/you last Sunday at St. Dunstan's, and I realized that you are my first child born since I've been baptized, two years ago. I was touched by the realization that we were both taking communion, that you could receive it even before birth, through me: 'Blood of Christ, Bread of Heaven,' and I was calmed, reassured, glad that we could share something I was unable to give my other two before birth. What is it like to receive the sacrament before birth? Some day, write a poem about it. The experience of our communion, yours and mine, blessed. But, you see, having a baby growing inside you is communion: you are my daily bread of heaven...

Provide a Special Way of Nurturing

Receiving thanks from our children for everyday nurturing is rare for parents. You can perform acts of service all day long and be completely taken for granted. Kids don't tend to thank you for the care-taking they come to expect—the shopping, bill-paying, cleaning, carpooling, cooking, and general managing of the details of their lives. There is something different, though, in what you give them in the diary writing, and they will respond to that. They know the diary writing comes from a different energy than the care-taking tasks require. It springs from a kind of nurturing they know you're not *required* to perform. They know the writing of the diaries is your attempt to spin straw into gold.

One unusually quiet afternoon when I was sitting on the couch in the living room writing in my daughter's diary, she found me and asked what I was doing. I told her that I was writing about her, catching up on some things in her diary. Silently, she took a pen of her own and scribbled a message on the blank side of the page on which I had been writing the following story. Her message said simply, *"m o m i s l o v e i n g."*

To Perri (age 6), November 25, 1998

"Diaries"

A few weeks ago, now that you can write—at least phonetically—you started keeping a diary that you write in before bed.

I did not know this until you and Lan got into a tussle over it at Hanna's where you spent the night a week (or two) ago for her birthday. You brought your diary, and amidst one of the boy-girl battles of the centuries between you/Hannah & Lan/Adam (who came w/ us to pick you up) Lan got a hold of it and tore out some pages in which you had revealed some not-so-very nice feelings about him.

This crime was discovered in the car on the way home and your wails and tears were not to be contained. You through [threw] yourself on the bed at home, and I came in to talk. . . .

. . . diarist to diarist, I told you that every diarist has to, at some time, deal w/ issues of having her privacy violated. But she cannot let this stop her from writing, because her diary is a safe and sacred place for her to speak her innermost thoughts and feelings, and she must find a way to keep it so.

For now, your idea is to get a diary that locks because you believe in the idea of a lock. So be it. Perhaps you'll get one for Christmas. I took you, for now, into my room and let you pick out one of my blank books that Dad gave me for my 40th birthday. . . .

Lan agreed to respect your privacy and leave your diary alone in the future. I showed you how to hide it between your mattress and box spring anyway, just in case.

And I promised, as a Mom, that I would always respect the privacy of your own diary. It's a sacred place.

So, keep writing, my dear.

Transform Photographic Moments into Relationship Histories

Why do you keep photos? You want to make quality time last—for the pure pleasure of it, because you are trying to catch hold of something that by its nature is ephemeral—a moment, a look, an action, a stage of development, an occasion, an outfit, or a relationship. You keep photo albums to chronicle visual portraits. A camera can make a treasured picture of a special moment in a relationship, such as your child toasting marshmallows around a campfire for the first time with a group of cousins and extended family outside a summer cabin. But diaries for kids are the narrative behind the still-life and the actions shots. They weave the picture into the story of a life. If you keep diaries for your children, chances are your grown child may someday open the diary and drink up these entries like vintage wine.

I didn't find the following story in my son's diary until many years after I had written it, and, like so many of my favorite entries, I had no memory of writing it down. All significant, bosom buddy, best friend, lifelong relationships *begin* somewhere, blossoming eventually out of tiny seeds. My son's relationship with his cousin Joey has blossomed since the time of this story into a best friendship of many years, so I was very grateful that I had captured the boys as they were just getting to know each other. It's the kind of story I imagine pulling out for them some day when one of them is preparing a toast to offer at the other's wedding reception:

To Landon (age 5), August 16, 1992

You were toasting your first marshmallows of the season with your cousins at the campfire in front of Grammy's camp when I heard Joey saying softly to his mother:

"It's really nice to see Landon, Mommy."

It was our first night together at Grammy's camp, mid-week in the first week of our vacation. We were all in the yard, sitting in the light of the campfire battling mosquitoes while you, Joey, Maelyn and Ben burnt your marshmallows in the fire.

"Why don't you tell Landon how glad you are to see him?" Auntie Jo asked Joey. "Okay."

You were totally committed to your marshmallows, bouncing excitedly to and from the fire with hot skewer in hand when Joey, full of affection for you, approached.

"Landon," he tried. "It's really nice to see you."

You didn't stand still long enough to even hear him. You, yourself, were talking excitedly about your flaming marshmallows.

Joey, absolutely determined, followed you to the fire and tried again:

"Landon, it's really nice to see you."

But as quickly as he found you you were gone, bouncing like a mosquitoe around the yard from one of us to the other.

Joey momentarily gave up and returned to his mother for advice.

"You know, sometimes people get so excited about something they can't hear us. Why don't you wait until a little later when you and Landon are alone and tell him then?"

But Joey, ultimately, was completely undeterred. He needed to tell you, perhaps knowing that if we wait to say something important the mood often passes and it never gets said at all.

Joey cornered you by the fire and said,

"Landon, would you please come inside with me? I have something to say that I don't want anyone to hear."

Finally, he had caught your attention and your curiosity was piqued. You followed him impatiently into the house. I could easily hear you both, just inside the screen door.

"Okay, okay, what'd you want to tell me?"

"Landon, it's really nice to see you."

A split second after the words were out you were bolting back out the screen door, and in a loud voice:

"Oh, is **that** all?" And then, to all of us who were 'round the fire:

"Oh, he just wanted to tell me how glad he is to see me."

There were marshmallows to be scorched and eaten, after all.

Celebrate and Honor Children and Childhood

More than anything else, you will find that keeping diaries and saving diary stories is a process that celebrates and honors children and childhood. These diaries allow children to maintain a connection to the child they once were as they grow into adulthood. They allow you as a parent to stay connected to the child you have raised. Diary storytelling shows you how to pay attention to the innocence, poetry, wonder, and wisdom of childhood, cherishing this time of exploration and limitless possibility. This process offers you a creative outlet that affirms your child's identity, self-esteem, emotions, and spirit.

Create a Storytelling Hearth in Your Home

When you keep diaries for your children, you are creating a storytelling hearth in your home, lighting the fire, keeping it lit. Gathering the family around you. Spellbinding family members with tales of their favorite protagonists. Teaching them to value themselves as heroes, as travelers and adventurers on life's journey. Write the stories, keep the fire, tend the hearth. When they leave, your children will take the diaries with them; and they will always return, return to the flame, and pass it on.

Using the Diary Door Openers

Within each chapter of the book you can find suggestions, inspiration, and guidance for writing your own diary stories and entries. As you read, you may find yourself stimulated and warmed up to write in your child's diary, so keep it handy. In addition, at the end of each chapter is a list of writing suggestions called **Diary Door Openers,** which address the specific themes and approach discussed in that chapter. These writing prompts are designed to spark ideas, motivation, and inspiration for you to write in your own blank book.

When you scan the list of exercises and choose one that motivates you to write through the diary door, remember that you are writing directly *to* your child as the audience and reader, not to yourself as you do in a personal diary. So, for instance, you write, "I watched you blink your eyes in the ray of sun streaming through the window," rather than "I watched him blink his eyes in the ray of bright morning sun streaming through the window."

Keep in mind that even though prompts or writing exercises may help you to recognize and open your mind to the possibilities of storytelling through the diary door, the best stories will arise from the rituals, actions, adventures, behaviors, and words of daily life with your own children. As you watch, listen, write, reflect, and respond to your children, they will provide all the inspiration you need.

Writing diaries for your children offers incredible rewards, but first you must begin. The next chapter shows you how to begin writing diaries for your own children and will answer many questions you may have about the process. Following are some Diary Door Openers that you may want to try before you move into the next chapter.

Diary Door Openers

1. Remembering *This* Day
    Towards the end of the day, sit down, relax, and close your eyes and review your experiences and memories of the day with your child, whether you are still pregnant with your first child, or you are living with a toddler, pre-schooler, or ten-year old. Open your blank book, write the date at the top of the page, and write one thing you *think* you and your child will want to remember about this day. It could be about something humorous your child said or did, a bit of enchantment you both experienced, a budding relationship that just began, or something new you learned about your child's development. Just begin writing, and see where the memory takes you.

2. Baby Gifts
    Begin an entry by listing as many baby gifts as you can remember that your child has received. Even if your child is older, you may recall some of the gifts as you begin to jog your memory by writing. After you have a list, look it over and choose one to describe in detail, including who gave the gift, a description of the gift itself, including what it meant to you to receive it, and what it seems to mean to your child. Is your child aware of the gift? Is it something useful and meaningful in your child's life today, or might it have more relevance or significance to your child in the future?

3. Gifts That Keep on Giving
    Close your eyes and take some deep breaths. Whether or not your child is born yet, project off into the future and imagine that she or he is leaving home, for college, for marriage, or for a new apartment. At the threshold of this rite of passage see yourself handing him or her a box in which you have packed all the diaries you have kept for your child since birth or since early childhood. Now, notice how you are feeling. How does it feel to offer this gift to your child? How do you imagine your child will respond? Go to your child's diary and write an entry about what you hope to give your child through this diary writing and what you hope to gain for yourself.

Chapter 2

Opening the Diary Door
When and How to Begin

They'll also begin the way most diaries begin:
all at once, with a rolling up of sleeves,
an intake of breath—and a here goes.

(Thomas Mallon, *A Book of One's Own*, p. xviii)

Just as you have probably longed to ask your parents, "What was I really like as a child?" your children will some day ask this of you. When you write diaries for your child or children now, instead of searching your memory later on you will hand them a collection of diaries in your own handwriting celebrating their lives from birth.

When to Begin

You can begin these diaries wherever you are in the process of parenting. If you are pregnant with your first child, this is a perfect time to begin. What better place is there to record the drama of pregnancy and childbirth?

But if your child or children are already born, you can begin now at whatever age or ages they are. It's never too late to begin. Start writing to your child today— at age two, at five, at ten. You don't have to try to fill in all the blanks of missed time. Just begin writing, because whatever you save before you forget will be a treasure for your growing child.

If you have already done some diary writing for your children but stopped because you lost momentum and feel as if you have fallen behind, then this book will inspire you to reconnect with the process and will give you many ideas to revive your enthusiasm and interest. What this book will not offer, however, is the opportunity to indulge in any guilt about not having started sooner or written more.

Diary writing nurtures us most deeply when we remove the "shoulds" about when to write and how much to write and encourages us instead to write what we feel like writing when we feel like writing it.

Grandparents, Godparents, and Other Special Caretakers

Parents are not the only ones who can gain and give satisfaction through this form of diary writing. Many children have the benefit of having grandparents who take a profound interest in helping to raise their grandchildren. Sometimes these grandparents have the additional benefit of more free time in their lives in which to keep the diaries. Whether you are aunt, uncle, godparent, or grandparent, if you have the desire to connect more deeply with a special child in your life, you may go through the diary door with special stories and a special point of view that the child's parents may lack.

If you are separated from your special child through absence or distance, these diaries can be a means of creating and maintaining a sense of connection and contact over time and across the miles. Whether you are observing and describing your loved one through phone conversations, letters, or email, the stories you save for this child will very likely be treasured by both your own children and your grandchildren. And, particularly if you are a grandparent or elderly relative, you may have many stories about your own childhood and upbringing that include a wealth of family history and diary portraits of other relatives who are no longer living. You may bring these stories through the diary door to share with your child and trust they will be valued long after you have gone. You may weave your family history stories into the questions and comments your special child shares with you.

If you hear about other people keeping diaries for children and look back many years and wish you had done that for your own, then perhaps you can begin now by keeping these diaries for another young child who has come into your life.

Though this book addresses parents specifically, most of the guidance within it can be applied to the role of grandparents, godparents, stepparents, foster and adoptive parents, and/or other significant nurturers of children.

Write Well by Writing about What You Love

This book is designed to help you begin writing diaries for your children with confidence, enthusiasm, and an open mind. It will help you approach the writing process in the same nurturing way you approach the arrival of a new child. It's important to pay more attention to content—what you put in the diaries—than to style. Your style will develop naturally over time. As your child grows, so will your writing skills if you focus on relaxing and enjoying this time with your child.

Diary writing to your children is a unique writing method that requires passion rather than polish. Remember that you have gone through the *diary* door, not the classroom door. You can leave your "critical English teacher" down the hall, out of the building, far, far away. You have the freedom in diary writing to cast strict rules of grammar and punctuation aside and to embrace freedom of thought and feelings. You are not writing for a grade, you are writing *for* your children *about* your children. You are writing about what you love.

When you write about what you love, you tend to write well. Whether or not you have any writing experience or talent, you may find that as you write to your children you will be astonished at the beauty and clarity of your own prose. If not, you can continue writing anyway because your children want you to, and they are not going to read these diaries at age five, fifteen, or fifty as literary critics, but as your children.

It may take you a while to become accustomed to the process and to develop a style that expresses your unique voice. Your voice and style will respond and develop in relation to your child's age and developmental stage. Your diary writing to your children may be sloppy and sentimental at times. So what? Just as often, it may be creative, inspirational, hilarious, and poignant, because that's the kind of writing that happens when you are writing about what is real and true in your heart, your mind, and your experience.

Why Diaries Are the Perfect Container for Childhood Memories

This room, this attic, this treasure chest, this world behind the diary door where your child is leading you is not a neat or orderly place and sometimes it's not a quiet or peaceful place. It's an unmapped world of frequent interruption, rapid change, exquisite beauty, and remarkable challenge. It is simultaneously a circus and a sanctuary.

Because the diary is, by nature, an unfinished, process-oriented means of expression, it is the perfect container for creative expression during the early childhood years. Distractions and interruptions are part of the reality of daily life with children. No other form of writing that remains unfinished is so sustaining. Letters that are unfinished generally don't get sent; book reports that are unfinished don't receive credit; theses that are interrupted delay the granting of degrees; manuscripts that are unfinished don't get published. But diary entries allow for interruption because they spring from, respond to, and respect the rhythm of real life as it is being lived.

Describing the joy of observing her grandchildren in their spontaneous play with the birdbath in the back yard writer Ellen Gilchrist wrote in her own published journal, *Falling through Space*, about both the allure and the challenge of writing about children:

> I wanted to write about it, but I didn't dare begin. I knew what would happen. The minute I got involved in my work they would sense I had stopped watching them and come running. I stood there thinking about what it would be like to be a young mother trying to write or paint or do anything alone in a house with small children. And yet life without them would be meaningless to me. (p. 36)

Unfinished entries may be frustrating, to both writer and future reader, but they are real and interesting too because they portray the reality of life with children. In fact, they can serve as proof of your availability and responsiveness to your children. Unfinished entries may intrigue rather than frustrate you and your child later on. The diaries are important, but not more important than time with your child. At the same time, the urge to capture the stories your children are spontaneously creating is compelling, and one of the things they want most from you is to *watch them in action* and respond to them. The diaries are a place to do that.

You don't have to be afraid to begin an entry because you fear you won't have time to "finish" writing. In the diaries for your children, the entry is finished when you leave it, not necessarily because you have completed it. You can always pick up where you left off when you have more time, and you may be surprised to find that you had more time than you'd hoped. If you have to suddenly leave off an entry to attend to a child, you can make a quick parenthetical note about what happened before you put the diary down if you have time.

How to Observe, Describe, Reflect, and Respond

By practicing diary writing you will learn about your child, learn about yourself as a parent, and learn to bring out the best in both of you. The four fundamental aspects of writing diary entries that you can begin using are—to **observe**, to **describe**, to **reflect**, and to **respond**.

Observe – Simply watch your child or children at sleep, at play, any time of the day. Write your observations down in the form of description.

Describe – Use your sight, smell, touch, taste, hearing, and intuition, and write down what you see, hear, smell, and feel in words and in a style that feels natural to you. Also, listen and write down your child's exact words, phrases, expressions, questions, and ideas—word for word, when possible.

Reflect – Let your thoughts and feelings surface in regard to whatever issue, theme, action, or story you are exploring. With this type of writing, you will be discovering your intuition and values and reaching for the wise parent within. Reflective writing may often surprise you with unexpected insights you gain as a result of writing the entry or story. You may recognize this as an "aha!" experience, where you are suddenly or gradually aware of greater understanding of what you feel, think, and need as a parent or of what your child may need from you.

Respond – Once you have discovered how you think and feel about a certain aspect of parenting through descriptive and reflective writing, you may begin to formulate a plan for change that you include in a diary entry. Writing about plans for change can be a means of making a commitment to try out a new way of responding to your child or children. Plans written in the diary can be reread, remembered, reviewed, and reevaluated as you continue to write over time. As you begin to write regularly, you will also find many opportunities to respond to your children about things they said or did that you did not think about or notice in the moment they were happening. In the quiet and creative moments of reflection, you may write to your present or future child an answer to a question you had previously ignored or you may find yourself telling a long story inspired by an observation you are recording or a line of dialogue you are quoting. Your responses in the diary will deepen your awareness as a parent and will also deepen your communication with your children.

You may be familiar with these types of writing from your own diary writing over the years. Throughout the rest of this book you can see many examples of using observation combined with descriptive, reflective, and responsive writing specifically applied to diary stories and entries about raising children. Don't try to apply these aspects as a formula to your writing because such an attempt may stifle your creativity and spontaneity. Throughout the book you can find many additional tools for diary writing and can learn creative ways for applying them in your own writing.

The Only Rule

Including the date is the only "rule" you should follow in keeping these diaries. Always write the day, month, and the year. Your children want to know dates and you will, too. The date is your reference point. Include whatever other reference points you want to include, such as the time of day, the day of the week, the place you are writing from, your child's age. Sign the entry, if you wish.

Choosing Your Notebook

This is where you strike a bargain between creativity and practicality. You are creating a family heirloom so you want a notebook that will stand the test of time and repeated handling. But, beyond being sturdy, it needs to be inviting and comfortable to write in, and the more portable it is the more writing you will do in it. Countless types and styles of notebooks are available everywhere these days. You may want to experiment with a few different styles before you decide what works well with your writing style and tastes. For instance, do you prefer writing on lined or blank pages? Do you find large pages intimidating and overwhelming, or do small spaces constrain you? Do you like highly decorative covers, or do you hope to design your own? Is it important to you that all the volumes in the collection match? If so, stock up with plenty from the start. If you've been keeping your own diaries, you may already have a pretty good idea of what works well for you.

For durability, choose a hard cover on both front and back and acid free paper. Beyond those essential ingredients, you may experiment and create. Spiral-bound notebooks open and lay flat, which is a nice feature. Choose a book that makes you want to open its door often. Above all, choose a diary that is portable so that you can carry it with you easily wherever you go.

Motivating Yourself to Write

If you are keeping diaries for your children or if you are thinking about beginning, it may be helpful to ask yourself—Why am I doing this? What do I hope to accomplish from the process? Think about what benefits you are hoping for yourself as well as what you are hoping to give to your children. This book offers you ideas about the potential benefits and rewards for both parents and children. But for you to write consistently and meaningfully to your children you will need to be aware of your own motivations, because the reasons behind your motivation contain your inspiration, and your inspiration is the energy that will drive your pen into the world behind the diary door. Someone in a writing group asked me recently how I stayed motivated to write regularly in the diaries. For me it's simple—I would rather squeeze writing into a place where it doesn't easily fit than face the nagging feeling of loss when a good story is neglected and forgotten.

If you want to explore your own motivation, try Diary Door Opener #3 at the end of Chapter One (if you haven't already done so) to explore the reasons behind your own desire to keep diaries for your children.

Finding or Making the Time to Write

There is no perfect time to fit writing into your busy day. Cultivating the habit of diary writing for your children does not mean that you will necessarily write every day or at the same time every day. What it means is that you will seize the moments that *can* be devoted to writing without taking time away from actually spending time with your children. Many of these moments will be unpredictable—moments squeezed through the cracks of an overly stacked day. If you make a commitment to the idea of keeping the diaries, entries will grow up as daisies often do through cracks in pavement.

How to Make Time for Writing during Busy Days

- When your child is small, put the diary in the diaper bag and carry it with you wherever you go.
- Write in waiting rooms of doctor's offices.
- Write on planes, buses, trains, or anytime you travel with or without your children.
- Write while your child is attending a dance class or is playing a sport.
- If you work outside the home, write on the commuter train to work or during your lunch hour.
- Decide that a story about something remarkable your child did or said will matter more in future years than how clean the kitchen floor was.
- Write while your child is happily playing. Even if she interrupts you, she'll be tickled to know it's all about her!
- Don't fuss about unfinished entries—interruptions are part of the rhythm of daily life with children and part of the process of diary writing.
- Keep yourself motivated by disciplining yourself to write when you feel most inspired rather than forcing yourself to write every day.
- Imagine how you will feel if your child says something you can't bear to forget and you fail to write it down.

Leave the Critic outside the Door

It may be a good idea to avoid rereading until the writing habit is well established unless you find that rereading really helps you along. If rereading makes you feel self-critical and self-conscious, stop and be gentle with yourself. Approaching the writing process in a gentle, patient, realistic way will help you keep your commitment to the process. Your children want you to keep your internal critic out because they will enjoy the diaries more if you give yourself permission to be creative, intimate, and spontaneous. Grammatical and spelling mistakes prove to your child that you're human. Perfectionism isn't necessary for interesting, thoughtful, creative diary writing—but permission is. Give yourself permission to write without worrying about whether your grammar, spelling, or sentence structure is perfect.

There is no need to edit, unless you think you have written something inappropriate. (Even so, give a questionable entry time and reflection before you delete anything.)

Listen to Your Tone of Voice

Just as you leave the critical English teacher who wants to read over your shoulder and red-mark your "errors" outside the door, so do you ask your critical parent voice to stay out of the diary writing. But how do you recognize the critical parent voice? The critical parent is the one who watches over your shoulder as you parent your children and barks criticism at you when you're not doing it "right." The internal critical parent makes you feel so guilty that you're not raising your children *right* that you decide that it's high time to whip your kid into shape so the critical parent will approve. So, you start barking orders and criticism at your kids about how they fail to live up to your expectations. Then you tend to make statements to your children that begin with—"You never," or "You should," or "You always." And when they hear these statements they run in the other direction.

The tone of voice you use in the diary will reflect your parenting style. There's a pretty simple Golden Rule to guide you behind the diary door—don't write to your kids in a way you wouldn't want them to write to you. And when the critical parent urges you to be perfect, gently remind him or her you're just human. Give yourself some time to sort out what expectations you are trying to live up to and whether or not these expectations are realistic or desirable for you and your children. Then work on the parenting issues you feel really matter to you and your kids.

If you want your children to read the stories with pleasure and gratitude, it's essential to be aware of your intentions and motivation to write to them. Stay conscious of the power of your voice and of the tone you use to tell your stories so that they will be appreciated some day. Nothing will be less appealing to your children than picking up the diary you have written only to find themselves being lectured to, criticized, judged, embarrassed, manipulated into feeling guilty, or ridiculed. Which isn't to ignore the fact that most parents at one time or another feel like criticizing, lecturing, judging, and manipulating their children. You don't have to deny these impulses, just put them where they belong—in your own private writing or in conversations with understanding adults, where you can resolve them and direct your most effective parenting toward your children.

When you reread your writing, don't proofread for spelling and grammatical errors that your children won't notice or care about. Reread to make sure your tone is appreciative, self-responsible, sincere, compassionate, and respectful of your child's individuality.

Pick up the Pen

Just make the time to sit down and write—that's the bottom line. You can read this book and get all the ideas in the world, but if you don't open your child's diary and pick up the pen, it will be like having a camera full of unused film. Diarists learn to write in diaries through practice and repetition. Diary writing is exploration. The blank notebook is like any gateway—you must enter to see where it will take you. You can't see the beach if you stand in the parking lot at the edge of the path that leads over the dunes to the beach. To find out whether it's windy, warm, or bug-ridden or crowded with naked bathers—well, these are questions you cannot answer unless you walk up the path, over the sand dune. Pick up the pen. Observe your children. Listen to what they are saying, watch what they are doing. Pay attention to how you are feeling. Start writing.

You do not need to plan entries, although you can make a conscious decision to pay attention to things you think you might like to write about as you go through the day with your child. Even if you are away from your children, even if you are separated from them by divorce or if you are living separately, you can find things to write about each day to your child. Writing to your child during a period of separation or distance can be an important way of maintaining the bond, coping with sadness or guilt, and showing a vital and continued interest in your child's growth and development. Tell your child a story about something you love and appreciate about her or him.

If you have started writing to your children at some point and then stopped, begin again now. Think about why you stopped and write an entry to your child about what you think happened and why you are beginning again.

How to Begin with the Story of a Name

Have you named your child? Have you told your child the story of the history or meaning of the name you chose? You can begin your child's diary with a story of her or his name. Your children want to know why you chose the names you did, and they want to know how their names connect them to their family history, including favorite people and significant events. They also want to know all the names you considered and discarded—all the names they might have had.

Somewhere near the beginning of each of my children's diaries is an entry that tells the story, like the following one, of how, where, when, and why we chose our child's name. Naming stories may also incorporate other themes, such as the story of a longing fulfilled, as this one to my third child does:

To Frances (not yet born), November 11, 1996

As soon as we bought the house . . . a year ago this fall, I conceived of you: my third child. I'm not at all sure how it happened that my life was off-balance. Many forces acted upon me to create the sense of yearning and craving that led us toward you. Perrin getting older, Billie having a baby . . . Perrin and Landon showering so much love and nurturing on your younger cousins . . . exposed to the new babies beginning to envision us having our own . . . me, approaching forty, watching the gap between Perrin and a "new one" grow almost to the point where I felt it would be too great . . . and very much the fact that a new name had sprung full formed into my psyche:

There was a new name to fill out w/ flesh and bones and life because from the moment it came to me I knew I would have this child. **How** *did I know?*

We all began to want you, very much: our first one to be born in New England.

I had named you, and knew you already when we discovered that you had been conceived. . . .

Frances, for Daddy, Helen Donahue for Nana . . . . Oh, Franny. I call you by name. **You** *are here.*

Writing about your child's name can be a beginning entry however old your child is when you start writing. And there may be more than one story about your child's name, because names change over time, and sometimes children grow special nicknames, like this one my son was given by his baby sister:

To Frances (age almost 2), March 28, 1999

. . . Did I tell you your name for Landon, whose name is too much of a challenge for you right now?

"Boy."

You say "Where Boy Go?" when he gets out of the car.

"Hi Boy!"

"Boy on Bus" etc. He likes this very much, the idea of you making up a name just for him . . .

If you keep these diaries over time and if you follow their stories long enough, you will make other entries about their names. What are the names your children play with as they try on fantasy lives? Your child might enjoy seeing herself involved in such creative play later on, as my older daughter does. The period of time when children playfully create alter egos is so brief, I'm glad I captured this story of my daughter's name and identity exploration:

To Perrin (age 5), November 21, 1997

Rushing around, getting breakfast, you are dressed in your green plaid skirt and shirt, purple tights plus green leggings, sitting on the kitchen windowsil, holding your little pink bear.

"I think I'll bring him to school," you say.

"Okay."

"I don't know what to call him . . . he doesn't have a name. . . ."

"How about Pinkie?"

"No ... I don't need to name things anymore ... I'm growing up. Sometimes ... you start to feel older and don't want to do the same things anymore...."

You wait in the cold icy driveway for the bus which never comes. I get in the car to drive you to school. At the car door you stand and looking in at me say:

"I am Magiera today. That is my name. You must call me that all day."

"All right, Magiera, please shut the door and put on your seat belt."

You do so.

"And a man named Kephron is picking me up tonight to go and buy my present for a boy named Landon" (who is sitting in the seat in front of you).

Looking at your face in the rearview mirror, I almost don't recognize you you look so different, this expression, dark eyes wide, mature.

"Landon, school is **boring**." Is that an English accent?

"I don't think so, Perrin, not exactly."

"I am not Perrin," you say in a chipped British voice, "I am a teenager. I am Anastasia. Anastasia is a princess, even though she does not wear a crown."

Your brother, mildly intrigued by this newest Disney creation humors you until it's time to get the heck out of the car, and then, he could care less who you are. He is Landon, the boy who does not want to be late for school.

Eventually, in their process of growing into their own sense of identity, children name themselves. When this happens, these are stories worth paying attention to and stories worth writing. Writing these stories encourages your reflection, and by exploring the story's meaning you may become aware of new boundaries and needs your child is expressing. Writing these subtle stories that your child slips into everyday life can allow you to express the tenderness and respect you feel for the way your child is changing. My son never cared what we called him until fifth grade, and then he found a name that fit. Writing this story helped me to recognize the important developmental shift he was making in claiming a new awareness of himself that was independent from how his father and I referred to him:

To Landon (age 10), November 9, 1998

"Lan"

Well, it's official. Your new name.

Your backpack has been fraying and disintegrating for a few weeks. I bought you one the day I bought your blazer, but you didn't like it. Last week you said you wanted one from LL Bean with a monogram, like lots of people at school.

And you wanted it to have "L-a-n" instead of your initials. This is what Mr. C calls you; has since the first week of school. Guess you like it. Guess it fits. Guess it's official.

I ordered the pack the next day. Why not? Sturdy, well made, easy to purchase, practical....

It was more than I expected, but not too much, because I knew how much you wanted . . . well, needed it. $24.95 plus $5 for the monogram. Black. First I told him all caps on the monogram. Rethought it. Guessed you wanted "Lan."

Found it wrapped in brown paper on the front step this afternoon. Knew you were hoping it would come today, as promised. You had worried as you left for school if I would be home when it came, and I said they'd leave it on the front step if I wasn't, thinking this would reassure you.

"But it will get all cold!"

"I'm sure it will be all right—it'll be in a box."

I unwrapped and admired it, leaving it in its plastic for you to open set at your place at the table for after school.

"Did it come?" [he asked in the car]

"Yes."

We dropped Perrin off at her friends and I asked if you'd come to the supermarket w/me before we went home.

"But I want to see my backpack first."

I managed to talk you into it, and soon enough we were back home where you moved right in.

"It looks small," I worried.

"Oh no. It's big. It will expand. It's plenty big," you said, setting the items that no longer comfortably fit on the table.

Later, Perrin came home after dinner.

"Perrin, have you seen my new backpack?"

Being someone who was not recently in possession of a new backpack, she was unimpressed.

The next chapter looks at diary writing as a rich storytelling medium to share with your child and to express yourself creatively as a parent. But first, try the Diary Door Openers below.

Diary Door Openers

Reminder: Don't forget to include the date at the top of the page!

1. What's in a Name?

   Open the diary, pick up the pen, and write the story of your child's name now including first, last, and middle names. If your child is not born yet, but you've decided on the name, go ahead. Tell your child the story of the history or meaning of the name you chose, including why you chose the name you did and where it came from. Do both parents have the same last name? Does the name connect your child to a person in family history? Does your child have a nickname, and if so, where did it come from? Tell your child about the names you considered and discarded.

2. Three Wishes

   Think for a few moments about what you hope this diary-door-writing process will bring into your life. Begin an entry by dating the page and listing three things you hope to get from the process for yourself. Then, list and describe three things you hope your child will receive, and three things you hope your future grandchildren might appreciate some day from your practice of diary writing for your child now.

3. Watch Me!

   Watch your child engaging in any activity for five minutes. For instance, if your child is not born yet watch and feel him or her kicking in the womb. If your child is a baby, watch him or her sleeping in the crib or drinking milk; or if your child is walking and talking, you might watch him or her playing with a favorite toy in the back yard. Write a one-paragraph description in the diary of what you see, hear, smell, taste, or feel as you watch your child.

Special Note *In Case of Miscarriage*

You may begin a diary for a pregnancy that ends in miscarriage and wonder what to do with the diary you began for a baby who will never be born. This is a very personal decision, and it may take you some time to decide what, if anything, to do with this diary. When you feel ready, one suggestion is to write an entry in which you say goodbye to this pregnancy as if writing to your unborn child. Putting your feelings about this loss on paper will help you to grieve, and sharing this entry with a supportive person may be a good idea. You may decide to bury the diary or to keep it in a special place. One woman I know decided to remove the pages of writing to her unborn child and save them as a keepsake in her own diary. The important thing is to find a ritual that honors your experience and offers closure that suits your needs. Closure with this diary may help you to open the door to a new one for a new child when the time is right.

Chapter 3

Once Upon a Time
Parents as Storytellers,
Children as Stars

You, like every human being, are a storyteller by birthright.
You are born with an endless supply of personal and
universal themes . . . Build a hearth within you . . .
In it your heart's wisdom may ignite and burn.

(Nancy Mellon, *Storytelling & the Art of Imagination*, p. 8)

In the world behind the diary door it is always Once Upon a Time. As parents, we are called on to become storytellers in order to entertain, to educate, and to enlighten our children. Stories of real life with our children provide plenty of dramatic action, conflict, and struggle, as well as opportunities for insight, enlightenment, and problem solving. There are the heroics, and there are the blunders. Yes, it's all there—the epic adventures of everyday life in the roles of parent and child, through the diary door.

Diary writing for children teaches us how to be more conscious of the stories we tell about ourselves, and of the stories we tell *about* our children *to* our children. This writing process offers us a unique way of saving these stories for the present and also for the future by placing them into a book of living history that may endure, for our children and ourselves, like classic literature. Diaries for children have a lasting value because they contain the roots of our children's lives as well as a larger story of family history across generations.

Of course, no one feels more passionately curious and concerned about the development of your children than you do. No one knows them so well or so intimately as you do. You can give them real and true stories to grow on. You can show them how they grow up in a web of relationships. You can give them stories of their own human struggles and triumphs.

Who will tell your children stories if you don't? They will be bombarded by stories their whole lives. Some of those stories you will choose for them, but many of them you will not. You may have very little control over many of the powerful stories that come their way because popular culture has invaded every aspect of our lives. Advertising billboards, radio disk jockeys, television and web-based commercials, movie moguls, and superstar performers will all be happy to tell your children stories about all the things they want them to buy. Advertisers will be very happy to tell your children who they are, what they need and want, where to get it, and how much to spend on it.

Only you can give them stories they can trust that are based on real concern for their welfare as well as on a deep and abiding love. The book of stories you save about who they are, what they do, how they feel, what they accomplish, and what they struggle with can be a book with wisdom that they carry with them into a wider world that's beyond your reach.

In this chapter, we explore the development of plot, character, and theme and other literary devices that spark the story-making process through the diary door.

Developing Your Storyteller Within

We all have a voice that floats up from our hearts through our throats and longs to say, "Let me tell you a story. . . ."

It's time to begin using that voice in your diary writing. You must ask yourself, what do your kids want to know? What do they *need* to know? What do they want you to pay attention to behind the diary door? What do you want to share with them in the diaries? These are the questions you will ask yourself over and over again as your children grow. To answer these questions with intuition, imagination, and insight, you connect with your storyteller within.

You may have grown up in a family or culture that nurtured your natural storytelling skills. Or, you may not have a chance to practice your storytelling art until you become a parent and gain an enthusiastic audience who begs you for stories. Children are always asking, and we are always telling them stories.

It's simple to write stories to your children. As simple as observing your children and describing your thoughts, feelings, and observations in the diary of what the two of you did together that day. As you grow in the role of parent, as your child grows, and as you grow in the role of diarist, your stories to your children will naturally develop in their complexity and depth.

If your parents told or wrote stories about you, think about the ones you treasure and use those as a guideline for saving stories for your children. Or, write the *stories you would have liked* to have been saved for you. You won't choose perfectly. There may be stories in the diary that they dislike at age seventeen but appreciate at forty. Trust that if you observe your children with interest, appreciation, curiosity, and respect, and try to tell the truth in a loving way, the diaries will have lasting value.

Whose Stories Do You Love?

Who is your favorite storyteller? It may be someone in your family, an uncle, a grandmother, a sister, or your spouse. He or she may be living in your neighborhood, or this favorite storyteller might be a teacher you once had, or a personality on television or in the movies, or a writer of children's books. This favorite storyteller of yours may be living or dead, but she or he lives in your imagination and in the stories you have saved in your mind and heart.

Relax now for a moment, sink into your favorite chair, take a walk or a long bath, and think about why this person is your favorite storyteller. Perhaps this storyteller has told you stories about how to live a good life, has given you a new perspective on what it means to be a human being or a new way of thinking about an old problem. One of our favorite family storytellers is my mother-in-law. She has a gift for telling stories about herself with a tone of humility and hilarity that reveals her own foibles in a self-respectful and endearing way. Her stories allow us, as listeners, to laugh at our own shortcomings, and they are often healing and inspirational.

If you lack confidence in your storytelling ability, you can imagine this model storyteller of yours leaning over your shoulder as you write and offering you her or his best tips. Start by trying to emulate this favorite storyteller's style, if you like. *If it helps.* If it makes you uneasy and self-conscious, though, try something else. Introduce this storyteller by writing a portrait in the diary that describes what you like or admire about the way he or she tells a story. Tell one of the favorite stories this person has told you, and tell your child what you like about the story.

Telling stories to your children through the diary door can be as relaxing and spontaneous as telling them at the dinner table or on long ride in the car. It can be as entertaining, as inspiring, and as enlightening as reading great literature. But how do you know where the story begins? How do you recognize the shape of the story?

Beginning, Central Core, and End

Stories have a basic structure: beginning, middle, and end. As the parent—as the diarist—you are like a theatrical director putting the spotlight on some person or action you want to show your audience. The beginning of the story describes on whom or what you are putting the spotlight in your own daily life. Following the action leads you to the core of the story, which is the theme, message, or central concern of the story—the core feelings, thoughts, or problem that involve you and your child. The action leads you *through* the core feelings or conflict and may be resolved in some way.

Sometimes the core of the story will contain a conflict, or sometimes it may simply be an awareness of a certain feeling, an observation, or an appreciation of something about your child. As you see in the following chapters, the core can be as simple as the discovery of a spiritual aspect of a worldly object. It can be a story about your child discovering the moon for the first time. It could be a story about an actual struggle with your child over an issue such as what to wear on the first day of school. Or, it can be a story about your internal struggle to sort out when and how to help your child discover that you are really Santa Clause or the Tooth Fairy.

This conflict, described in the diary, may be resolved or left unresolved, just as problems are often left in fiction and in life. You do not need to neatly wrap up the stories you write in diary entries. They are part of a process, not a finished product. There is room behind the diary door for complexity, paradox, future discovery, and contradiction. The story is finished when it feels finished for the moment, when you have a sense of closure, or when it has to be finished simply because you have run out of time to tell it! The diary stories included in this book give examples of simple and complex diary stories, and of many places in between.

Recognizing Themes

Writing regularly or on a daily basis allows you to notice repetition and development of themes. Consciously and unconsciously as you keep the diaries your writing will be driven and guided by the questions and ideas that are important to you and your child. As the content of the diaries grows and you and your children reread them, these themes will emerge as surely as they do in literature, creating a portrait of what guided you and what you learned as you raised your children. These themes may lead you to harvest a deeper, more symbolic, poetic, or spiritual meaning contained in the stories of growing with your child each day.

Themes are much more likely to reach out and grab your attention as a *result* of your writing than as a planned and deliberate exploration. Themes of everyday life may include such issues as connection versus separation, holding on versus letting go, the pressure to hurry versus the satisfaction of slowing down, teaching versus being willing to be the student, being easily accepted and understood versus struggling to fit in, or learning to be vulnerable versus playing it safe. There are limitless personal and universal themes to explore in your diary writing.

Protagonists and Auxiliaries

Protagonist is a literary term for the central actor in the action of the story, the person whom the story is really about. The protagonist in drama is the star of the show. In novels and short stories the protagonist is the one around whom the action revolves, the main character whose development embodies the theme or message of the story. In psychodrama, the protagonist is the person in the group who offers a personal experience, wish, goal or conflict to explore with the support of the group through spontaneous acting. In storytelling, the protagonist is the hero or heroine who embarks on a quest that leads him or her and the listener to a meaningful personal discovery.

In diaries for children, who's the star of the show? Well, most of all, your child is. What's your role as the parent, the storyteller? You're a narrator, giving shape to the story, reflecting and commenting on it. Sometimes you're the co-protagonist, because you're growing right along with your child. Sometimes you tell stories to your child about other significant people in his or her life who are the protagonists for that particular story. The other players in diary entries are the cast of auxiliaries who may have a significant or peripheral role in the action. They are brothers, sisters, teachers, neighbors, playmates, bullies, grandparents, or strangers in the supermarket—they are the people with whom your children interact in their world.

Building Character

In the diaries, you create portraits of your child in action over time. Your stories aim to bring out the best in him, and give him direction for building character. You tell stories of celebration to reinforce the best in your child's character development. When your child shows integrity, you capture this. When she doesn't, you help her see where she went wrong and point her in the right direction—without criticizing, judging, or blaming. In diary stories, children are the heroes and heroines on their own journeys into adulthood, and you show them that they have the inner resources to face their dragons and to discover and trust their own talents and gifts.

Developing Plot

One characteristic of diaries is that sometimes they read like good fiction, creating thematic tensions and suspense—one never really knows how it will all turn out. Sometimes this happens naturally without any effort on your part. But you may also create a suspenseful story by writing when you and your child are waiting for the outcome of an important event, and then writing again once the outcome is known. Pay attention to how your child seems to feel about the event, how she handled the success or disappointment, then write about what your child or you as parent have learned.

You can tantalize your child with the plot of a story in a variety of ways, even though, ultimately, she may know while reading the entry how it all turned out in the end. Try starting with the end of the story—the successful accomplishment—and then go back and describe the obstacles your child had to overcome to get there.

Using Titles

You can create titles when you know you are going to write an entry around a particular theme or event. Or, after you've written an entry and found that you have done this you can go back to the top of the page and add a title if you like. Titles may add a cohesive quality to the entry, creating a container around an important theme or subject matter. They may add an artistic element and catch you or your child's interest when rereading the diaries later on.

Past, Present, and Future Tense

Any story can be told in the present, past, or future verb tense: "You dance, you danced, you will dance, if you dance. . . ." Tense is a stylistic concern that can be fun to experiment with. Using different tenses to write to your children in the diaries can create different effects. There is no right or wrong way to do this. Writing a story that happened in the distant past as if it is happening in the present can add a feeling of immediacy that draws your child—your reader—into the action and excitement of the moment. Writing in the present tense about the moment as it is happening can help you to tune into your five senses and use them to engage your child more fully with the story you are trying to tell. Recollecting, observing, and describing the past can offer you an opportunity to reflect and to help you and your children gain a greater understanding of the meaning of the story. Writing conditionally about the future allows you to imagine, to project, and to add an intriguing "what if . . ." spin into the story.

Audience and Point of View

Like a fiction writer, you can experiment with writing from a different point of view. Reverse roles with your child by imagining that you are standing in your child's shoes or looking at the world through his or her eyes. Write what you imagine to be your child's point of view about something your child is experiencing. This may be particularly fruitful when writing about infants, who use only body language and sounds to communicate their needs and feelings. As in all literature, point of view defines whose story it is. You can reverse roles with one of your child's favorite possessions to tell the story from its point of view. Just step into the role and speak from "I." For instance, your child might be enchanted by your imaginative portrayal of how his favorite stuffed animal feels about *him*.

Writing Dialogue

The most cherished passages to reread contain your child's own words. Kids spontaneously create the spectacular dialogue that keeps these diaries fresh, funny and fascinating reading for years to come. Children particularly enjoy the contrast of their early innocence and ignorance with the more sophisticated understanding of the ordinary reality they soon learn to take for granted. Capturing quotations of these early, childlike beliefs will delight and fascinate your children as soon as they are old enough to grasp that they were not always as savvy as they are now. Sitting together on the couch reading the diaries before bed, you will belly laugh when you come across amusing dialogues you saved for them.

One of the most gratifying discoveries I have made as I reread the diaries with my children is to come across quotes of things they said when they were *very* young, innocent, and wonderfully, spontaneously imaginative. When my son was four, I became pregnant with my second child, which led to many amusing exchanges among my son, my husband, and myself. Pregnancy is a magical and mystical experience that stimulates the imagination of a child in amusing ways. This exchange was recorded the morning after it occurred while it was still fresh in my mind. I first read it aloud after my daughter (the one in the womb at the time) was old enough to appreciate it and laugh about it, too:

To Landon (age 4), October 10, 1991

Last night I came home from the office [where I had been seeing psychotherapy clients in my private practice] after Daddy had put you to bed, but you were very talkative so we visited for some time. You kissed the new baby [through my belly] and tried to get "her" to kick for you by jostling my belly.

"I think she's sleeping, Land."

"Are **you** sleeping too, Mommy?"

"No!" I laughed.

"Maybe she's seeing clients."

"What? How could she be doing that?"

"She's seeing baby clients in your tummy," you explained.

"My goodness, how did they ever get in there?"

"They just did."

The secret to capturing dialogue or quoting your child for the diary is simply to pay attention and listen very carefully, making a mental note that you want to preserve what your child is saying for the diary. Visualize yourself writing it down, and make the entry as soon as you can within the next twenty-four hours while it is still fresh. Placing the dialogue or the quote in the context of what was happening at the time by including a variety of descriptive details will help you remember it clearly. If you lose the actual words, don't attempt to write it as a dialogue, but paraphrase to capture the essence of it. If you can, jot down some notes after your child has spoken, being careful to avoid being obvious. If your child knows you are writing down what she says, she may become self-conscious and shut up or start performing, all of which will spoil the natural, spontaneous effect you hope to achieve.

You cannot save enough of these amusing anecdotes to satisfy your children's— and your own—craving for them later on. Keep the diary and pen handy. Use them.

Playing the Role of Reporter

As you keep the diaries, you may want to try observing your child's activities from the role of the reporter—writing as if you are an arts, news, or sports reporter.

When your child begins playing team sports, you will be in spectator seats of ballparks, soccer fields, skating arenas, and every other place sports are played. This is the perfect time to bring along the diary and write to your child. Writing up the game *as it is* happening, with the outcome still unknown, and focusing on your child's involvement can be an exciting and fun record for your child. Also, it can help you cope with your normal parental anxiety about your child's performance. The diary writing can help you relax and pay attention to what's really important to you and your child.

You can write a feature story about your child, including:

- How your child seems to feel about the sport—passionate or indifferent?
- Who her friends and rivals are on the team.
- The coach's style, including any positive things he or she says about your child.
- The positive things other parents or kids say about your child.
- What your child is accomplishing easily and what your child is struggling with.
- Who your child reminds you of—perhaps a family member or a celebrity who played the sport.
- How he plays—his style.

Inevitably, as you watch your child develop the physical and emotional skills necessary to participate in individual or team sports, you will find your own parallel process of emotional development occurring. Many issues from your own childhood sports days are likely to remind you of your own successes or struggles and concerns. Whether you were the star soccer player or you sat on the sidelines and watched your brothers play (because only the boys in the family were supported to play sports, perhaps), this can be a wonderful time to share with your child some of what you learned about yourself in the sports arena over the years.

The competitive playing field is a microcosm of our world today. It's a place where we are chosen or not chosen, stretch ourselves and soar or fall flat on our faces, encounter our rivals with assertiveness or passivity, live up to our own or other's expectations or fall short, stay committed or drop out. And it's the perfect place to discover and reflect on life's lessons for any age.

It can be hard to watch your children trying to learn something new, particularly when it involves the additional risk of trying on these new skills in front of a group, some of whom are rivals or authority figures, like coaches, and countless other parents. Standing on the sidelines, your own unresolved vulnerabilities rise to the surface and need a healthy outlet. For your kids, participating in sports is often not a comfortable way to stretch themselves. The diary is the perfect place to show your support and to assure them that *at least you* are watching them with compassion, concern, appreciation, respect, and sensitivity.

The Season of Stretching

When you approach your child's activities as *story*, you will find yourself paying attention to the natural development of plot, theme, character, conflict, and resolution that can potentially elevate what occurs in ordinary, everyday life to the realm of meaning-making for both you and your child.

I wrote the following diary entry to my son during his baseball game one Saturday morning when I had the unusual experience of getting to watch his game without any siblings present—just me sitting on the grass with the diary. I did not open the diary intending to write a story exploring the theme of the anxiety of performing in a new role. But since my son's anxiety about striking out had been mounting, I found myself feeling anxious for him over the last few games, and I found that writing in the diary provided both an outlet and a container for my feelings. Certainly, talking to other parents who are watching the game is also an appropriate outlet. Conversations with other parents provide much needed support, encouragement and opportunity to vent, but when they are over they may evaporate into thin air. Sharing through storytelling in the diary leads you into unexplored territory, where you may find important insights that are preserved for both you and your child.

In most diary entries, you have no idea what you will discover about your children or yourself until you begin to write. You can count on being surprised with many discoveries as you write to your children. For instance, when I picked up the pen and put the spotlight on my son's baseball game I discovered myself smack in the middle of a parallel growth process, and I realized that my anxiety had a lot more to do with whether or not *he* would get a base hit. This is an entry where both child and mother are the protagonists. When I observed, described, and reflected on *his* anxiety, I encountered my own. Writing the entry helped me get to the core of an issue, achieve perspective and understanding that related to the plot of his own life, and gain some resolution to my own anxiety. This entry is written in the present tense, as the action of the game is unfolding:

To Landon (age 10), June 14, 1997

A real summer day, warm enough for sleeveless even before we get here to watch the game, and now a 4th of July type of warm, delicious breeze blowing across my bare legs.

Striking out—the tough lesson of the season for you. I talk to the other mothers of third-grade Minor Leaguers, and I think that's the theme. I'm not sure you can see how much you have grown from this season; it's so tempting to measure growth by success in its most obvious form—base hits, runs home, balls caught and thrown w/precision. And you have achieved some of this, here and there, a little bit from time to time.

But I know you can't measure the growth of this season that way, because the growth is in the misses, the growth is in the **striking out**, the attempts to hit, the repeated **attempts** to hit the ball, and the long way back to the bench to watch the next batter up.

I know this, because it's just where I am with my writing. This is the season of my first writing year in the freelance minor leagues. Some hits, some misses. But my process w/ the Quarry piece defines the experience. I began writing it exactly two years ago; read it to everyone at Dad's surprise birthday. Made countless revisions. Read it to my writer's group, made countless more. Submitted it, a year ago . . . she sent it immediately back:

"A nice read, but not right for **The Mother's Voice**."

Strike out.

So, I re-wrote and revised some more. Wrote another cover letter, and mailed it....

Almost immediately, it came home to my P.O. Box. The editor, like your constantly encouraging coach, had scrawled in red ink at the bottom of my cover letter:

"Good luck!"

Good luck? What did **that** mean?

Strike two.

. . . I stuffed the piece back into its folder and filed it for the long fall and winter, and suspected it would die a quiet & peaceful death there.

I'm not sure what made me pull it out of the file yesterday, but I sense it has become something of an inevitable summer ritual to swing at it. I spent a few hours revising it yet more. . . .

. . . It will be ready for the mailbox Monday.

*So, this is what I mean about the season of stretching, the season of strikeouts. I know I can't learn from the Quarry piece unless **I send it out**. It is dead, sitting in the file doing nothing. But it's **not** dead if [they] shoot it down, do you see? It lives in the mailbox, going or coming back, it lives in motion, it lives in the swing, it lives if I keep working on it, whether it's a home run or not. Because I'm facing failure, and I'm trying.*

What amazes me about you this season is that you haven't given up, and you haven't overreacted. One of the coaches sons—a 4th grader struck out last week and left the game to sulk behind the dugout, and his mother was unable to coax him back into the game at all.

And you've made some brilliant walks that have led to some runs completed. The whole team knows how well you can hit, because you proved it in your second game w/two base hits.

You've really overcome a lot of emotions that could have de-railed you this season, and I suspect that's what's most important—learning how to manage the feelings through the learning process of a new role. . . .

Wait—you're up! Number 5! What's going through your head? Your heart? Two and 0, one strike . . . .

"Take your base!" [you walk to first] No outs. A runner in front of you, you must move. In position, you're ready . . . you're going! You're there—2nd base stolen. No one on 1st, you don't have to run, you stay put, wisely, but the third base runner is off, out, and now a long drive past second, you're off, touching third, you speed toward home,

You're there. You see? You're there. You're home safe.

Diary Entries versus Diary Stories

Does every diary entry have to be written as a story? No, not all diary entries will be stories. You may include simple observations, and slice-of-life moments where you are capturing your child's or your impressions of a particular moment. You are free to include fragments of stories. For instance, you may take a vacation with your child and include only your impressions of watching her take her first plane ride rather than the whole story of the vacation. Beware of your expectations when you are keeping diaries for your children. If you think you can only write about the vacation if you include every detail of every day, you will overwhelm yourself and quickly lose your motivation to write.

Writing a diary entry does not mean you must sit down and retell everything that happened in a single day. If you find yourself at a loss for what to write in your child's diary on a given day, you can write a brief, spontaneous portrait or a description of a loved one. This may not be a whole story of a person's life, but it's a valuable *piece* of description or reflection on your part that fits into your child's life-history, just as character descriptions in novels are a basic element of the whole story.

Perhaps there is a single impression you want to save from the day or the week, such as when your son, who has always struggled with shyness, shares his last cookie with a new friend in the playground. An exchange of a few lines of dialogue never to be uttered in the same way again is a diary entry that may have a long life if it captures something funny, charmingly inexplicable, or precocious that your child said. If, when you sit down to write in the diary, you are not feeling particularly energetic or stimulated, you can report on a week or a month of gains your child has made in the form of a list. This is the unique freedom that diary writing offers through its form. Diaries make room for all of our moods by offering a method or a tool that will allow us to capture something worth saving for our children later on, without restraining our spontaneity and creative storytelling when it is available to us.

So, let's say that at the end of a long and exhausting parenting day you pick up your child's diary and find that the *only* sentence you have the energy or motivation to write is this (fictional) entry:

February 19, 1999

> Today you cried hysterically when the refrigerator repairman came to fix the fridge and the only thing I could find to settle you down was a pint of melted chocolate ice cream even though it ruined the outfit I had dressed you in for your two-year-old photo portrait.

This brief impression from the day may not tell an insightful or inspirational story, or uplift you or your child by discovering something important about the great themes of life. But it certainly leaves an impression, and it keeps you connected to the writing process even when you're too tired to go another step *for today*. In writing diaries for your children, there is room for both the routine and the spectacular and everywhere in between. The key is to sit down even when you are tired or bored, and write *something*.

Make Your Own Home on the Frontier

Diary entries consist of a variety of styles and content limited only by your own exploration. You will discover as you keep your own diaries a whole world of possibilities that has not been captured in this book, because only *you* can find it by writing yourself, by growing with your children, by writing your own stories, rereading them with your children, and continuing to write. If you are a single or divorced parent, your stories will reflect these challenges to your parenting. If you are raising a child with a significant physical challenge or illness, these themes may play a role in the diary. You have an ethnicity, a spirituality, a family history, family values, and family challenges that are uniquely your own. You have a wealth of perspective to share in your own stories that cannot be revealed in the one family's diary history included in this book.

What you will find in this book are entries that flash pictures, draw a map, and tell stories about one family growing together through the diary door. They are small footsteps on the edge of a frontier. Use what you like, leave the rest, find your own world through the diary door. Make yourself at home.

The next chapter looks at the importance of writing birth stories for children, but first, try some of these Diary Door Openers.

 **Diary Door Openers**

1. Make the Laughs Last
   If your child is speaking already, quote something funny or unique that she or he said today. For instance, did your child ask you an intriguing or funny question? Describe the context in which your child was speaking, and add your own comments if you like.

2. Playing Reporter
   Take the role of reporter at your child's sports game, class, or activity and respond to the prompts on page 46 in a diary entry to your child. If you choose, you can add your own reflections about what this reminds you of in your own childhood memories or something that is currently happening in your own life that seems to parallel or mirror your child's experience.

3. The Plot Thickens

   Think about something your child is experiencing that is not yet complete. Even though you are as of yet unaware of the outcome, describe in detail or list the series of events that have led up to this point in time. What do you and your child hope or expect will happen?

4. Favorite Storyteller

   Who do you think tells great stories and why? Write a portrait of this person for your child and include one of the stories she or he tells, particularly one that seems relevant to your child's life. Is there a designated storyteller in your family or circle of friends? Does this person tend to tell stories orally or in writing? What have you learned about yourself as a storyteller over the years? What special skills or attributes do you bring to the storyteller's role? Which ones would you like to work more on developing?

5. Making Friends

   Observe your child making a new friend. Describe the verbal and nonverbal cues they give each other. Do you have a sense of where the friendship might be leading or what it might offer your child?

6. Role Reversal

   Write to your child from the point of view of your child's favorite stuffed animal and describe your feelings about being connected to and loved by him or her.

Chapter 4

In the Beginning
Writing Creation Stories for Kids

The stories we tell about ourselves accumulate into a
sense of self, an identity, the most personal of mythologies.

(Jo Salas, *Improvising Real Life*, p. 21)

The first heroic quest for any child is the process of being born. Whatever the specific details are, whatever challenges we face or blessings we receive, this is our first, big story. Have you been told your birth story? If so, perhaps this is a story of celebration that parents or grandparents tell you again and again to reassure you of the special place you have claimed in the family. Perhaps it is a story that lets you know how your birth enriched the lives of your loved ones in wonderful ways.

Perhaps you don't know your birth story because no one ever told you about the day you came into the world. Even if you grew up with one or both of your natural parents who were there when you were born, you may not know your birth story. Adopted children who grow up and spend years seeking information about their birth parents have enlightened all of us about the fundamental human need we have to know our origins and our ancestry, and to have an awareness about what the beginning of our lives was like. We need to feel wanted and welcomed into the world by our mothers and fathers. If your birth story remains shrouded in mystery—for whatever reason—you may still long for a feeling of connection with your roots.

Has either of your parents ever told you the story of when, how, and where you came into this world? Have you ever longed to ask your parents—*Where did I come from? Where was I born?* Do you know whether you were you born in a hospital or at home? Was your father there as well as your mother? Were you born unexpectedly and easily, or after prolonged labor? Who was the midwife or doctor? How much did you weigh, what time you were born, who was president, what was the weather? What were the complications and challenges as well as moments of hilarity and surprise? I recorded in detail my daughter Perri's birth story three weeks after she was born. Rereading this entry, I realized that many of my observations had been long forgotten, so discovering details in this excerpt years later makes me laugh and feel grateful that I took the time to write them down:

To Perrin (age 3 weeks), April 10, 1992

. . . *Walking into the waiting room of the maternity ward, I saw the back of a woman in bare feet, a baggy plain robe, and she was slightly hunched over and looked quite haggard and I thought for a moment, where the hell am I that they've got this old lady hanging out looking homeless, lost and miserable and as we walked through the room, I saw a man sleeping on the waiting room couch and the woman's face was actually young, and I got it in a split second that scared the hell out of me:*

This is no bag lady; this is labor.

I was afraid that's where I was headed, too. . . .

Your children—age five, ten, twenty-five, or fifty—want to know their birth stories, too. It's important to their sense of self-esteem and identity to know *why* and *how* they came into being, to know that they were wanted, and to know *how* they were welcomed into the world. Your description of the Big Event and your memories, if they are preserved, may become the stuff of legends that nurture your children as they grow. I never would have remembered this entrancing part of Perri's birth story if I hadn't written it down when it was fresh. I did not then know that she would grow into a young girl who would find delight and significance in the idea that fairies attended her birth:

To Perrin (age 3 weeks), April 10, 1992

. . . *I slept fitfully most of the night, watching the clock, waking every 15-20 mins, feeling the mild, but quite noticeable contractions, wondering when they would prove definitive. I concentrated on **resting**, saving my strength. I dreamt at times. At one point I dreamt that two teenage fairies were so excited about this birth that they "took over" dealing w/ the contractions so that I could get some sleep. (I did!)*

Stories about their conception and birth may help your children to grow up feeling whole and connected to their roots, and perhaps to some of the best parts of themselves.

Fostering Self-Esteem

Writing your child's birth story is a rewarding way of honoring your child by shining a spotlight on your child's entrance into the world. This story may lay a foundation for your child feeling cared for and attended to in life. It's difficult to imagine a child who would be uninterested in the dramatic retelling of her birth. All that action and attention focused so completely on her! In a birth story, your child gets to be at the center of the universe with you, as my daughter was with my husband and me on the way to her birth:

To Perrin (age 3 weeks), April 10, 1992

[on the way to the hospital] . . . I insisted your Dad, who always looks his best— to change his ratty, holey sweatshirt—how dare he come to your birth in a crummy sweatshirt!

It was warm & dark and silent on the street. No one in the world but you and me and Dad. . . .

Peak-of-life moments are fascinating for all those involved in them, and birth stories can be fun to write. They so conveniently contain all the elements of good drama—action and adventure, sympathetic characters involved in noble pursuits, pain, conflict, struggle, obstacles to be overcome, catharsis, comedy, heroic figures, and often, though of course not always, happy endings. Even the tragic moments may be worth recording for loved ones, and retelling them can have a profoundly healing effect. You don't write a child's birth story to make it seem like a perfect, predictable, neat, and orderly event, because all births have obstacles, complications, and unexpected challenges. You write to show your child how you overcame the obstacles and grew from the struggle while attending to his needs in all the ways that you could.

In writing a birth story, you may be thinking about the future and imagining your child about to become a parent. Perhaps you are hoping your child will gain wisdom, courage, and confidence from your shared experience. But in writing your child's birth story, you are also thinking about the past and your own birth story. If you know your birth story, you may be thinking about why you cherish it and following the clues to know what to include in your child's birth story. If you don't know your birth story, you are thinking about what was missing for you that you can now offer to your child. You write the kind of story that would have helped you to feel welcomed into the world.

Conception and Pregnancy Stories

One place to meet your child in the diary is at the beginning of your child's life while you are pregnant. If you write in the diary to your child while you are pregnant, you may find yourself, as I did, writing a story about discovering the pregnancy:

To Landon (5 days before birth), November 29, 1987

. . . As I began writing tonight, I'm remembering that night in early March, as I drove up Rt. 495 from work—late—and in a sudden, joyful, intuitive moment, I knew I was pregnant with you. I missed my exit! And the next day the test was even unnecessary proof. I knew you were there. . . . I wanted you to have this book as a record of our love for you, and I'm writing tonight to set down for eternity that we love you so much and you are not yet here. And I'm writing to wish you a safe, calm and joyful delivery into this world where you will be welcomed with so much love—all your grandparents and great grandparents and aunts, uncles, cousins. People have been calling, impatiently for weeks to find out if you are here yet!

As shown in the previous and following stories, writing my children's conception stories was intuitively linked with my desire to share the reasons I was keeping the diaries, as if my children could not be brought fully to life until I had prepared a place for their *stories*:

To Frances (7 months before birth), September 9, 1996

. . . Your sister was with me, about two weeks ago, when I bought this journal for you. In the car, leaving, I mentioned it to her . . .

"I just bought a journal for the new baby," I said.

"But the new baby can't write yet!" she exclaimed. . . .

*I want to know as soon as possible if you are a son or daughter. . . . Some time after I bought this journal and I was writing about having you in my own, I realized how much I want to bond with who you are **before** you are born, and that it's hard for me to get to know you w/o knowing this fundamental core of your identity—your gender. . . .*

One of the main—certainly not the only—reasons I have kept journals for all of you (three now!) before birth is so that I can begin, well, to deepen the process of communication and intimacy, to build a solid relationship before you are born. And it's difficult for me to imagine sustaining the communication w/such a large question mark as my audience. Son or daughter is so much more intimate and concrete than "child." Don't you think?

You know I began planning you almost exactly a year ago? I told your Dad I was sure I wanted to try for a third, and he agreed; on my birthday he agreed. . . . It was a surprise—a happy surprise to realize in early August, that I got pregnant w/you in mid-to-late June! Almost exactly to the date when, five years earlier, I got pregnant with Perrin. . . .

Writing as a Tool for Delivery Warm-up and Preparation

In telling a birth story there is your warming-up process to attend to with all the ramblings, reflections, and digressions that surface as part of your preparation for the Big Event. There is the anticipation to celebrate and the anxiety to calm. There are the expectations, both positive and negative, that accompany you and your child on the journey. Writing to your child before giving birth, for either a father or a mother, can be a way of centering yourself and emotionally preparing for the challenge ahead. Walking, and then writing about my walks in my late pregnancy with my daughter Frances, was a way of relaxing, grounding myself, and creating sensory experiences that calmed and soothed us both in preparation for the delivery:

To Frances (2 months before birth), February 14, 1997

*In a rush, I return home from driving P & L to school to have time for **our** walk. It is snowing, hard, but pleasantly. We get Emma [the dog] and set off up Brush Hill. We enter the woods at Brush Hill after the red cape. There is a dust of snow over icy patches; I'm careful not to fall. It is the silent kind of snow that isn't really silent at all—it brushes against things. But it is silencing in the sense that it is a gently focusing sound—shutting out all others.*

I like these walks alone with you. It is one of my rare quiet moments, like this, when I can give you my undivided, sustained attention; I can think about what condition we are in together, I can think about the changes to come.

It is grey and lovely and wet in the woods. The snow is stuffing the pockets of the bushes and trees. The stream gurgles around the icy rocks.

You are coming soon. . . .

In preparation, there are changes in the family to anticipate and there may be needs and wishes of siblings to manage in this transition. Diary writing gives you a chance to preserve the wonder and delight of siblings who are experiencing the pregnancy also, in its suspenseful, tense, or gratifying moments. Sibling relationships begin in pregnancy, and moments of introduction may be honored in the diary writing, as this one is between sisters:

To Frances (2 months before birth), February 14, 1997

. . . For the last two or three nights I have read to your brother and sister in my bed, well, to all three of you, really, because it's a very active time of day for you. You are wide awake, one of the crowd. You become, for some time, much more interesting than the book. I bare my belly for them, and they fight over you, whose hand gets to go where. Perrin gets lucky. For months I have been guiding her hand to your kicks, your movements, and she has always waited patiently where I've placed her hand, but failed to feel you. Partly, it's that she doesn't know what to expect, but also, she gets distracted easily. So, it has become a great frustration.

*Until, the other night. You moved **very** distinctively for her. She pulled back her hand in shocked, giddy joy!*

"I felt it!" She squealed. "I felt it!" We laughed and laughed. And then she did it again, and you touched her, and she squealed in delight again. In those moments, you were born for her. . . .

Writing as a warm-up to birth can be a way of tuning in to your inner wisdom about how to nurture you and your child through the process. It can be a way of clarifying what you need and what's important. It is an opportunity to say to yourself and your child a few, final words from this stage of your relationship that is about to change rapidly and irrevocably. Birth is a rite of passage for parent and child, and writing from the threshold of change can give you a chance to say goodbye to the past and welcome the future:

To Perrin (1 day before birth), March 13, 1992

I'm hoping this is my last day of wearing my white baggy cotton pants and Black & White maternity top that Grammy bought for me last summer.

Landon was a little grumpy this morning; overtired. So, when I asked him if he wanted his sister born tomorrow he said,

"No. In one week."

That's kind of how I was feeling this morning when I woke up, and so Daddy and I had a long talk, which helped. You know, Perry, every single day of my life, I thank God for bringing me together with your Dad. . . .

So, I awoke this morning feeling nervous, distressed, ambivalent, discouraged, guilty ... all about this induction, but talking to your Dad, getting his support really helped get me back on track and helped me turn my focus back around to the joy.

"I think we can go in tomorrow and really just have fun having this baby," he said. And he is right. It will be fun and full of joy....

Anyway, your Dad, for a time, felt we'd be fine with just one child, but he knew how important it was to me, so he always kept an open mind, but asked for time, and asked me to keep mine open to the possibility of having just one. We knew that we would only do it if we could both have our whole heart and soul in it. So, we waited....

I believe it was some time in February, one year ago, that Frank came into the kitchen one evening where I was cooking, and, out of the blue said:

"Well, I'm ready to commit to having a second child."

And that's where you began, or, rather, the plan for you began....

We had a nice, romantic lunch at Bentley's a little while ago. A time for us to connect and prepare for tomorrow....

Safe, happy journey Perry. I have loved having you be part of me. Tomorrow, I will love the first stage of a life-long process of letting you go.

God bless you, my dear.

Writing Birth Stories—Welcome to the World

Writing a birth story in your child's diary serves to welcome your child into the world and gives you a chance to describe the world that you have brought your child into. Writing a birth story gives you a chance to share any details that you hope to preserve for yourself and your child about this fascinating, once-in-a-lifetime event.

There is no right or wrong way to write a birth story to your child, and there is no right or wrong time to write it. You write it when you have the opportunity and the inclination. You may also write it in many different ways and styles over your child's lifetime. Even if your child is five, ten, or twenty years old, she or he may still want to have this story from you. It's never too late to tell your child his or her birth story. You may not remember everything, but what you have lost in details you may have gained in perspective.

Birth is such a profoundly life-altering event for both parent and child that it may be difficult to have the time or energy when it is recent to find a way to write at length and coherently about it. My birth stories to my children vary greatly in length, style, details, and how soon after the birth that they were written. They don't conform to a pattern or formula that dictates what to put in and what to leave out. They express a message of love and gratitude to have them in my life that affirms my desire, and the desire of significant others, to welcome them into my life, the family, and the wider world, as this simple birth story for my son does:

To Landon (1 day old), December 3, 1987

*Hello Landon. Welcome! You are a beautiful baby, and I wish you could have seen your Dad's joyful face when you were born. We're **so** happy to have you here, safe and healthy and happy. And we're delighted to discover that you are a boy.*

*Your grandma and grampa Dummar waited here all night for you to be born. Daddy and I came into the hospital on Tuesday around 3:00 pm. (the day **after** you were induced) and you were born at 7:15 a.m. I'm afraid it was a rough journey for you after all, but sweetie, you're hanging [in] just fine. After your Dad brought you to the nursery, your Gram and grampa just stood in the window, looking at you, and crying and crying, for they were so happy to see you, safe and sound. I think they both wanted a boy this time!*

My Mom, your grandma Burke, arrived last night and, of course, she fell in love with you too. She's going to stay and help me take care of you for a few days. All my family—my Dad & Dusty, Karen, Jo, Bob wish they could be here to see you too, but they will meet you in a few weeks when we go North for Christmas.

You have spent quite a bit of time with me today, eating and sleeping, hardly crying a bit, and I just napped along side of you, jumping (a bit nervously) every time you coughed or sneezed. I love you so much. Thank you for coming!

Daddy and Gram B are coming soon, and I know the first thing Dad will want is to hold you in his arms.

I love you, sweetie

Writing your child's birth story in the diary is just the beginning. The next chapter shows you how to make diary entries of everyday life. You may want to try Diary Door Opener #1 on writing your child's birth story before you move on. For adoptive parents who may not be present at the birth, Diary Door Opener #2 helps you to write an adoption reception story.

Diary Door Openers

1. Writing Your Child's Birth Story

   Have you written your child's birth story? If not, you can open your child's diary and do it now. You may have been too busy to do so just after the birth; but that doesn't matter, this tale can be told any time. You don't have to remember every detail. The process of writing will revive your memory.

   One way to approach a specific entry you want to make in the diary around a particular theme such as a birth story is to sit quietly for a few moments and relive in your memory the events from your own point of view—as mother or father.

   Fathers—whatever role you took in the delivery, you have a unique perspective on your child's birth, you play a valuable role in the birth of a child, and you have a powerful story to pass onto your children. What was it like being a participant/witness? In your role as observer, you are less preoccupied with physically managing labor and delivery and therefore may have more opportunity to observe a larger picture of the event. Perhaps you saw or felt things that remain a mystery or are unknown to your child's mother. You can describe for your child the ways you were directly involved and the feelings you had.

   As mother or father, spend some time thinking about questions such as these: Where were you when labor started? What were you doing, thinking, feeling? Were you ready? What had the wait been like? Did you go to the hospital? How did you get there? Was it a home birth? What was the time of day? The weather? Where were other members of the family? Did you call anyone? Who?

   Pay particular attention to the potentially comic details. Was all this new for you, or had you been through it before? What were your hopes and fears? What were you wearing? Who were the doctor/midwife/nurses? Was anything missing? Was it a false start? Mothers—what did giving birth feel like?

   You may want to include details such as a description of what were the medical interventions—anesthesia? Were you expecting a boy or a girl? What was the birthing room like? How long did labor last? What was it like to see and hold your child for the first time? Was the child nursed or bottle-fed? (Your child may be interested in how and why you made this choice.) How long did you stay in the hospital, and who came to visit, bringing what? Then, of course, there is the homecoming. What was it like leaving the hospital and arriving home?

When you're ready, date the entry at the top of the page and start writing directly to your child as if he or she will someday be reading this story. Use as much detail as possible in your description. Just let it flow from your heart. You might want to leave yourself some time for reflection after writing the bulk of the entry. For instance, is there anything you would change about the birth if you could? Why? What would you want your child to know about giving birth if she or he becomes a parent some day?

You may not be able to write everything you want to in one entry, and that's okay. Write as much as you have the time and energy for and know that you can continue later.

2. Writing Adoption Reception Stories
    Although it may never fulfill your child's need for a birth story if your child is adopted, there is a story to tell about the process of your decision to adopt, the application process, and your first meeting. There is a reception story for your child to treasure about when you brought your child home for the first time. You can include a variety of details when writing your story, such as where you were when you got the call about this special child who would become your own. What was the journey to receive your child like? What do you know about your child's birth parents or life before the adoption? Were you present at the birth? Did you make a journey to another country to meet your child? Who welcomed your child into the family and how?

    Telling your child a story like this in the diary will help your child feel at home in his or her new family and will allow you to preserve your memories of a special event. Remember that it's not just parents who can write diary stories for children. My sister, who accompanied my other sister on her trip to Korea to adopt her son, actually kept the diary of the trip and described the first meeting between mother and son.

    Perhaps you have access to a birth story or an account that is written by your child's birth mother or father (or you write the account that was told or passed along to you). Your child may very much appreciate having access to that story in the diary as well.

Chapter 5

The Wisdom of Children
Capturing the Beauty, Mystery,
and Meaning of Everyday Life

. . . It goes so fast. We don't have time to look at one another. . . .
I didn't realize. So all that was going on and we never noticed.
Take me back—up the hill—to my grave.
But first: Wait! One more look.

(Thornton Wilder, *Our Town*, p. 108)

Emily, the protagonist in Thornton Wilder's 1938 play *Our Town*, about domestic life in a small town in New Hampshire, captures in her after-life realizations the essence of a primary motivation behind diary writing. As Emily grows in the play from her role as daughter and young girl, to girlfriend, wife, mother, and spirit after her death during childbirth, she makes a painful discovery about how agonizingly short life is.

Looking back at her life on Earth from her new perspective among "the Dead," she teaches us to *pay attention* to the beauty, the pleasure, and the meaning in the mundane experiences of everyday life. Asking to return for one last look at her life on Earth, she chooses to go back and relive an ordinary day, where she watches herself experiencing her twelfth birthday. As she sees her mother preparing breakfast for her younger self while she receives a birthday gifts from her father and the boy next door she will some day marry, Emily, as spirit, realizes how blind human beings can be to the simple pleasures of ordinary family life:

> . . . Goodbye, good-by, world. Good-by, Grover's Corners . . . Mama
> and Papa. Goodbye to clocks ticking . . . and Mama's sunflowers. And food

and coffee. And new-ironed dresses and hot baths . . . and sleeping and waking up. Oh, earth, you're too wonderful for anybody to realize you. . . . (Thornton Wilder, *Our Town*, p. 108)

When Emily then asks the Stage Manager, who is the narrator, "Do any human beings ever realize life while they live it?—every, every minute?" he answers, "The saints and poets, maybe."

Saints, poets, and diarists, maybe. Diarists *try to*. Parents who keep diaries for their children are trying to realize life while they live it. Diaries for children pay attention to clocks ticking and to Mama's sunflowers and to sleeping and waking up.

Embrace the Enchantment of Daily Life

You don't have to be a parent for long before you are shocked by how quickly infants become kindergartners, and kindergartners become college students. Diary writing helps us slow down and appreciate every moment we have with our children. Children naturally approach life at a slower pace then we adults do, and if we follow them they teach us to pay attention to the beautiful and simple things in life. Some days over the course of a childhood contain momentous events or long-awaited accomplishments that you want to save in the diaries. But the diaries also allow you to find meaning and make magic out of the mundane. Diary writing to your children helps you grow young again and stay young. Savoring stories in the diary slows the passage of time.

Your child's innocence, amazement, ability to be aware of the moment, and sense of discovery can be inspirational. If you listen carefully, observe, and write about it, each of you can continue to gain pleasure and inspiration for many years to come. After children learn to speak, you will find that they often speak poetically—inventively or ingeniously or beautifully—about everyday events and occurrences that you have grown accustomed to. If in growing up you have lost touch with your ability to be enchanted by the world, your child will remind you how easy it is. In their innocence, children reach for the impossible, and they want to take you with them. Listen to your child, and when your child speaks imaginatively or poetically, record it:

To Landon (age 2), March 12, 1990

Putting you to sleep tonight, you reluctant as **always**, *sitting on my lap in the rocker, chatting, wide awake and lightheartedly rebellious against the days end, questioning:*

"Mommy, where's the dogs [that live next door]?"

"Sleeping."

"Where's the moon?"
"Outside."
"Where's the sun?"
"Sleeping."
"Where's the stars?"
"In the sky."
"I want to touch them."
"I would like that too."
"I take Mommy's hand. . . ."

It's amazingly easy to forget the charming beliefs your children create about where babies come from. These fascinating ideas, however much they are appreciated in the moment they are uttered, are in danger of being forgotten quickly by you both as children learn the "facts of life." And yet, these ideas may contain grains of truth, or at least a poetic outlook about sexuality that is worth preservation. My son shared these ideas despite the fact that he had been given many of the facts about where babies come from the year before during the pregnancy and birth of his sister:

To Landon (age 6), February 5, 1994

Tonight, after Burger King, on the way to the office, you say, looking up at the dusky sky:

"You know, there are a lot of babies in the sky—they're just invisible."

"Oh really?"

"Yeah. All over the blue part of the sky. Then when God wants to he has magic, and he just shoots them into your tummy."

"Oh really? And how does God decide who to give babies to?"

"Well, if you don't want one on the outside, but you really do on the inside of your heart, then God gives you one, 'cause that's what's true."

Memory Sculpture—Preserving the Moment

Writing about a special moment is a perfect way to give it a permanent shelf life. Many moments of childhood may live beyond the diary door if you take them there and leave them there in the form of a brief description or story, like this one on my birthday:

To Landon (age 8), October 26, 1995

Awaking from a bad dream around 6:45, I become conscious of you and Dad chatting about me. It's my birthday. You are rustling and bustling in the kitchen. Shortly, I hear the three of you come into my room. It is one of those moments where I wish I could stop time and be forever in my bed as my children and husband approach w/delight to sing me Happy Birthday. To just freeze that sense of being treasured forever. Not having a memory of that kind of welcome at my birth, to have it now, w/so much love from the three of you, feels completely fulfilling.

The three of you climbed in bed w/me. You had cooked me an English Muffin, which I let you eat. You gave me your card and gifts you had wrapped for me—your watch and a few other miscellaneous items from your room.

I wanted my birthday to last longer!

This heavenly encounter with my daughters occurred as I was making dinner one night while my older daughter watched her baby sister in the baby swing:

To Perrin (age 5), July 1, 1997

. . . You stood staring at [baby] Franci as she swung back and forth, toward you and away from you. Then,

"I wonder what heaven looks like?" you ask.

"I'm not sure . . ."

"I've seen it before," you said. Then, smartly, with a grin, "I should have made a video of it!"

*(Sometimes, **this** is what heaven looks like to me, standing in the kitchen with you.)*

You can write a "snapshot" of a moment that catches your child making a quintessential childlike gesture she or he may soon outgrow. Perhaps this gesture captures an important aspect of your child's personality or future interests that will develop as she or he grows. Since this story was recorded, many summer gardens have come and gone, and my daughter Perrin has discovered that, like her grandfather and her great-grandfather before him, she has a green thumb and is a natural gardener:

To Perrin (age 3), May 21, 1995

"Garden Romance"

Our first real weekend of summer. Warm, sunny and fragrant. Just perfectly delightful.

After Landon's 9 am baseball game I took you and Landon plant shopping. . . . Then we went to Grampy to plant.

You helped with the pepper plants and the onions.

"Can I kiss them?" you ask after placing them in their holes and patting them in. You kiss them.

As we're leaving the garden, when we're all done for the day, and the soil is watered, I see you kissing the little lettuce leaves that Grampy planted a couple of weeks ago.

Appreciation and Positive Feedback

Just as you are taking the time to write down the positive things you feel about your children, make sure you take the time to write down the nice things they say about you and their other parent. You can never get enough appreciation in life, and their words of praise are very pleasant and uplifting to reread:

To Landon (age 9), April 30, 1996

. . .After our last day at the beach [on vacation] I heard you say to Dad:

"You're the only father that all kids want to play with. They all want to play with you more than any other Dad."

When children spontaneously express the positive things they feel about you, these quotes are balms to soothe tired spirits that you may need during the more challenging moments of raising children:

To Perrin (age 3), August 1, 1995

Early this morning you had climbed into bed with me and Dad and rolling restlessly over in your sleep you said:

"I really like you, Mom."

I think you go to heaven and sleep with the angels.

Reading the diaries during a present or future time of stress in your relationship with your child may be a way of reclaiming positive feelings or aspects of the relationship that once worked well between you. It can also help you to keep the conflicts your are experiencing with your child in perspective.

Car Quotes

Children will often give you their opinions and ideas while you are riding in the car. Listen carefully, and record the best of what they tell you before you forget.

To Landon (age 6), February 5, 1994

...While riding in the car you overheard Daddy say the word "sex," and you started saying that he had said a "bad word."

I said, "Sex isn't a bad word. Sex is where babies come from."

You said, "That's not where babies come from."

*"Then, where **do** they come from?" I asked.*

"From artists," you said. "They draw them then paint them and then they put the picture in your tummy and it turns into a real baby."

*"Oh—where did you learn **that**?"*

"I just knew it."

Philosophy, Words of Wisdom, and Everyday Advice

Never record your advice to your children in the diary. You can take it for granted that unless they have given you some unusual evidence to the contrary, children of any age do not want to be lectured to. Save the lectures for when they *have* to listen to you, (such as when they're seat-belted into the car). Restrain every impulse to lecture them, *particularly* any time you turn out to be right. Your child will not read a diary to be told "I told you so." Your child will run in the other direction if you write an entry that contains a "you should. . . ."

On the contrary, *always* record your child's advice to you. And take it. Their advice will be right on the mark, and you have developed the maturity and humility to swallow your pride and absorb any good advice you can get wherever it comes from. Your child's innocence will contain a lot of wisdom that you yourself once possessed, and one path toward recapturing that wisdom is to make it concrete through your writing.

Sometimes children offer advice in the form of comforting suggestions. For instance, even at a very young age my son seemed to know exactly how to lift my spirits when I was feeling down:

To Landon (age 4), March 12, 1991

Daddy is away for the week and Grammy B. [maternal grandmother] has been with us a few days & left today. After leaving her at the airport riding in the car, I told you I felt sad and you said:

"Don't feel sad Mommy. I'm here. Just look outside at all the things."

Other times, your children will catch you when you're acting badly, and their advice will reassure you that you've raised them with the right values even if you occasionally forget them yourself, as I did one Mother's Day weekend:

To Perrin (age 6), May 10, 1998

. . . We were driving up Green Lane and Grammy B. was saying she was feeling guilty for not going down into the basement to help Billie watch her kids while she worked at the fair. I was giving my Mom my opinion in a rather . . . controlling way, not even conscious of how awful I sounded. And, just as I was speaking, from the back seat you interrupted me:

"Mom, you shouldn't fight w/your mother on Mother's Day!"

*. . . I hope I only have to be corrected like this once. And I hope you never speak to **your** mother like that!*

Through diary writing we don't just observe our children. We realize that they are always observing us and that they absorb what really matters to us. They begin to know us very well, and they give us feedback when we most need it. They have a remarkable, intuitive ability to refresh us with their encouragement. Because I invest a lot of energy in making up stories that I hope will please and entertain my children and their friends, my son's unsolicited feedback about my storytelling, recorded in my daughter's diary, encouraged me to keep at it:

To Perrin (age 6), March 9, 1998

. . . I finished and printed the blueberry story for your birthday. Fifteen out of sixteen children have said "yes!" to your party.

Landon said yesterday after church on the way home as we were discussing plans for your story,

*"You need to take your stories and pass them down from generation to generation until some day they're as famous as **Little Red Ridinghood**."*

Children can be wonderful teachers, and they share their wisdom with us at surprising moments. They have a knack for giving us just the encouragement we need in the moment that we need it, as my son did on the eve of one of my new adventures:

To Landon (age 11), January 6, 1999

. . . On the ride home from swimming, discussing tomorrow's schedule, I mention that I'm starting my singing class tomorrow night. This leads to a remark by Perrin that her friend took a singing class and now she sings too much.

"You can't sing too much," you insist. "Singing makes you live longer," you say authoritatively. I have no idea where you got this lovely idea, but I like it. Maybe this explains why you have been singing more in church this year, kind of like your life depends on it! . . .

There is no denying the fact that, as parents with responsibilities, challenges, and conflicts in relationships and roles, we sometimes become exhausted, preoccupied, impatient, and stressed by our children's needs. We're tempted to tune them out at times, but diary writing reminds us that there are times when tuning them *in* instead can be the solution to our own need for refreshment. When we stop and pay attention through the diary writing to what's important to *them*, we may get a message we need to take for ourselves. One reminder children regularly give us, if we stop and listen, is to slow down and pay more attention to the beautiful and mysterious things in life that we may be taking for granted. My son, even at age two, taught me this with one word that he had just learned how to say—"Loon!":

To Landon (age 2), July 27, 1989

*Tonight, you discovered the moon. . . . You saw it for the first, joyful time, and once you **grasped** the moon, it was all you wanted . . . even though it was 10:00 p.m. and Papa [Dad] and I were at the end of our strength on the end of our day, both just home from work. Papa had taken you up the street a bit to wait for my car, and on the way he introduced you to the moon, that was full.*

When I came home, after a quick meal that you watched, you started coaxing me off the couch w/ a funny word I had never heard you use, and you were pointing toward the door, "Loon! Loon!" I followed you, and we went to your bedroom window and you showed me the moon you had just discovered.

*I put you to bed to the tune of **Moon River**, and even then you pointed, wanting more.*

*After you slept, I thought of writing, and then of **not** writing, and it was only then that I realized the joy you must have been feeling, the joy you almost missed communicating to me in my exhaustion and preoccupation of a long working day. I felt so **old**, and so ashamed to almost have missed realizing your joy . . . how far I've grown from my first real glimpse of the **moon**.*

Thank you Land, for showing me the moon and reminding me of what a wondrous, beautiful thing it is.

Your children will grow up and be adults and they may be parents themselves some day. Writing in the diary is a way that you can share with them what brings you comfort during stressful times in life. Tell them about some of the things you do to care for yourself, and tell them how you cope. Show them, with a story:

To Frances (age 1), December 14, 1998

After Daddy puts you to bed, I walk in the cold, dark night. It is starry, thoroughly worth the effort.

There is nothing in the world more comforting than a walk on a starry night.

It is a time when one cannot be anything but close to God, in the presence of the infinite, the eternal, the lights of heaven in the blackness.

Always walk for peace.

You can use the diary to give your children a sense of your personal philosophy, explaining why you do the things you do. Later, they will have a chance to both understand *and* disagree. Even if they disagree with your ideas, they may gain reassurance, at least, from the awareness that you thought deeply about what you were trying to do as a parent. You can tell them about the important things you've learned in life, as if you are speaking to a future friend who might like to hear your best ideas about how to live well. You can tell them about how you have come to some of the decisions you make about parenting them. When I was pregnant with my third child, my son wanted to be present at the birth. I explained in an entry in my daughter Perri's diary about our decision to invite them both, even though she ultimately decided she did not want to be there. Writing this entry helped me to clarify my own decision making process, as well as to leave a story in the diary that showed we wanted to include her if that was her choice:

To Perrin (age 4), December 13, 1996

*You know I plan on having you and Landon w/ me for the delivery of the baby? At least if you want to be, and all is going well. So far, you seem to want it very much. At first I wasn't sure about including both of you; I thought you might be too young, or that the two of you might be too much to handle. But Daddy and I discussed it and we both immediately saw that there was no way we could have just **one** of you. This is an experience we want you to have together. This is an adventure you will share w/ each other, and a story you will have for Franny.*

*I can't really think of any reason **not** to have you there. Both of you are old enough to behave in this unique environment. And all of us need to bond w/ Franny; the closer we all are to her in the beginning, the easier it will be. Landon so much wanted to be there at **your** birth. Perhaps it was a mistake not to, but for some, per-*

*haps many reasons I did not have the confidence. Maybe Dr. Wolff discouraged me because it was unfamiliar to her. Or perhaps Landon **was** too young—you are a year older for Franny than he was for you.*

But more than that, I did not have the confidence of a satisfying delivery yet— you provided me w/ that. . . .

*When I **had** you, I **had** you, and I had you my way. . . .*

A birth is truly a family event; . . . It can be. When I was pregnant w/ you I involved Landon many times in my OB appointments, and now I'm doing the same for you, because I want health care to be a familiar, safe process for you all. And because I think it's a wonderful learning experience about a major act of life.

I just want to share it with you.

Spirituality

Your child's spiritual questions and observations will begin as soon as she or he can make a sentence. As soon as they can form sentences, they will begin to ask questions that you, despite decades more searching, may still not be able to answer completely for yourself. Even if you have ready, self-assured answers, you may find that their questions intrigue, excite, or even disturb you. Their questions may provoke thoughts and feelings for you to wrestle with. And you may find that your children have some answers for you, or that their innocent or inventive point of view offers new possibilities for your own understanding.

You can show them how they wonder about the afterlife and what concerns them spiritually. Some of the most charming entries of their early lives contain my children's spiritual questions and concerns, like this one, when my son began considering his own mortality:

To Landon (age 4), July 13, 1992

Daddy and you went out together Sat. afternoon to fix the red car and see the chimp farm. In the course of the afternoon you got a balloon which you soon lost to the skies which prompted you to ask Daddy:

"Daddy, when you die and go to heaven, do you get all your balloons back?"

In the diaries you can show them how they wrestle with *your* mortality as well as with their own. Show them how *you* wrestle with their questions, as I did when my son surprised me with his challenging and relentless probing about questions I had never had to answer for a child before, and had only begun to answer for myself:

To Landon (age 3), October 10, 1991

. . . Just as we sat down to eat you asked, out of the blue:

"Mommy, when are we going to die?"

"Not for a very, very, very, long time until we're very old."

"How old?"

"Very, very old."

"Why does God make us die?"

"To make room for new babies on earth."

. . . Daddy was putting you to bed and you were still concerned, wondering if when you die you have to leave your toys?

Daddy said no, they go to heaven.

"But how do they get to heaven, how does God get them there?"

Daddy was stumped, so he brought you in here, and you asked me.

I was stumped, momentarily. Then I thought, and thought and thought.

"Magic," I said.

You were satisfied.

You can show them how, in their attempts to make literal sense of the abstract, they skip off into spiritual possibilities, as my son's imaginative questioning did:

To Landon (age 3), November 4, 1991

. . . Today, it was your new jacket that stirred up questions of God.

"Why do they call it my windbreaker? Does my jacket break the wind? Does God send the wind down? Does God send the people back to earth from heaven?"

When their questions sneak up from the back seat of the car and grab you, pulling you out of your daily planning and preoccupation, listen carefully. When their curiosity inspires you to find the divinity in the day, you can show them where their questions led you with the story. For instance, my daughter Perrin always seems to save her most probing questions for car rides. When she asked me the question about God that initiated the following entry, I had no idea where it would lead us. But I put forced myself to put aside all my thoughts about what I was planning to do once I dropped her at school and let my search for an answer to her question lead us on an unexpected journey of discovery:

To Perrin (age 4), November 18, 1996

"How God Speaks"

I am backing the car down the driveway taking you to school [pre-school] and you ask,

"Mommy, does God speak like us? Like our voices, you and me?"

"Well, I don't know, what do you think?"

"Tell me!" you say angrily.

"Well, I can't tell you. You have to find out for yourself. God talks to each of us differently. I don't know what god might sound like to you. . . ."

"Oh." And then we were rounding the bad Brush Hill corner just as a young deer did a dancing hop across the street to join the other two deer heading up into the woods. I stopped the car so we could both have a good look, and they stopped just inside the winter shelter of the trees, which, isn't much, and watched us too.

"I wish I could touch one," you say. . . .

"You know, I think God just spoke to us, Perrin."

"When? How?"

"With the deer. That's one of the ways God speaks to us is to slow us down to see the beautiful and unexpected things she has made." We are heading down Green Lane now, past all the brown, bare bushes and the Grape vines and bittersweet that run wild over the old stone wall in front of the orchard. . . .

"But sometimes the best way to hear God talk is to just be quiet and **listen**."

We are silent for a brief moment that is long enough for you.

"I don't want to listen, I want to see some more beautiful things."

Now we're pulling into the driveway of the church, and straight ahead I see the white and black bare-branched birch, so I stop the car:

"Like the birch tree? See how the top half is shining, lit by the light of the sun, and its branches like arms are reaching up to god?"

"God made the birch tree for us."

"And see that?" I ask, pulling the car into the parking spot. "That birds' nest on the bare branch above our heads?"

"I see it!"

"God made the branches bare so in the winter we could see all the birds nests and be reminded that the birds will come again in the spring. . . ."

"No, God made the branches bare so the birds could **find** their nests!"

"Yes, that too."

At the door, you resist:

"I want to stay outside and see more beautiful things."

"But there are beautiful things inside too. We have to look for them. I know, follow me." We hang up your coat and pass the door to your classroom. I am hop-

ing....yes, the door to the sanctuary is wide open, and we step quietly onto the red carpet in the silent room. You go to the candles in front of the altar, and you are standing on the spot where Daddy and I said our marriage vows.

"Do you know what happened here?"

"This is where Landon and I were blessed!" You are confused, remembering your Baptism, thinking it was here because of the candles.

"No, Dad and I were married here."

Suddenly, you are running up the steps behind the altar, standing at the lectern, trying out the microphones which are a silent disappointment.

"Its time for school," I say, and walk you to your class....

In the next chapter, we explore more challenging aspects of daily life with children when mishaps and mischief lead us down a more adventuresome parenting path. In the meantime, try some of the following Diary Door Openers in your own writing.

Diary Door Openers

1. An Ordinary Day
   Think about an ordinary day with your child when she or he did something that caught your attention and made you stop and notice something that you otherwise would have missed seeing, hearing, tasting, touching, sensing, or feeling. Describe the scene, writing in the present tense even if it happened in the distant or recent past. Allow yourself to spontaneously reflect on why this was particularly moving or meaningful for you.

2. Memory Sculpture
   Write to your child about a moment when you were in a heightened state of awareness about some pleasurable aspect of parenting that you wish could have lasted longer. Using descriptive language, preserve the moment by capturing it in all its exquisite detail.

3. Wise Child
   Tell your child a story about the best piece of advice she or he has given you this week explaining what you learned from his or her sharing. Have you attempted to put this advice into action in your life?

4. Spiritual Questioning

    Write to your child about a spiritual question, idea or belief she or he has shared with you recently. How did you handle it? Do you agree? Has this question or observation helped you think more deeply or differently about a belief or value you hold? Write, and see where the exploration leads you.

5. Solid Stances

    Write to your child about three of her or his most solid opinions at this time of life, whether or not you agree with them or support them. Observe and describe, non-judgmentally, how these beliefs seem to influence your child's actions.

6. Nature's Classroom

    Observe and describe your child experiencing some aspect of the natural world, whether it's encountering a spider in the bathtub, planting in the garden, or taking a walk in the woods or through the city park. Look for a story to tell your child about this encounter that has a beginning, middle, and end, and a theme, symbol, message, or feeling that you both discovered.

7. Drinking from the Well

    Describe something you did today or this week (with or without your child) that nurtured you and revived your energy or spirit and refreshed your outlook on life. Reflect on why this activity helped you.

8. Sharing Values

    Choose one value you were raised on that you try to incorporate into your own parenting philosophy today. Include a memory from your childhood when your parents, grandparents, or caregivers acted on this value that helped you discover its worthiness.

Chapter 6

Comedy, Mishaps, and Mischief
Writing Adventure Stories
of Daily Life

Tom disappeared under the bed just in time.
He crept to where he could almost touch his aunt's foot.
"He warn't bad," said Aunt Polly, "only mischeevous . . .
He never meant any harm, and he was the best-hearted
boy that ever was"—and she began to cry.

(Samuel L. Clemens, *The Adventures of Tom Sawyer*, p. 146)

Children like adventure stories. They like fast action, suspense, surprise twists, comic mistakes, and heroic rescues. If these exciting plots are pulled from their very own childhood, if they get to play a starring role in these dramas, so much the better. If you look for these stories in everyday life, if you write them and save them, your children will read, enjoy, retell, and treasure them for years to come. And so will you. Writing diary stories helps to transform distressing or irritating events into family lore and family laughter.

Writing about the Mishaps of Daily Life

What child doesn't like a good disaster story? Every household with children experiences mishaps routinely so there's plenty of opportunity for storytelling here. Disasters or accidents that turn out all right in the end can read like slapstick comedy and become the stuff of humorous family legend. These are stories that were scary or annoying or painful to experience, but because they turned out all right make you laugh out loud to read them later on. It's parents who play the fool most often in these stories, to a child's delight. There is nothing your children appreciate more than your sense of humor. They will help you, if you let them, make comedy out of the little disasters of everyday life.

Every new parent encounters the moment of a child's first accident and all the guilt, sadness, shock, and concern that go with it. Children learn very early on that mere mortals are rearing them. Admitting this fact openly to yourself and to your child can be a way of creating more intimacy with your children. Writing about the accident through the diary door can be an additional way of comforting both you and your child. This is one of the ways diary writing will nurture you both. Writing the following entry to my infant son in the diary as if he could actually listen to my feelings about this first mishap helped me to put the stress behind me:

To Landon (age 1), April 5, 1988

. . . Well, my dear, we had our first accident with you last night, but you'd never know it from your happy-go-lucky mood today. I almost hate to tell you about it, I feel so awful. (It's taking me longer to recover than you, my dear!)

Daddy was on the phone in the kitchen and you were on the bed w/me. I thought to myself, I need to pack him in w/pillows so that I can go to the kitchen for some water. But, the next thing I knew I was standing in the living room and I heard you cry suddenly, shriek in a way I had never heard you cry before. In a split second my heart fell to the floor and I panicked. I knew, in a split second, that my baby had fallen onto the floor. I yelled—screamed—for your Dad as I ran past into the bedroom and around the bed to the other side where I found you crying and scooped you up into my arms. Then Daddy took you and I followed him around wringing my hands helplessly . . . then we called the Dr., and while Daddy talked I had you back on the bed smiling once again.

The Dr. told us what to watch for, but intuitively I knew you were okay. We kept a vigil anyway for an hour sitting on the edge of the bed with you rocking yourself to sleep in the swing, peaceful once again.

Oh, my Land, I thank God so much that you're okay, and I feel so awful about my carelessness. You can bet I'm more careful today!

I love you so much, Land. Don't ever get hurt again—you scare your Mom & Dad so much. . . .

Recognizing Mishaps as Wake-up Calls

Accidents and mishaps may serve as a wake-up call when we reflect on them in the diaries. Writing about them as story may help us recognize their underlying meaning, connect us with our inner wisdom, and bring an awareness of any need for change to prevent recurrence.

Falling flat on my belly nine months pregnant with my third child was a frightening experience. But, in retrospect, it was also very funny, and it was a story that I imagined my daughter Frances would enjoy some day as part of her birth legend if I saved it for her in her diary. On one level, it's a simple story about an unexpected accident that could happen *any* day of the week with young children. But, on another level, it's also a story about how great and wondrous long-awaited events in life are often accompanied by mishaps, accidents, or unexpected problems that serve as a way of waking us up and making us more conscious of the need for change. The task for the newly born first child is to get his parents to make room for a child in their adult-centered lives. But the task of a second or third child is to get her siblings to make room for her in a system that is already running their way. This story about an accident may also be a cautionary tale about a family that needs to slow down, pay more attention to what it's doing, and make room for a new member who is bringing a whole new set of needs and feelings into the system and who will change it in a variety of welcome and unwelcome ways.

To Frances (3 days before birth), April 7, 1997

. . . Picture a spring-like, sunny Friday afternoon in our front yard, Perrin, Landon, & Dusty [cousin] playing happily outside w/o their coats on. It's almost 4:00 p.m., and I am expecting Daddy home any minute to take us all to buy the new car he has picked out for me. It's a surprise—he won't tell me anything about it.

While the three of them play, I go out to clean out my car—the Caprice, because we need to trade it in. Landon has gotten the Little Tikes car out of the garage and is giving Perrin & Dusty rides down the driveway by pushing and holding them from behind and they roll. Preoccupied w/the bags of toys and trash I am collecting from my car, they roll past me almost unnoticed.

But suddenly, I'm aware that the game has changed. Landon has moved on to other amusements and yet, the car is rolling by me once again, this time too fast down the sloped driveway toward the street. It is Perrin at the wheel, and little Dusty, out of control, in charge of pushing.

Frantic, I see that Perrin will careen out into the street at full speed, and I yell aloud, to Landon, I guess, "Stop her!" I yell again as I try to run, but now, like a heavy weighted out-of-shape dwarf, I realize my feet cannot sustain the momentum produced by my brain to move like a bullet down the driveway, and so, my feet in protest **give up***, they just* **give up** *on the rest of my body and I am the victim of gravity, an awkward, uptight terribly silly and angry looking very pregnant woman sprawled flat on my stomach in the driveway, while Perrin & Dusty roll across the street safely to the other side.*

My knees and elbows stinging (but not as much as my face) I return to the house *in a flustered, angry, hurt, embarrassed rage and burst into helpless tears—helpless because my body has failed **me**, and I feel like I have failed Perrin, Dusty, but especially, **you**.*

I've never fallen nine months pregnant before. I'm shocked and terrified. Have I hurt you? Are you okay? The three children come in, I bark angrily for Perrin & Dusty to go to time out, Landon to call Daddy . . .

*. . . It turns out that they would like to check you out, just to be safe, so when Daddy gets home, he and I go to the OB unit where we stay three hours, w/me hooked up to the monitor, then, an ultra sound to prove you are all right, and you are. I **know** you are, but we must prove it to them.*

I don't mind; it's a rare moment for me to relax and get cuddled a bit by Dad. The car will wait. . . .

Providing Comic Relief

Just as humor is used to break the tension in the middle of a serious scene of a play, short story, novel, or poem, it can be used in diary writing to provide comic relief. Children have wonderful senses of humor and a thorough appreciation of the ridiculous.

Writing about the little mishaps and disasters of everyday life helps children learn a fundamental coping skill of life—using humor as a way of getting through the predictably unpredictable, difficult moments of life. Laughter is the perfect antidote to these minor stresses, for both parents and kids. The family will bond around funny stories that are always available for tension relief as long as they are retold in the spirit of respect for everyone's feelings.

Younger children love their stories graphic and gross, retold in gory detail, and they will continue to tell these stories themselves in great detail ever after. My children love this story about their lives with their new sister because, like the little comic she has since grown into, her antics make them laugh hysterically. *I* like it because rereading stories of my momentary stresses—when the last thing I feel like doing as a mother in the midst of a mess is to laugh—reminds me how quickly those stressful moments pass. The story allows me to look at myself in the role of mother with some distance and perspective and to take life's little disasters a lot less seriously:

To Frances (age 2 months), June 9, 1997

. . . Tonight, on the way home from watering plants at Dusty & Billies, you started screaming in the car fiercely. I pulled over on Green Lane, finally, to feed you, thinking you couldn't wait. Instead of being hungry, I found you bathed in poop that had

exploded out of your diaper and seeped up through your bathing suit, spreading onto the car seat where your hands, wildly flailing in your furious discomfort, got covered w/it and spread it all over your face.

*Landon, leaning over to check you out fell back against his seat in a faint, and almost **lost** it, and Perrin slid over as far as she could go and watched, and I stood against the hot exhaust of the car running w/my dress unbuttoned trying to find rags to clean you with, swearing under my breath, as people out on a pleasant evening's stroll strolled by.*

Capturing Heroics

Children often try to help when these mishaps occur. Diary stories can catch them trying to perform heroic acts whether or not they are successful. I wrote the following "disaster story" for my daughter Frances because, as the first significant accident of her pre-toddling days, I knew that it would be remembered also by her sister and brother as a significantly stressful event. I wanted to show her how her older brother, even though he wasn't actually successful in preventing her fall, had tried to save her. We all like the reassuring feeling that someone played a heroic role in our lives when young. I wanted to tell a story about the role he often plays in her life as someone who is concerned for her welfare and as someone who tries to protect her. I also wanted to express that, even though our busyness and distractibility made us imperfect caretakers, we still cared deeply and showed her feelings great concern.

When writing these stories, you can place them in the context of normal daily life as it is being lived in the moment, describing what you were doing, what they were doing, what the weather was, and who else was present. Adding this sense of atmosphere will capture a flavor or texture that you and your children will remember and perhaps enjoy. These stories also offer miniature portraits of people in roles, like my daughter Perrin, who may someday be interested to read that she was already writing poetry when her sister was just a baby. Sometimes what seem like insignificant details add greater meaning and resonance to a story, particularly as time passes:

To Frances (age 9 months), January 23, 1998

"Stair Stumbling"

I was frosting gingerbread cookies. Daddy came home to get his present ready for Grammy B.L. and Grampy Mike, a large screen TV hiding in the garage. Perrin and Landon had been bickering for the last hour, Perrin screaming because she couldn't get her words right for the poem she was writing. So when Daddy came home before dinner and scooped you up and Perrin & Landon followed him like the Pied Piper, I was relieved to have a quiet moment to myself w/my gingerbread ladies and men.

Soon, Perrin returned from the cold garage, and Landon too, both chatting to me as I frosted. Then, in the back of my mind I heard you chatting, calling out in your own language, somewhere off in the distance w/Daddy.

"Where's Frances?" I asked Land.

"Isn't she w/Daddy?" Then, I panicked, because your calls, though not urgent, were unusual. Something was wrong! Where was Daddy? Landon got to the basement door first and saw you where we dreaded—halfway up the stairs all alone! He reached for you, calling to you to stop, but of course, you did what was completely natural when you saw your frightened brother above you reaching for you—you leaned up and let go, just as I got to the door behind him, and I saw you flip backward, tumbling to the bottom, and I screamed in horror, slipped down the stairs on my rear end and almost fell directly on top of you where Landon was collecting you at the bottom. Still screaming in anger and fear I scooped you up, Daddy came and discovered his error, everyone came running and we all cuddled you, and you stopped crying and screaming well before I did, I'm afraid. No damage. Just a terrifying warning to us all. Grammy and Grampy arrived then and we had lots of joy giving them their house-warming gift, and you ate more gingerbread cookies than can possibly be good for you.

Writing Mischief Stories

Every child plays Tom Sawyer or Eloise from time to time. Writing mischief stories can be a stress reliever for you and also a source of future amusement for you and your child. These are stories that celebrate children's curiosity, creativity, and adventuresome spirit, even if these aspects of their personalities occasionally lead them astray. These stories capture your child's mischief in the lighter sense of the word, referring to the times when your child's playfulness misfires and causes you annoyance. Writing these stories reminds us that children learn through playing, investigating, stretching their imaginations, and following their curiosity, often without thought to the consequences of their exploration. Sometimes they pursue an adventure that may be beyond their developmental ability or may express a normal childlike wish to assert their will beyond our pragmatic limit setting.

We want to support their imaginative play, boundless energy, and wish to explore beyond safe boundaries, but we fear for their safety or dread the consequences of their inevitable mess making. Writing these stories is a way of dealing with our own mixed feelings about our child's playful misbehavior, venting about the pressures of caring for children from a humorous perspective. Writing stories about mischief in the diaries has often captured the charming side of mischief making and has given my children and me an appreciation of their need to occasionally follow their own curious and assertive impulses against my wishes.

This story I had completely forgotten until, years later, I found it in my son's diary; it made us both laugh. I had forgotten so many of the feelings and concerns that my potential second pregnancy posed for my son and the rich emotional response that he continually expressed throughout this new phase of our lives:

To Landon (age 3), March 12, 1991

*. . . Daddy totally thrilled me w/this news a couple of weeks ago. One Sat. morning he came to me & said he was ready to make a commitment to a second child! Yippee. You and I are **so** happy. . . .*

You have been upset from time to time, though, because you want your very own baby in your tummy, and the first time I told you this could not happen you burst into tears and cried for five minutes. Now, you cry less each time I tell you it's not possible, but you still blame me:

"You won't let me . . . [have a baby]"

*You have also, on occasion, been known to threaten and manipulate me with the new baby. One day we were home together in the kitchen fixing lunch, I think, and you wanted me to juggle the fruit in the fruit basket. When I refused, you told me if I didn't you would tell God not to let me have a baby. When I **still** refused, you carried your apples into the living room and shouted up at the ceiling:*

"God!? Don't let Mommy have a baby cause she won't juggle with me!"

Bedtime can be a great source of mischief stories. What child goes to bed willingly and smoothly? What parent doesn't struggle desperately to find the formula and to set the limits that will end the evening in a mutually relaxing way? If reflecting on your methods and your child's response in the diary doesn't help, at least it may offer some laughs later on, when your child has outgrown the phase of avoiding sleep at all cost:

To Landon (age 3), April 2, 1991

I rub your head, tuck you in, leave, confident that you are now down for the night.

Then, sitting on the couch reading, I slowly become aware of the feeling that I am being stalked. Going to your door, cracked, I see the laser gun aimed directly at my feet, dead on.

I force the door open as you try to push it shut. I pick you up, place you standing in your bed, try to convince you to lie down.

"No! Wait! Something's the matter with me!"

"What?"

You stare ... concentrate hard.

"The bed."

"What about your bed, what's the matter w/it?" I ask, gently trying to coax you down.

"Wait! Let me think of something!" You said, quite seriously, pursing your lips.

I wait.

"Nothing," you surrender, drawing a complete blank.

We laugh as your head hits the pillow.

Mischief as a Developmental Marker

Children's mischief may represent more than curiosity, unchecked desire, veiled emotional expression, and self-will run riot. Mischief may also reveal signs of your child's developmental growth, playing with boundaries as a means of preparing for new freedom and the idea of greater independence. Playfulness is a healthy skill for exploring new challenges. I wrote the following story for Perrin as a way of capturing her in a creative, courageous, and playful role. Writing regular portraits of your child in action allows you to be *aware of* and to celebrate transition and growth as it is happening. When children are ready to grow, they will test the limits. The limit testing allows us both to mutually warm up to change through a balance of giving and taking. The story shows me trying to respect yet contain her courage without extinguishing it while I managed my own fears of her moving forward to a new stage of independence:

To Perrin (age 3), October 4, 1995

It's a rainy morning, but warm, not too cool; it's a light, fresh rain.

Driving back from dropping Landon at school you are thinking about what you will do this morning—you are thinking about riding your bike.

Last week I was worried about you going too far down the street in front of the house, so I took the chalk and drew a line across the sidewalk showing you how far you could go and wrote:

"S – T – O – P!" to send you back to the safe area. You weren't too happy about this boundary being drawn on your freedom.

So, this morning, from the back seat I heard,

"Mom? Will the rain wash the sidewalk?"

"I guess so ..."

"Good," you say.
"Why? Then what will happen?"
"Then the line will be gone, and I'll be free!"
"Oh, really?"
"Yes, the rain is my friend!"

Mischief and Memories

Of course, there are many times—perhaps *too* many times—when what looks like pure mischief—*pure, inexplicable, outrageous craziness*—to you is simply pure play to your children. Mischief stories often include portraits of playmates, best friends, the best of times. Observing and writing these stories about your children will reconnect you with memories from your own childhood, and you may want to include some of them in your child's diary.

Writing this next story about my son and his best playmate, cousin Joey, made me remember my relationship with my cousin Debbie, who played this ideal role for me in childhood. Suddenly, I remembered all the delicious mischief we had made, oblivious of our parents' concerns. Many times we couldn't resist breaking all the rules, like staying up all night and foraging through my aunt's generous makeup supply to play beauty parlor—a memory of purely blissful childhood adventure. Or running naked through a sprinkler in the yard on warm summer evenings or hot, daring summer afternoons—certainly not something our parents would have approved of. But these were the best of times. Writing about cousins playing made me wish I could have back just one day of my childhood with Debbie, and I realized that my son was currently enjoying something that I could only long for—a part of my childhood that is gone forever and much too soon.

As angry as I was at the moment my son and his cousin made mischief in this entry, saving it as a story in the diary allowed me to view it, on reflection, as a way of honoring the deep bond between my son and his cousin. It's a portrait of blissful, imaginative childhood play that transcends the practical barriers of real life, including mothers who lose their patience from time to time in the midst of it. Writing it allowed me to see the world more from their point of view:

To Landon (age 9), May 5, 1996

[cousin] Joey overnight.

. . . *Riding home in the car I hear you two playing w/your battle trolls, creating scenes of danger and rescue. In the midst of it all Joey says:*

"There's a house in my neighborhood for sale."

"Mom?" You ask. "There's a house for sale in Joey's neighborhood. Can we buy it? I'll chip in my own money!"

Later, it's raining lightly, but warm; you and Joey go out into the backyard while I bake a coffee cake for church. I look out the window into the back yard from time to time. You're just swinging happily, it seems. I am surprised at how long the swing seems to entertain you.

Later, dressing in my room, I notice that the bushy rhododendron in front of the swing has been hacked to pieces, branches and leaves litter the whole general surrounding area.

My blood boils.

I set you two to hard labor picking up stones in the grassless front yard.

Later I find out that you were playing that the leaves of the bush were each worth a million dollars and the swinger was trying to steal them from the yard where the neighbor was guarding them.

Mischief as a Mirror

Mischief stories can also act as a mirror, reflecting our best and worst parenting qualities. We all have bad days as parents. If we are honest—if we want to gain the most we can from this diary writing—and if we are using the diary for reflection about our parenting skills, then we are willing to catch ourselves when we're acting badly. We write so that we can reflect on those times when we may not be acting up to our own standards. Measuring ourselves against the ideal parent who lives in our imagination, we come up short. We own our bad behavior so that we can learn to change it. We all have days when we lose our patience and find ourselves reacting out of anger instead of thinking through a mature and reasoned response to conflict. If we're lucky, our children may offer us healthy alternatives for coping with the stress they cause us, as my younger daughter, who possesses both charm and wisdom, frequently does:

To Frances (age almost 3), March 6, 2000

A mischievous morning w/ you. It's Monday. Boy misses the bus. Perrin misses the bus. We drive her to school. You run away from me many times before I can get you in the car.

At the bank, you refuse to stand in line w/ me and you keep exiting through the heavy glass door into the vestibule. Then you lean your face against the glass and smile at me while I wait for the teller to take me. I can't help smiling back.

At the post office you refuse to wait w/me and you keep threatening to run out the door into the parking lot. By the time we get back to the car I am quite irritated w/ you, and in an impatient, critical voice I am attempting to lecture you about the dangers of parking lots.

"Take a bref, Mommy," you urge me from the back seat as I prepare to back the car out.

"What!?"

"Take a bref, Mommy. Take a deep bref."

"Oh! Oh, take a deep breath. Good idea. Thanks."

I am grateful that you have calmed me down!

After we drop about twenty books at the library, I try to put a tape in the tape deck so we can sing on the way home, but it's not working.

Peering inside the cassette player, I see a pile of pennies. Daddy let you hang out Sat. in my car while he washed it, and now I see that you have used my pile of pennies to break everything in my front dash that you could get to.

"Take a bref, Mommy," you tell me. "Take a deep, deep bref. . . ."

The diaries are also a place where we need to catch ourselves acting our best. Just as we often celebrate our children in the diaries, we get to celebrate the best of ourselves. On days when we manage to meet the mess with humor, zest, creativity, and an attitude of spontaneous fun, on days when we actually *do* live up to our parenting ideals, we need to include these stories in the diary, as I did in the following entry. Children love nursery rhymes, often because they glorify or make a game of mischief. Maybe your child's mischief is a nursery rhyme in the making, like this one I saved from a long, cabin-feverish, winter day at home with young children:

To Frances (age 10 months), January 18, 1998

. . . One afternoon early last week, I was busy doing stuff around the house, Perrin was under a blanket watching TV, and I was letting you crawl around the family room.

I came into the family room at one point and found you sitting on the hearth in the ashes of the unlit fireplace, dusty with soot from head to toe, and grey dust around your mouth and lips where you had stuffed handfuls of ashes.

I picked you up, laughing to Perrin and said:

"Ashes and soot
ashes and soot
for breakfast, lunch, and dinner
Ashes and soot

Ashes and soot
They're making me grow much thinner!"

Perrin and I laughed at our new nursery rhyme all week, most of our mirth coming from the vision of you sitting deep in ashes and soot, enjoying your snack.

Mischief as Adventure—
Tales of Quests Taken, Threatened, or Thwarted

Going through the diary door with your child and looking at the world from his or her point of view allow you to see your child's mischief as an important opportunity for adventure. We all hunger for adventures, and we also hunger to return home from them. This is the nature of the hero, his or her calling, and of the quest. Writing these stories for your child before she is able even to process or understand them can help both of you discover the meaning, purpose, and growth in the adventure. Writing about your child's return is a way of helping her see what taking the adventure has taught her about herself and about life.

"I'm Running Away!"

Many children threaten to, make, or execute a plan to run away from home, usually around the time that they are entering kindergarten. Some attempts may be more dramatic or adventurous than others. But however the impulse or plan is executed, this is a developmental milestone that deserves attention. Your child may need to know that these are normal feelings—everyone feels like running away sometimes—and they also need help in finding a way to change their minds while keeping their dignity intact. Diary entries made at these times can help you achieve this feeling of normalcy.

I wrote this entry because, even though I could not remember why I left, or why I came back from my own first attempt to run away from home, it was an emotionally significant experience for me, as it is for most children. I wish I could remember more about my own running away story. The diary assures Perrin that she will have hers, brief and unspectacular as it may be:

To Perrin (age 5), July 1, 1997

. . . .Then, bedtime, inevitably, a major battle. Angry, dealing exasperatedly w/yours and Land's resistance, I blow up, rant and rave about my need to have some time to myself. You cry and throw yourself dramatically on your bed. I kick your toy debris about to make a path to the door. While tucking Landon in, I see you exit your bed-

room, talking to yourself, planning. You are wearing a short sleeve black T shirt, no pants . . . no shoes, but your purple backpack is slung across your back.

I meet you as your hand reaches the knob of the front door.

"Where are you going?"

"I'm going to live at Dusty's."

It doesn't take too much to dissuade you from exiting into the dark and mosquito-filled evening. . . .

When you write running-away stories for your children, keep in mind that your child may very much like to hear the story about *your* first attempt to run away from home. Do you remember? Writing a story about your first runaway attempt will help to normalize for your child the scary feelings that surface when they first realize home is not always the perfectly safe, secure, ideal place they wish it would be. Maybe your story will help them know that it's okay to feel like running away and to come back home once again and talk the problem through with a good listener like yourself.

Narrating a Mischief Story from Your Child's Point of View

When you write from the third person point of view, as an objective narrator might, you can imagine your child's thoughts, feelings, motives, and perceptions, as if he or she is a character in a fictional tale. Of course you can't *literally* enter your child's mind. But you can try to imagine your child's experience as a means of better understanding your child's feelings, needs and motivations.

One nerve-wracking summer morning, my daughter Frances at age two suddenly disappeared from her seat on the couch with her brother and sister in the blink of an eye while I was making lunch in the kitchen. The only evidence I had of her sudden departure was an item of clothing she had been wearing at the time that I found discarded at the threshold of the back door. After solving the mystery, recovering from my own terror, and harvesting the lessons her adventure had to offer me as a parent, I retold this story in her diary, taking the role of the narrator, as a classic adventure tale of her youth. It's one of her favorites:

To Frances (age 2), July 26, 1999

There's No Place Like Home

One day, when Frances was two, it was a beautiful, summer day. Her mother helped her put on her bathing suit and promised they would go to the beach right after lunch. But, while she was sitting on the couch watching TV with her older brother and sister, Frances felt a funny tickle in her tummy, and felt a strange feeling of longing that seemed to be calling her outside. "Why, I miss Mari!" she thought.

Mari was Frances' best friend in the whole world, and she lived nearby. Visiting Mari in her backyard sandbox was Frances' favorite thing in the whole world, next to going to the beach. And so, she had an idea. Why not go to Mari's sandbox, where she was sure to be playing on such a fine day, and play with her? So, Frances went to the back door. My, how warm it was outside in the hot sun. She opened the door and went outside. Nobody even noticed!

"Ahhhh!" Outside a warm breeze tickled her skin, and she felt free, free as the birds in the garden who could fly wherever they liked! Frances walked past the garden, and right to the path that led through the brush to Mari's house. "I'm on my way!" she thought, bravely. "I know Mari will be so happy to see me!" At the other side of the path, she crossed the neighbors' lawn that led to the street that she would cross to Mari's house. When she got to the street, she looked both ways, and crossed, and hurried across Mari's lawn, peering around the bushes at the sandbox. "Mari?" she called. But the sandbox was empty. The back yard was silent except for the birds.

Frances, who had felt so brave through the woods and across the street, began to be afraid. She stood in the hot sun, staring at the empty sandbox. Now, all she could think about was the empty space between her brother and her sister on the couch and her mother in the kitchen making lunch. More than anywhere else in the world, Frances wished she was home.

Home seemed like such a long, long way away, and Frances felt as if she were going to cry. She started walking quickly up the driveway, and across the lawn, feeling lonelier than she had ever felt in her whole life. Suddenly, through her tears, Frances saw her mother running toward her with open arms, and her mother was crying too. Her mother scooped her up and squeezed her too tightly, but Frances didn't mind. She couldn't answer all the questions her mother was asking, because she had a lump in her throat. All she wanted was to go home. And, so they did. They walked back through the neighbor's yard, back down the path, and there in the back yard waiting to hug her was her brother and sister. She was home. Home! Home safe! And it was time for lunch.

There are many ways that children have adventures. In the next chapter we look at how diary writing can keep track of milestones and rites of passage in your child's growth and development. But first, try these Diary Door Openers in your own diary.

Diary Door Openers

1. Accidents Happen
   When did your child first learn that she or he was being reared by mere mortals? Tell your child the story of an accident or mishap that turned out all right in the end. What did you and/or your child seem to learn from it?

2. Wake-up Calls
   Mishaps can be wake-up calls. Have you had any lately? What did the mishap wake you up to?

3. Comic Relief
   Daily life can be full of comic details when we are able to keep our sense of humor intact. As you go about the day today, notice some of the comic possibilities. Sit down later and include some of them in your child's diary.

4. "I'm Running Away"
   Every young child executes a running away plan. Describe the events leading up to this journey. What did your child seem to be running *from* and running *to*? How did you handle the return? If your child's adventure reminds you of a time when you ran away from home, or planned to, you may be inspired to include your own adventure here.

5. There's No Place Like Home
   Describe a time when your child seemed particularly relieved to be home once again. Why? Where had your child been, and what, if anything, did she or he seem to gain from the experience of leaving home?

6. Capturing Heroics
   Write about when your child acted quickly, nobly, generously, or skillfully to help another child, person, or a pet.

7. Mischief Making
   Children's mischief making can be a call for our attention. Write a story about your child's mischief that highlights one or all of the following:
   - Your child's imaginative thinking
   - Your child's creative attempt to capture your attention
   - Your best or most creative, spontaneous response
   - Your child's point of view of the mischief—the why's and how's and thinking that led to the mischievous behavior

Chapter 7

Milestones, Achievements, and Rites of Passage Affirming Kid's Accomplishments

"There is no hope for me," she said, sadly,
"for Oz will not send me home until I have killed
the Wicked Witch of the West; and that I can never do."

(L. Frank Baum, *The Wizard of Oz*, p. 114)

Milestones

Milestone: A stone marker on the road to show distance; an important event or turning point in one's history or career. (*The American Heritage Dictionary*)

Children will expect you to remember the times, dates, and stories behind meeting their milestones, pursuing their accomplishments, and participating in the rites of passage that mark their young lives. They have a natural desire to understand and value the unique ways in which they grow and develop. They want to know *when* they took their first steps, what their first words were, and when they used the potty on their own for the first time. Through the diary door, you build the entries and stories that stand as the stone markers on the road of childhood.

When your children are taking steps that mark momentous occasions in their personal history, you may be so awake and aware that you assure yourself that you could never forget the details of how, for instance, your child said "Da Da!" for the first time. Sadly, you *do* forget, and you don't realize you've forgotten until it's too late and your child is begging you for details your memory has treated carelessly after all.

In the diary, you can record milestones, pay attention to your children's unique process of achievement, and attend to their rites of passage in ways that transcend the brief notes that are often in baby books. Diary storytelling allows you to place these events and occurrences within a context of interesting details about their lives. The inclusion of dialogue, sensory description, portraits of the significant others, and plot development allows you to create interesting stories about your child's achievements or new experiences as she passes out of one phase into a new phase of her life. The milestones and accomplishments you write about in the diaries do not have to be momentous—your child will appreciate you celebrating the "small stuff." Has your child just clapped his hands for the first time? This can be as exciting and interesting as your child mastering difficult music on the piano at age five, climbing a mountain at age eight, or walking without you to school for the first time. You can include all of it.

It's important to remember when writing these stories, however, to avoid comparisons with other siblings or children. Statements like, "You learned to walk three months sooner than your brother!" will encourage competition and may engender self-esteem struggles between the siblings. Diary storytelling leads you to discover what is unique and exciting about each child's accomplishments. Diary writing encourages you to be truly appreciative—and to be cautious to avoid implying that your child's achievement just doesn't measure up to some expectation. Children want to feel that they are meeting milestones long before you ever expected them to. What can you write that will enhance your child's pleasure in having this moment of triumph preserved? Every child meets milestones at his or her own pace, and often when least expected, as my daughter Perrin did:

To Perrin (age 16 months), July 21, 1993

*Daddy said he put you to bed tonight in your crib, closed the door, heard you crying, checked on you and found you standing at the **door** trying to get out! Sixteen months and you climb out of your crib already!*

Firsts

Baby books typically provide you with lists of milestones and achievements about which to make notes. One such book I have contains a one-page list of "firsts" (which covers the first five years!) with room to record only one line of text about each. Baby books are often organized around the idea of *firsts*—recording the time when a child does, says, or experiences something for the very first time. Through the diary door, there are unlimited possibilities for writing creative and fulfilling entries around first experiences for children as they grow throughout the years, because children never stop encountering new challenges, new phases and stages, and new beginnings.

Some *firsts* are physiologically ordained and may be predicted, sought after, and anticipated by anxious parents. Whether you are eagerly waiting for your child to meet these specific developmental milestones or not, the actual achievement of them will almost always catch you by surprise, and that adds another element of delight to the experience for both parent and child. When my daughter Frances rolled over for the first time, she happened to perform this feat on our town's beach. In writing the diary entry I thought she might some day appreciate the fact that one of the casual bystanders who was observing her milestone was a well-known marathon runner who lives in our town and who happened to be sitting nearby observing her:

To Frances (age 3 months), July 2, 1997

... **Milestone:** *You rolled over for the first time yesterday. We were at Farm Pond, second day in a row sitting comfortably in the shade at the furthest edge of the beach next to Bill and Gail R. Perrin was in the water having her lesson. Bill and I were watching you twist and turn, and finally, just after Perrin ran up, after I had looked away for a moment Bill yelled, "She did it!" And there you were on your tummy! Landon came soon, quite sad that he had missed it. But you performed for him tonight instead.*

You won't be able to capture *all* of the milestones of your child's rapidly changing development, but certain moments in your observation and awareness of your child's daily growth will tug at you until you take the time to write them in the diary. The first time that a small child sees her reflection in the mirror, recognizes who she is, and calls herself by name may not be an event that can be predicted and caught on film, but it can be noticed, appreciated, and captured in the diary. This *first* for my daughter Frances tugged at me until I wrote it down:

To Frances (age almost 2), March 28, 1999

... *Friday night we were in my room rumbling on the bed and then I was walking you to bed. As we walked past the mirrors you caught your reflection, pointed and said: "Franci!"*

This is the very first time you said your own name. What a delight. I ran and told everyone who came running, but you would not repeat your performance. ...

A diary entry about a milestone may also tell a deeper story, connecting you with such universal themes as the awareness of time passing and the desire to feel connected to generations who came before you and who will come after you. In rereading the children's diaries, I notice that any time I write during a trip to Laurel Lake, a place in New Hampshire where my family has gathered in cottages now for four generations, I am flooded with memories and emotions. These entries spark a desire to reflect on the meaning of place or setting within the context of my family history. The diary writing is one way to give children a sense of past, a personal history, and a path of continuity. I can never remember off the top of my head what year my husband, brother, and sister-in-law bought our own cottage at Laurel Lake, but when I reread this entry I remember that it was at the very end of this special summer of *firsts* for Perrin:

To Perrin (age 4 months), July 19, 1992

I have come to treasure the early morning; a time to be quiet by myself, but near my loved ones, to read my daily meditations; to write. I love the first hour of the morning because it is so full of hope and possibility. No surprise to me that both of my babies were born in the morning!

You sleep, bundled in your white and pink sweat suit beside me as I sit here writing on the picnic table Daddy built our first summer here when Landon was a baby.

*How I have missed the smell of these pines. The paper is getting spit on by them. I see the tops of the pines, and I watch you closely, guarding you from the mosquitoes, which are bad, this year. I listen for sounds from Aunt Virginia's cottage, hoping to share an early morning coffee with her while Daddy and Land sleep soundly in the double bed and Pam and Hanna sleep **tightly** in the bottom bunk. Uncle Bob must have crashed at Aunt V's. Grammy Burke arrives this afternoon w/ Grampy.*

Your very first trip to Laurel Lake. (If you don't count last summer when I was... pregnant with you.)

Our family has been coming here for generations I can say. Your Grammy has been coming here since she was just a little girl, and every summer since. And, of course, with a few summers missed here and there, now have I, and now has Landon, and now, will you?

During certain periods of their young lives, children grow so rapidly and accumulate first experiences so frequently that it can be challenging to keep on top of this process in your memory and awareness, let alone in the diary. When this happens, you can bring the diary up to date quickly by summarizing milestones and accomplishments in the form of a list. I did this with an entry that is continued from the previous one about the Laurel Lake trip, when so much happened at once for my daughter Perrin that I wanted to save:

To Perrin (age 4 months), August 4, 1992

In the three weeks of our trip, you did all these things:
- *Rode your second plane*
- *Cut two bottom teeth—your first*
- *Met all your cousins, for the first time*
- *Wore your gold lame bathing suite at Laurel Lake*
- *Watched your Dad & Uncle D. get a trophy in the Laurel Lake canoe race*
- *Rolled completely over for the first time*
- *Put your feet in Laurel Lake & Farm Pond for the first time*
- *Sat up on your own w/o falling over*
- *Sat in your new jumper seat*
- *Spent an evening in Quincy Market & got your picture taken*
- *Rode the ferry to Martha's Vineyard*
- *Visited the cottage on L.L. that we are hoping to buy w/ Billie & Dusty*

Milestones can be markers of certain aspects of your child's identity, as we discovered during our first summer at Laurel Lake with our third child:

To Frances (age 3 months), July 15, 1997

*. . . Sitting on the dock early yesterday morning, beside the still lake and the last sounds of the owls, watching the orioles flit from tree to tree, I say to Daddy, who is holding you—just the three of us awake—"You know, she is our only child **born** while we've owned the camp, and the house. . . .Our only child born in New England"*

"Our Yankee baby," he says.

Yes.

The water was quite cold, so I didn't let you swim.

In baby books, you are told what to notice and record about your child's development. But, in the diary, how do you know what the important milestones are that your child will hope you save? Well, you know your own child better than anyone else. You intuitively know the big stuff, know whom they love and admire, know what they dream of, hope for, look forward to, and struggle to achieve. You know what matters to them now, and you have a sense about what will matter to them later on.

When a child is ready for her or his first overnight stay away from home, this can be a momentous event, opening a door to new freedom and new intimacies beyond the parent, child, and sibling relationships. Neither one of you is likely to take it lightly, but rather to see it as an important emotional milestone that gives your child the reassurance that it's okay to sleep away from home. Whatever kind of first-overnight adventure your child has—full of ease or emotionally challenging—writing the story about it will help you to connect with the important needs and feelings that both you and your child may have about it. I knew this long-anticipated first overnight with an older cousin would be a treasured milestone for my daughter Perrin. The matter-of-fact tone of this simple entry reminds me that by the time Perrin was ready for her first overnight, she was wholeheartedly ready and there was no holding her back. The theme I captured then has remained consistent over the last five years of these overnights with her cousin Maelyn—she's always ready to go, and never ready to return home:

To Perrin (age 4), May 3, 1996

> You are ready for your first overnight at Maelyn's w/o me or Landon. All day you have been asking if you can stay four nights instead of one.
>
> Maelyn calls in the late afternoon to tell you what dolls to bring. We drive over in the rain and you sleep on the way. Dinner for all of us at McDonald's, and a perfunctory kiss goodbye.
>
> I will see you tomorrow afternoon whether you're ready or not!

Birthdays as Milestones

Birthdays offer an opportunity to stop, reflect on, and summarize all that has happened over the past year in your child's growth and development. If you are writing regularly throughout the year, however, you may not feel a need to make special birthday entries to bring things up to date. But if you're not, then birthdays are an excellent time to open the diary and write your child a story about that special day that involves your observations and reflections about the significance of the event.

However, you may find, as I have, that you become so caught up in planning, shopping for, and creating birthday celebrations that you neglect the diary writing on these major occasions. That's okay. You may want to wait and write a birthday entry during calmer times after the birthday storm has blown over. It wasn't until four days after my daughter's third birthday that I managed to find the time for a birthday entry:

To Frances (age 3), April 14, 2000

Daddy, as promised, woke you Sunday morning (which we treated as your birthday even though it was the 9th) by going to your bed, kneeling down, and whispering in your ear:

"Wake up, Frances. It's your birthday!"

You had asked very specifically for this.

Perrin gave you her present first: a lifelike baby doll w/ a pacifier. You took the thing out of her mouth because you assumed she hated it.

A little later we gave you your birthday ritual. We put you on the birthing chair which was layered w/ colorful scarves and put the birthday crown on your head and let you hold the birthday wand. We lit your birthday candle and Joey and Landon blew bubbles at you. We paraded around you three times and sang happy birthday. We gave thanks for your birth and acknowledged your namesake, Nana, w/ her picture and your other grandparents with theirs.

You sat quietly, in awe, drinking all the attention in. Boy [Landon] gave you his card & gift—the promise of a trip to Frosty's and the playground.

We gave you your long-awaited gift—the trampoline. In a moment Daddy had it assembled and all of you were jumping like monkeys.

Then it was time to rush around and get ready for your party. Perrin and Dad assembled all the food, and soon your guests began to arrive bearing gifts and fuelled w/ a wild energy. . . .

Milestones Contain Slice-of-Life Portraits

When you write about their milestones in the diary, you give your children what they need and are asking you for *and more*. Writing about them in the diary gives details about milestones along with slice-of-life portraits. You give them the milestones in a context that may relate their accomplishments to other significant events in their lives that you may all find interesting later on. I suspect my daughter Perrin will appreciate this milestone that includes a birth notice of a cousin who becomes a bosom-buddy playmate:

To Perrin (age 7 months), October 29, 1992

You have a cousin! Baby Dustin the 3rd! Eight pounds one ounce born around 3:00 a.m.

Daddy yelled: "Watch mommy!" and held you up and let go of you and you took three steps completely on your own!

Language Milestones

The depth, breadth, and quality of the diary writing expand when children begin to develop language. They provide their own fresh, funny, intriguing, and provocative dialogue to enrich the stories of their lives. Language that begins as sounds and babbling soon develops into first words, like those of my daughter Perrin:

To Perrin (age 17 months), August 29, 1993

Nana came to a Roast Beef Dinner. Her 80th birthday is in two weeks.

You are afraid of thunderstorms, and we have had a couple of beastly ones in the last few days, sending you, me and Land into hiding in my room. You, who never sits still except when sleeping, sat on my lap with your hands around my neck and your head buried in my chest. When it's over you of course recover quickly.

You say "shoe," and "Pooh" and "no" and "mine," and when you see something you like (whipped cream on your apple crisp tonight) you say "ooooooooooh!" You say "baby," "dolly," "Barney," "Banana," "Nana," "Grammy." You love to talk on the phone, and you have a temper tantrum when we get you off.

Soon enough, sounds, babbling and first words transform into three-word phrases that make increasing sense, bringing possibilities for deeper and deeper intimacy and connection with your child. There may be no sweeter words to a parent's ears than a child saying "I love you" for the first time:

To Frances (age almost 2), March 5, 1999

Of all the new words you are saying—and there are many—probably the most gratifying to each of us is,

"I love you!"

Another phrase you've mastered is "Happy Birthday!" Yesterday, to Perri's delight, as we were in Daddy's car doing some shopping for P's birthday and discussing her party, you said from the seat next to her:

"Happy Birthday, P!"

Right on time you are making three-word sentences, and purring like a little copy-cat, you mimic every word that comes out of our mouths toward you.

. . . . Frances, you are like what I think they call a diviner—someone who uses a divining rod to search for sources of water underground to find the place to dig the well. You're a love diviner. You find the love in people and love it out of them right down to the very depths of the well inside.

You're a lover. You have Nana's blood in your veins. You have Nana's spirit. Nana was a lover. Nana, even after she had her strokes in the nursing home [and couldn't call any of us by name] would cup my face in her hands and say:

"I love you up to the sky!"

. . . This is the kind of thing **you** *do, Frances. Sometimes you come and cup my face in your hands and say urgently:*

"Mommy!" *and stop my heart dead in its tracks because to be noticed this deeply is startling, it takes my breath away. It can be arresting to realize how important a person I am. You make me so.*

I pull myself up by my bootstraps in awe of this, your love for me. This is a deep, deep well I fall into, loved and being loved by you. . . .

Achievements

Achievement: Something that has been accomplished successfully, especially by means of exertion, skill, practice or perseverance (*The American Heritage Dictionary*)

Your children work hard to accomplish certain things, and they expect you to notice and appreciate their efforts when they do. Accomplishments that come easy to one child can involve overwhelming struggle for the next child. Keeping track of your children's achievements in the diary is a way of showing them that you really see how hard they are trying and that you appreciate how important certain successes are to them. These stories may later serve as proof to remind your children at a difficult time that they are capable of achieving goals. Perhaps they will be stories to share with *their* own children someday.

These stories of achievement, when written in the diary, offer you greater freedom to explore and expand your thinking than the brief record that may be kept in a baby book. In the diary, there is the story you *intend* to tell, but you may also discover an unintended story that springs from the same source. When you place your child's achievement into the context of her or his daily life, you may be pleasantly surprised some day to find that it contains a larger story. For instance, the reporting of one milestone may capture a multigenerational story about other achievements in the family, as does this one to my son Landon about riding his bike alone to his friend's house for the first time:

To Landon (age 5), September 12, 1993

Tomorrow is Nana's 80th birthday, so Daddy and I went out to her birthday party at Bon Appetit. We brought home cake which you and Perrin hungrily gobbled after having brushed your teeth. Tomorrow we will go and wish Nana a happy birthday in person w/ you and Perrin after school.

You had a big day on Sat.: you scored the first goal of the season for your team, and went on to score another. Your team won. Daddy was substitute coaching.

But Friday was an even bigger day—you finally rode your bike completely on your own, up to Jason's and back. You've been high on it all weekend, smiling proudly at your new accomplishment. . . .

Uncle Dusty just called to tell us that he and Grampy won the President's Cup Tournament at the Club. Uncle Dusty has only been golfing for five months!

The achievement of certain milestones may involve fun for the whole family as this entry about my younger daughter learning to snap her fingers does:

To Frances (age 2), November 5, 1999

Last weekend, Daddy was carrying you to the car and he heard a snapping sound at his ear.

"What's that?" he asked.

He looked at your fingers and realized you were snapping! He set you in your car seat and we both looked at you in amazement.

"Who taught you how to snap your fingers?" we asked. You looked at us staring at you and said,

"P." [Perrin]

"Oh! Oh! P taught you to snap your fingers!" We all rejoiced.

But you were missing P terribly, because she spent two nights at Hannah's. All weekend we got you snapping those fingers. Perrin was even surprised to come home and find you doing such a good job.

Landon said, "Wow, I didn't start snapping my fingers until I was about seven!"

Your dainty fingers don't look sturdy enough to make such a big sound!

Milestones and Accomplishments as Assessment Opportunities

As you are recording certain milestones, you may find yourself evaluating what the accomplishment of this particular milestone means in your decision making about your child in the future. Does this mean she or he is capable of moving on to greater challenges? Writing in the diary can help you reflect on what the accomplishment of this milestone might mean to your child and how it might guide you in your decision making. Any time we support our children to take on challenges and risks in working toward accomplishments, we're taking risks in our own decision-making skills as parents. I seem to have written the following passage as much to myself as to my daughter Perrin, as if I were relieved to realize that the risks I had supported her to take were well-grounded and had paid off:

To Perrin (age 4), June 10, 1996

Yesterday, it was warm and muggy and overcast. A heavy day, that I rather enjoyed. Every time I walked into your bedroom, the air was thick w/the scent of the celebratory pink roses that overflowed the vase by your bed. It was as if the memory of your recital was trapped by the canopy of moist air hanging in the house. I was glad, and very surprised at how pleasant and happy the busy week felt upon completion.

*I never thought we could get through it all! I was surprised by how well **you** got through it all. I started the week dreading all the pressure, but by yesterday was left w/ only feelings of delight in your accomplishment, and the flowers—your congratulatory flowers spread around the house in cheerful bunches kept reminding me of a wonderful sense of completion about the dance year.*

*. . . I watched your performance from backstage—as good as the night before— no jitters, just concentration, and from the perspective of looking out **at** the audience, I was struck by the magnitude of what you had done—you were facing a large audience taking a significant risk, and you didn't seem nervous! How amazing to achieve this ability to face an audience at such a young age.*

Really, all my doubts about this dance class & performance have been destroyed. . . .

There are few absolutes in this parenting process, and few parenting decisions that involve the complexities of supporting your children to take risks come easily. One gift of reflective writing in the diary is that it allows you to assess what you have learned about the decisions you make as a parent. Diary storytelling also offers problem-solving opportunities.

Milestones and Problem Solving

The most reflective and helpful entries seem to be unplanned. Rarely do I sit down, open one of my children's diaries, and begin writing with the intention of solving a particular problem. What I begin with is an urge to tell my child a story, and often I'm not even certain what the story is about until I begin to write it. It's not necessarily a conscious decision to report something specific in the diary, but rather a response to an intuitive desire to open the diary door and find something I'm not even consciously looking for. Often, the story begins, as the following entry does, with a simple description of something that happened during the day, like a routine trip to the hairdresser. Writing about this haircut helped me recognize that a mile-

stone had been met and led me to an insight about the need to be more spontaneously attentive to my daughter's needs:

Frances (age 2), December 22, 1999

. . . Haircuts yesterday for you and Land.

*. . . At the haircut place—Snip-Its, you sat drowsy and dazed as the nice lady cut
your hair prettily for Christmas—a nice, clean trimming.*

*Putting you to bed, I read "The Night Before Christmas," then turned off the light
and cuddling you in a blanket as I rocked you, we sang "Away in a Manger," then two
rounds of "Silent Night."*

"Mommy?"

"Yes."

"I have a question. That boy pushed me!"

*You were referring to a little boy in Snip-Its who seems to have come up and
pushed you off the top cube where you had been sitting. I saw you land on the floor,
and I guessed that he had pushed you by the look on your face of hurt. You were not
hurt physically, but you had certainly been de-throned.*

*I called you over, gave you a hug, asked what happened. Then we were called for
our cuts and I forgot all about it.*

You didn't.

*. . . As I sat rocking you in the darkened room, listening to your story and your feel-
ings about the boy who pushed you, I realized what a milestone this was—our first
real bedtime problem-solving talk!*

*Tuck-in time has been a lovely, important ritual for me w/ the other two for many,
many years—still is. It's a time for feelings to be uncovered and explored, soothed
and comforted, probed and sometimes resolved.*

*Intuitively, as if you'd been healing your hurt feelings for forty years, you seemed
to know exactly what you needed to do to feel better.*

*"Ring Ring!" you said, putting your pretend phone to your ear. "Boy, don't push me
again . . . . Okay Mom, you talk" you said, handing me the phone.*

*"Boy, you really hurt Frances feelings. She doesn't want you to do that ever again.
She's friendly and she wants you to act like a friend."*

*We went back and forth like this for quite awhile while you settled your feelings.
. . . Listening to you, I became aware of your needs, realized, perhaps, that I had not
properly helped you address them* **in the moment***. Perhaps I overlooked your need
to speak to the boy directly? Perhaps you needed to tell him in-person how you felt
& set the boundary w/him. I think this is one of my greatest challenges, speaking up
to people who hurt me in a spontaneous and assertive way. It's a terribly important*

skill to have in life. Just because I don't always do it as well as I like it doesn't mean
I can't help you learn to do it well.

Milestones in Emerging Sexuality

Sex is something children ask questions about and share opinions on as soon as they can say a three-word sentence. The diary is the perfect place to begin paying attention to your child's growing interest in and awareness of his or her sexuality. Writing about sex to your child can help you break through some of your own shyness or self-consciousness regarding sex so that you can feel more comfortable addressing your child's concerns about sex at every developmental stage. The diary is a perfectly appropriate, private place to reflect on your child's sexual development.

If you wait until your child approaches puberty to talk openly about sex and sexuality, you and your child may simply be too embarrassed to get over the hurdle. You may use the diary entries and dialogues early on with your child to normalize the process of talking about sex, to clarify and communicate your values, and try to understand what information your children need and what developmental transitions they are experiencing. There may be a respectful *and* fun way to write about sexual development, as there was, unexpectedly, with my son one spring day:

To Landon (age 10), May 1, 1998

I was pretty shocked by what I saw out of my kitchen window a short time after you and Alex got home from school.

First, I heard giggling coming from the driveway. Girlish giggles that might have come from Perrin and Tory, except their [there] was a quality of determination, or purposefulness to the giggles that I knew would not come from your sister, who would be giggling from pure pleasure, rather than as an enticement.

I looked out the kitchen window.

Girls. One on a bike, both at the end of the driveway looking up at me—or rather, the front windows where they wait to catch another glimpse of the two of you when your ears catch their drift.

I tell you. You both groan, but then you are out of the door in a flash, and very soon ask if you can go for a walk.

I don't see you for an hour or so—seems you went and hung around her [the girl's] house for awhile outside. This is the very first boy/girl encounter that I have witnessed you in. I suspect Alex is the instigator; he has been more interested in girls.

Now what? . . .

Illnesses and Health Challenges

Every child encounters illnesses and health challenges as he or she grows. Childhood illnesses can trigger emotional responses in both of you. The diary is a place where you can explore your child's ways of dealing with discomfort and pain. You can write about how you and your child deal with sickness, whether it is occasional or a chronic condition. You can keep track of significant illnesses that may be useful later in a medical history. Perhaps with increasing use of the chicken pox vaccine, cases of this classic childhood illness will become as rare as measles by the time my children, who each had the disease, become adults. Maybe that will make this story more interesting to my daughter later on:

To Perrin (age 5), January 24, 1998

"Chicken Pox"

It is grey and rainy, all the snow left on the ground is soggy and slushy. More like a late March day. I will tell you the story of you getting the chicken pox:

On a Wednesday afternoon, a week before Christmas we had your first stained glass cookie making party. We invited seven of your best friends. . . .

. . . so, we made cookies, everyone went home, and you complained of not feeling well, a headache, and you did feel warm. But it wasn't until Thurs. night, tucking you in, that I discovered the problem. Stretched out on your bed you complained of itching. I looked at your thighs, and was quite alarmed to see a strange rash. Then my eyes travelled to your abdomen where it seemed to be spreading, and after a moment or two of puzzlement I finally took evidence from every area of your body and had no difficulty determining that it was Chicken Pox! Chicken Pox the week before Christmas! And I realized we may have sent home a lot more than cookies w/your friends! (I called them all and laughed w/their mothers.)

*The first day wasn't too bad. But you cried quite a bit Thurs. when you discovered it—"I don't want Chicken Pox!" I think it was scary for you because you had seen the kid in your class come back to school all ugly and pock marked. It **is** a distressing thing to suddenly see your nice smooth skin break out into ugly sores (I know only too well from my years of acne). The promise that you needn't return to school until well after Christmas comforted you a bit. . . .*

Saturday was a miserable, itchy day for you, and even you—of boundless energy—didn't rise from the couch all day.

Except to bathe in oatmeal. Sunday you had to miss Aunt Jody's Christmas party, but since you got to eat black raspberry ice cream for breakfast, lunch and dinner, you hardly minded at all.

By Mon. you were quite better, happy to be home from school, Tuesday it snowed heavily and you wandered outdoors, and Wed. Santa Claus came! . . .

Rites of Passage

Rite of Passage: A ceremonial act . . . any ritual that marks the transition from one stage of life to another . . . an initiation rite. (*The American Heritage Dictionary*)

There are many kinds of rite of passage stories to attend to in the diary writing that will be gratifying for you to write and your children to read. These are stories that capture children, in both small and large ways, approaching doorways or passages in their experiences and development that bring them to the threshold of closed chapters and new beginnings. These stories of transition and initiation may involve cultural rites of passage that are often developmentally based. There may be religious ceremonies that honor rites of passage, like a baptism, a First Communion, or a Bar Mitzvah. There are stories about rites of passage that are gender-based, such as your son's first shave or your daughter's first period. Your child may treasure stories that celebrate these special occasions in the diaries later on. There are also family rites of passage, which have to do with accomplishing milestones that may have a particular meaning to your own family. Perhaps they have been handed down for generations, or perhaps you have created and introduced them to bring a greater awareness of the importance of ceremony and ritual in your own family. Writing about them as diary stories can add to the sense of purpose and meaning that you hope to evoke through these rituals. There are also personal rites of passage, which may have meaning only to you or your child. You can write about all of these experiences through the diary door.

These rite of passage stories often mark a physical change or the accomplishment of a new ability in your child, but their greatest significance may be the emotional or psychological changes they represent for both you and your child. Writing about them in the diary can help you be attentive and responsive to your child's transitional feelings, needs, and issues that surface with the change of status or role, as well as to your own.

For instance, the loss of baby teeth and growth of permanent teeth that typically happens around the time children start kindergarten or first grade corresponds with the many social, biological, emotional, and cognitive changes for a school-age child. Of course, whether it's nature or some other influence taking its course in the first lost tooth, there's always a story to tell about *how* your child loses it that she or he may be interested in later on. The ritual of the magical, nocturnal visit of the

Tooth Fairy never fails to add an intriguing element of enchantment to any story about losing teeth:

To Perrin (age 4), July 5, 1996

*It was about three weeks ago that I put you two to bed on a weeknight, hoping you would fall right asleep w/o much effort—on **my** part. Dad was away; I was tired from a full day. Lorri had called me earlier during your story time, and I asked to call her right back. We were in need of a long, reconnecting talk.*

After tucking you each safely in bed, I heard Land ask what I was planning to do. Foolishly, I told him, and I retired to the family room couch to talk.

Noises in the outer reaches aroused me to know that the two of you were up....

Soon, deep in conversation w/ Lorri, the two of you interrupted me w/ some urgency.

"Perri's tooth is bleeding!" I hung up. Yes, it was, but not badly. You weren't particularly hurt, just a little concerned. I wasn't concerned—it was just a touch of blood—until I heard the story of how it happened.

You were playing Dog and Fish. You put one end of the jump rope in your mouth—you were the dog, and Land held the other—he was the fish. The dog was chasing the fish who was swimming away and pulling on the rope. At some point the fish accidentally fell which pulled so hard on the rope that it knocked your top front tooth loose.

I certainly wasn't ready to see you lose a front tooth, so I urged you to stop wiggling it, hoping it would re-settle and last another year. For a couple of weeks you favored it, avoiding bagels, and we all tried to ignore the discoloration it assumed as well as the gap it left by its new slant.

A week ago I took you to the dentist, and finally had to realize the tooth was on its way out; no need to pull it, but it would go momentarily. We all began to accept that it would go soon.

Yesterday I took you & Land to D.Z. [Discovery Zone Play Area], and again, you came running up to me to tell me your tooth was bleeding. I sort of tried to pull it, but this is not my thing:

"Daddy will pull it," I said, and you went off to play.

Standing in line for the fire engine rides [at the 4th of July celebration] . . . a bit later, Daddy was holding you to say hello, and suddenly we all noticed your tooth was gone!

You must have swallowed it!

So, even though you didn't have a tooth to put in your little tooth container under the pillow, I had you put it there anyway when you went to bed, very excited, and quite hopeful.

As always, you climbed into Dad's & my bed in the middle of the night, so you woke there. As I was showering, you ran into the bathroom shouting and gleefully waving a dollar bill, smiling with a gap-toothed grin:

"She came! She came! The tooth fairy came!"

I've been grieving a little today, though, because this tooth-losing is a rite of passage. It represents how close you are to being school-age, how far you've come from babyhood, and when your very first teeth came in.

I'm not sure I'm ready for this!

Whether or not we feel ready to accept it, our children will move forward. Over and over again I have found that diary storytelling helps me to acknowledge and accept my own feelings about my children growing up and moving into new phases. The writing process allows me to express and accept feelings (without judging them) that may block me from facing the normal, emotional losses involved in change, freeing me to be open to the gains that will surely replace them.

Honoring Family Rites of Passage

Families create and pass on rituals and rites that have to do with their unique interests and opportunities. These rituals, elaborate or simple, formal or informal, gain significance through history and repetition as they become embedded in the family culture.

These rites of passage may be dictated by chronological age or by some risk-taking or achievement. Your children know what these initiation rites are—they have probably watched older sisters, brothers, or cousins pass through them, win the approval, move to the other side of the invisible bar that allows them to feel included in something they have reached for. They mark a passage, within the immediate or extended family, into a new status for your child.

In our extended, multigenerational family, learning to swim at the small sandy beach at Laurel Lake is a ritual that each child grows up with from the time she or he is able to toddle off the beach blanket to the place where sand meets water. Every swimmer is aiming for the same destination from this beach. There is a huge, flat-surfaced, copper colored rock that serves as a perfect raft for as many as ten people and lies mysteriously under less than a foot of water directly out from the beach about as deep as the chest of one's father. There are no formalized swimming lessons at Laurel Lake, but rather coaching, modeling and encouragement from swimmers of every age who take on the responsibility of helping each child achieve the basic skills required to swim for the very first time to the rock completely on one's own. This initiation rite signifies a new freedom and a new status—a swimmer who no longer needs supervision to get to the rock has been born. When my daughter gained this status, I made sure to make note of it:

To Perrin (age 4), July 8, 1996

You sleep, exhausted. Pink-cheeked and hoarse from over-tired crying, you fell asleep in my bed, moist from a shower, (not the bath you wanted). Two days of constant swimming and sun and walks from our cabin to Grammy's to the beach, over stumps and rocks in your barefeet—you're pooped!

But I must tell you about your swimming yesterday. Saturday you went happily to the rock w/Grampy, leaning on a blue floatie. But Sun. I knew you were ready, w/Maelyn there, to go yourself. So, I took you to the rock, stood back, and w/in minutes you were swimming successfully on your own to and from the rock. So, there!

Another rite of passage in one long weekend! . . .

There may be significant experiences that you remember fondly from your own childhood that you want to pass down to your children. The tradition of the annual grange fair was still thriving when I was growing up in a small rural town in New England that was becoming less rural every day. Years later, after I had returned to live in the town with my husband and children, the town held a revival of the old grange fair tradition as part of its 325th anniversary celebration, and I had the opportunity to share some childhood rituals with my daughter. Whether the experience was more meaningful and gratifying to me than to my daughter only time may tell, but writing about it completed the circle for my having changed roles from daughter to mother:

To Perrin (age 7), October 1, 1999

The afternoon before the Grange Fair—a Friday—you came home for us to bake.

*Together, as Frances sat on the bar stool w/ persistent, flowery hands which she would **not** keep out of your dough, we made your first, from-scratch loaf of white bread to enter into the fair.*

*I'm not sure how old I was when I made **my** first fair loaves w/ **my** Mom, but it was a ritual I felt determined to replicate—as long as you seemed interested.*

Of course, you had no direct rival—we had no idea who else might enter—but I was always trying to beat Michelle B., my next door neighbor, who always seemed to be entering the same items as I was. I think she often beat me, alas.

Anyway, Grammy B. was very good at helping me learn to cook. I helped her preserve her pickles.

We kneaded the bread, and set it aside to rise, which I thought you'd find very exciting. This is the fun part about making bread—being aware of all its stages as it turns from flour and yeast into bread. Then you made your brownies, all by yourself, really, because this is a recipe you have mastered. TV on the couch w/ Landon was a welcome break after this, so I had quiet time in the kitchen to work on my own entry—frosted hands & feet w/ fingernail polish.

Finally, by about 9 pm the bread was baked, tossed from the pan on the butcher block, and sliced into.

"MMMMM!" I can't believe how good this tastes," you said as you consumed piece after piece of the extra loaf.

Sat. morning, around 8:30, I began to get all our items ready for entry . . . The day before I had been to the garden and knew I had many beautiful tomatoes and eggplant left.

It was raining heavily, but I ran up and collected a huge basket of vegetables. I found three nearly perfect eggplant . . . I washed them, grabbed the bread, brownies, cookies, et al. . . . and drove up to the Barber reservation and made the entries in the rain.

. . . Later, the sun shone as we picked up Grammy and hurried to the fair. After 11:00, they finally finished the judging. Little Dusty had entered potatoes that he had helped to grow in Grampy's garden. . . .

Under the tent were all the entries w/ pumpkins, hay-bales, and scarecrows all around as decorations.

As we entered the tent, a friend of mine . . . ran over to me, grabbed my arm and pulled me over to the tables of bountiful vegetables, tomatoes, radishes, squash, and grapes and apples and fruits of all kinds.

"Look—you're eggplants have won!"

I looked up at the prominent display of my three eggplant sitting in their basket, adorned w/ a big, bright, flashy yellow ribbon that read:

"Best of Show."

. . . Rushing across the tent, we went to the children's table where we found your brownies first w/ an Honorable Mention ribbon. (They only gave out first prize w/ honorable mention). . . . Then we found your bread w/ a blue first-prize ribbon!

. . . My beautiful tomatoes got a first . . . and my decorated cookies got honorable mention. . . .

Perhaps you can see that, though you seemed to enjoy the fair, it was really **me** who enjoyed it most. "Little" Kelly has been jumping up & down for joy. . . .

There are countless milestones, achievements, and rite of passage stories that can be written about your own children and families, and this chapter only hints at a few of the possibilities. The next chapter looks at the ways that we try to encourage, support, and capture our children's creativity through diary storytelling. But first, try these Diary Door Openers.

 Diary Door Openers

1. Making Note of *Firsts*
   Make a list of *firsts* achieved by your child over a period of time, like a week or a month, and allow this process to warm you up to a longer story about one of these significant achievements.

2. First Words
   Begin an entry, "Today you said . . ." and see where it takes you.

3. Filling In *Firsts*
   Ask the person who witnesses one of your child's *firsts* in your absence to write the story about it for you in the diary or to give you enough details to write it yourself.

4. Birthday Rituals
   Write about one thing you do to honor your child on his or her birthday. Where did you get the idea? How did your child feel about it?

5. Initiation Stories
   Think about a moment when your child stood on the threshold of embracing a new role or stood outside and apart from something she or he wanted to achieve or be included in. Describe your child's process of becoming or belonging. Reflect on what was gained and what was left behind for each of you.

6. Sacred Family Places
   Describe a place where your family goes to connect more deeply with each other and with the environment, or to relax, reflect, and revive spirits, nurture the soul, and have fun. If this place doesn't yet exist, imagine it, and describe it for your child—and perhaps you will find it some day.

Chapter 8

Creative Juicing
Nurturing Creativity in
Parents and Kids

Only the creative are free.

(J. L. Moreno, *Words of the Father*, p. 122)

W e crave opportunities to be creative, and so do our children. We want to nourish their creativity and offer them opportunities to explore all their own talents and gifts. Diaries are a place in which we can be creative as parents as well as a place where we can capture stories of our children's creativity in action.

Diaries Provide a Safe Play Area

Diaries provide a perfect environment for supporting creative expression. One primary reason we write diaries is that diary writing honors the creative process and offers freedom to experiment and expand our thinking, feeling, and imagining. We look beyond predictable and restrictive categories to write out of the box, between the lines, and through the looking glass, giving ourselves permission to nurture our own creativity as well as our child's creative process. Through the diary door, we get to follow our spontaneous storytelling to see where it leads us. We get to follow our children's stories to see where they might be going and what doors their risk-taking and mistake-making might be opening for us as well.

Diary writing provides a safe place to play, experiment, and dream without fear of making a mistake—like a child in the sandbox with a shovel. The blank page is like the empty sandbox—with each blank page of the notebook we get to start from scratch. We can dig, sculpt, sift, shape, build castles and tear them down, and smooth it all over with a new day, a new entry, a new story, a new beginning.

Making a Mess and Making Mistakes

The challenges we face in encouraging creativity in our children are problems that most of us as parents continue to struggle with daily as adults. Is it okay to make a mess? Is it okay to try something new if it means I might make a mistake? We might find that as adults we continue to encounter the same obstacles that blocked our creative risk-taking as children. We might find ourselves thinking about how we handled our creative impulses, activities, and explorations as children. How did other people typically handle them? Were we encouraged or allowed to make a mess? How did others, like teachers or parents, treat us when we made a mistake? How did we treat ourselves?

Our children need to know, just as we constantly need to be reminded, that creative expression involves risk-taking and all the potential glory and failure that go along with it. To create means to originate—to make something or do something that is uniquely our own. We have little or no control over the response to our creative endeavors. To be creative, we have to allow ourselves to be vulnerable and we have to be willing to encounter the emotional and intellectual risks involved in creative expression. We need to be allowed and to be willing to make a mistake and to make a mess. We need to learn to face the risk that even though we may be seeking approval, we may find only criticism and harsh judgment about the quality of our work or ideas.

We need to be willing to have faith in ourselves and to make a commitment to a creative project even though we can have no assurance that it will be worth the commitment in the end. We need to maintain trust in the creative process and in ourselves even while voices of self-doubt and insecurity urge us to give up and stop wasting our time. Diary writing is always there to offer support as we encourage our child's creative process and embrace our own.

Parents as Supportive Narrators

Through diary storytelling we want to encourage and support our children's creativity as well as to capture and preserve stories of their creative expression in action. We write entries that will help to give our children the skills for dealing with risk-taking and overcoming blocks to creativity. As narrators who observe our children's risks and challenges, we provide the emotional safety that will allow them to risk vulnerability in creative endeavors by giving them a foundation of appreciation of their natural and acquired talents and abilities.

We honor our children's stories of creative expression in the diaries by following the same impulse that calls us to display their artwork and save it in boxes in the attic. We're proud of their creations, and we want them to know how much we enjoy their originality and imaginative sculpture, paintings, collages, and drawings. Imagination is the most important problem-solving tool they possess, and our children will need to play with it their whole lives. Our words, actions, and stories give them permission to use it.

We also simply want them to have fun and we want to have fun, too! Playfulness is a quality we naturally possess in childhood that we usually have to work hard at re-introducing into our lives in adulthood. Diary writing gives us permission to be playful and to appreciate the playfulness of our children. One way children play creatively with their futures is to imagine what they want to be when they grow up.

"What I Want to Be When I Grow Up"

Once, we imagined what we wanted to do when we grew up. Maybe we are doing it now. Maybe we *wish* we were. Perhaps we appropriately left dreams of what we could never realistically achieve in the past with other childhood illusions. Our children, like us, will seek their true callings in life. They confide their dreams, goals, and wishes to us, trying them on for the first time with us as their first career counselors. My daughter Perrin began to discuss her career plans and goals with me when she was four. Where she got the idea that she might need to have the freedom to explore more than one major career in life, I'm not sure, but I really appreciated the creative idea she came up with to solve the problem of wanting to *do it all*:

To Perrin (age 4), February 25, 1996

... "Mommy, what do you want to be when you grow up?"

"A writer."

"Oh, I want to be . . . a ballerina."

"Oh, that's nice."

"And, in my second grown up, I'm going to be a fire trucker . . . No, a doctor. And in my **third** grow up, I'm going to be a dresser."

"A dresser? What's that?"

"Like Linda! A dresser!"

"Oh, a hairdresser! Sure."

"Mom, am I going to have a second grow up?"

"Sure."

Most children spend time planning their careers in early childhood. Though their plans may go through significant revision by the time they graduate from high school or begin to work or attend college, these early projections may be signifi-cant. Whether or not my son will achieve the career goal recorded in the following entry, it must be important to him to attend to because he keeps repeating it as he commits himself more and more to playing the game he loves and is good at:

To Landon (age 11), July 20, 1998

...Yesterday as we all piled out of the car to shop at Bradlee's you said:
"I know what I want to be when I grow up."
"What?"
"A professional soccer player."
You met the Revolution at Babson [during summer camp]....

Prior to this, when my son was eight, his goals were much more abstract and much less specific. Rather than giving me clues to his future, his career plans seemed to reflect the developmental themes that he was struggling with regarding good and evil and power versus powerlessness. One evening, he and I went for a leisurely stroll when he began shyly telling me his plans as darkness fell around us:

To Landon (age 8), March 29, 1995

...Towards the end of the walk you ask me, kind of giggling—actually, it was just after you said, out of the blue, "I wish there was never any danger, and I wish we could all live forever," you asked,
"Mom, if you think about something that you want to happen over & over for a few years, does it happen?"
"Usually it does," I say.
Giggles, shyly. "Oh, well then I've been thinking that I want to fight bad guys...."
Giggles; A moment or two later,
"The problem is I haven't seen myself winning!"

Some childhood wishes may be based on pure whim, fantasy, or wish fulfill-ment, like the one above. Some are momentary passions and others cling to chil-dren persistently, perhaps pointing them in a natural direction toward doing what they're best at or finding a way to do what will really make them happy and fulfilled in adult careers. Recording your child's career hopes, plans, and dreams can help guide them and explore the possibilities. That they will reflect on their career choices as adults is a given. The diaries you keep for them now may later remind them of dreams they may have left behind in their childhood that are worth reclaiming in adulthood. My daughter Perrin seems to have lost the belief that she will get "second and third grow-ups," and continues to struggle with the theme of being faced with too many competing career goals:

To Perrin (age 7), November 2, 1999

. . . You came home cheerfully, and played w/ Katie & Frances as you do every Monday. At bedtime, as always, your juices started to roll. We had been sitting on the black couch, me coaching Landon his vocab., you patiently sewing a baby blanket by hand. But then I had to put L—who was tired—to bed, and you wanted to read Harry Potter.

"Meet me in front of the fireplace," I said, because Daddy had built a fire in my bedroom.

But, we never got to Harry Potter. In the bathroom you started chatting to me non-stop about your career plans, and though we did sit in front of the fire, we never read. You had too much to say, too many dreams to encounter, and conflicts to resolve.

"Mom, there's too many things I want to be when I grow up. I just don't know how to choose. . . ."

- *Singer, definitely a singer*
- *Teacher, definitely a teacher*
- *Writer, poem maker, writer of children's books*
- *Clothes designer & sewer*
- *Artist*

"Maybe I could do a different one every day . . . no, some of them have to be done every day, let's see. . . ."

You got out a yellow legal pad and started making a schedule, trying to figure out a way to work each of them into your day.

"One of the good things, Perrin, is that you already do a bit of each of these every day."

"I know, but I want to do them professionally!"

Dreamers and Dreams

Recording and exploring your child's dreams are another way to support your child's creativity and to explore your own creative challenges as a parent. Diary stories of your child's dreams can be simply funny or charming anecdotes, like this one my son shared with me during a period of time when his father was traveling regularly on business. This entry tells the story about how much he was missing his Dad:

To Landon (age 8), May 23, 1995

You nudge me awake.

"Mom, Mom, I dreamed about Daddy," you say, hugging the king size pillow in your arms.

"I dreamed he came home and brought me a present, and this pillow was the present, and I was hugging it and then I woke up and saw it was a pillow."

Or, dreams may be fascinating descriptions of the concrete and abstract realities that interest and disturb your children. Just as adults are often intrigued, inspired, aroused, disturbed, or frightened by their dreams and nightmares, so are children, and they may need your help dealing with their feelings. Perhaps all they need to do is vent about the dream, and then you may make a record of it for them after they share it with you. It's worth recording dreams and images that your children may discover later on as adults that have important symbolic or psychological meaning.

In a practical sense, your children may need your help creating strategies to cope with scary dreams, or they may develop a creative strategy on their own that you want to record for them so that they can feel a sense of power in resolving their own feelings and problems. I recorded the following dream for my son because I was so impressed with his spontaneous ability to learn to manage his threatening dreams in a new way:

To Landon (age 8), November 28, 1995

"Dream Power"

Early this morning before sunrise, you woke me with the whimpering of a bad dream. I said something to comfort you and we both fell back asleep until the alarm.

After I woke you from a heavy sleep, you told me that you had prayed to God to help you after you woke up from your nightmare and after you fell back asleep you went back into the dream and God kept giving you great ideas about how to change the dream to come out happy, which it did.

In any case, dream themes, images, and plots may be quite interesting for your children to interpret on their own later on. And children's dreams can change their lives, help them solve problems, or get in touch with important feelings. Their dreams may teach them important life lessons, like this one that I kept for my son when he was obviously struggling to deal with his feelings of rivalry with his sister. I wanted him to have a memory of how his dreams could help him resolve some of these feelings in a positive way. Both children had come into my bed in the middle of the night because of bad dreams and had fallen back asleep in the crowded bed:

To Landon (age 10), February 25, 1998

...You go back to sleep and I finally do also, but only to be awakened shortly by you again, apologizing, but needing to shake another fresh nightmare from the bed, because you are frightened and emotional.

I reach across the sleeping Perrin to comfort you. You tell me little snippets of a "white man" who opens doors very very quietly and sneaks in, and it is Perrin whom he gets ahold of....

"Mom," you say quietly. "I think God taught me a lesson w/this nightmare. I guess I really do love Perrin after all...."

Writing dreams down for your children is another way that you can seek to understand and be attentive to your children's emotional lives, picking up on clues to their struggles and psychological needs. Saved in the diary, a dream may become a fascinating story-within-the-story, enriching your child's sense of personal history from early childhood the way authors use dreams in fiction to enhance the theme, plot, and psychological development of the characters and the story. For instance, what would a classic story like *The Wizard of Oz* be without a dream?

Facilitating Your Child's Creative Process

We all struggle with the creative process, dealing with our warm-up, or lack of warm-up, to a creative task or project. You can write stories about your children's creativity to show them the natural parts of the creative process, such as dealing with boredom and lack of ideas, to fears of taking risks, mistake making, or the pure zest and joy of a creative impulse followed and brought to fruition. I wrote this story in my son's diary, I think, to give both of us encouragement through a difficult transition when we were new in town and I was trying to dramatically reduce the amount of television he was consuming in his diet. I was bored with his television watching and he was bored without it. This is the story of how we both solved the problem creatively one afternoon:

To Landon (age 8), June 10, 1995

"Instead of TV"

*You came in the door from school expecting to watch both **Transformers and Power Rangers**, but I said No....*

Well, you are persistent, of course, and you hounded me pretty hard for 10-15 minutes but I held my ground.

*Fine. You gave up the battle. But, then, **what was there to do** if you couldn't watch TV?*

I suggested you write a letter on the computer to Auntie Karen to thank her for a copy of the Jurassic Park photo she had sent you. The idea of typing—yourself—on the computer intrigued you. I showed you what to do and you managed the letter nicely. We faxed it, which intrigued you even more, but left me feeling hopelessly inadequate that I couldn't even begin to explain how we could send a copy of this letter across the country to be in Karen's hands w/in moments.

*We returned to the computer since you were all sparked up for the next project you had in mind, a father's Day Present. This time you had me sit at the computer while you dictated a story you made up as we went along about the origin of Father's Day. Then we printed it, bound it, and you ran up to your room to illustrate it page by page. Now your book sits in a plastic cover waiting on the mantelpiece for Dad to get home. You missed both **Transformers and Power Rangers**, and you couldn't have cared less, and Dad will profit the most by that loss.*

Our children are naturally creative given the space and the opportunity to play with spontaneous, creative ideas. Writing about creativity in the diaries can show you ways in which you may be inadvertently blocking or accidentally freeing their creative impulses. One way I find that I block their creativity from time to time is to fail to give them a place and supplies for making a mess. But when the craft items are put in front of them and I get out of the way, interesting things happen:

To Landon (age 8), January 27, 1995

. . . After dinner we were all in the kitchen and while I made whoopi pies for your school birthday celebration this week you and Perrin were playing with craft stuff at the table. I looked over and saw that completely spontaneously and out of the blue you had created a paper cross and then drew and cut out a Jesus and hung him on your cross. I asked if it was going to be part of our Christmas decorations [for the next year] and you suggested we hang it on top of the tree, and perhaps we shall. Then you went on to draw and cut out an anatomically correct Jesus, complete w/body parts and veins in a kind of see-through Jesus!

Some creative ideas may be worth exploring more in theory more than in action. Not all of my daughter Perri's creative ideas are worth carrying out, but I always enjoy listening to her exercise her imagination:

To Perrin (age 7), October 1, 1999

... Late yesterday afternoon, you, Frances and I headed over to Bob & Pam's for dinner. From the back seat next to Frances you said:

"Mom, here's something I just heard on TV. You take some of that cheese, that watery cheese ... what's that called?"

"Feta?"

"Yeah. Feta. You put it in a strainer and let it drip down overnight."

"Okay."

"Then, you cook it w/ that stuff, that hot stuff you sprinkle in?"

"Chili powder?"

"No ..."

"Tabasco?"

"Yeah. Then you cook it for a while, then you shred some zucchini, and you put it in and put it in the refrigerator for seven hours ... I mean ... an hour ... I mean, well, a few minutes...."

"Then, you take that sugar—what's that sugar they put on french bread?"

"Confectionary sugar?"

"Yeah ... Mom, I didn't really hear this on TV ... I'm making it up, but I think it sounds good, don't you?"

For the next ten minutes of the ride you expanded this recipe to include cocoa and carrots and God knows what else until you were distracted, or bored, or you had lost your appetite, as I had.

Nature's Classroom

Children often encounter the great creative themes, questions, and problems of life through their experiences with nature. Through nature they learn about the life cycle and wrestle with their own questions about how the universe seems to make sense or confound them. Stories of creative activities don't always involve *creation*. The themes of failure, death, and destruction as natural parts of the cycle of creativity may be illustrated by stories of your children's encounters with nature, like the one I had with my son and daughter when we found a bird's egg fallen from its nest:

To Landon (age 7), May 22, 1995

"Egg Shell"

You want to go to the park after dinner ... so we ... go to the playground at your school, you, Perrin & me. After we play, you suggest we take a walk through the "out-

door classroom," a swampy area where we walk down a steep hill into the woods surrounding this swamp. We take the path around, you and Perrin ahead. As I'm walking by a tall pine I notice a little beige and slightly blue egg at the foot of the tree. I call you over and you are thrilled to hold the little egg. You don't seem to understand at all that the egg is dead. There is a pin hole in the egg, and the yellow yolk is spilling out. But you cradle it very gently and talk about keeping it warm so it will hatch. I suggest you keep it simply to bring to school and show your teacher. It takes the whole walk back to the car to convince the two of you that, though it **is** a bird egg and it would have hatched into a bird had it not fallen out of the tree, there is positively no way we can bring it back to life now.

You sit in the back seat, holding your egg.

"I wish when eggs fell out of trees they would bounce and land right back up in their nests, then they wouldn't have to die."

And,

"So, is it a rotten egg now? Is it going to stink?"

From Perrin:

"Let me smell it, let me smell it!"

I know you are thinking of **Charlotte's Web** which your teacher has been reading you, and the little exercise you brought home just today where you wrote that your favorite part of the story was when the egg broke, and you backed it up w/ a drawing of the cracked egg and the gas from it in the air surrounding Wilbur.

Walking in the house you ask:

"How did it fall out of the nest?"

"I don't know, perhaps the wind blew it . . ."

"Birds build their nests w/ sides to protect them from the wind."

"Or, perhaps it got pushed out . . ."

"The mother would never do that!"

"Or, maybe another bird stole it and dropped it . . ."

"Birds don't do that to each other's eggs."

I'm sorry tonight that I just don't seem to have enough answers to your grief about the bird who will never be born; the possibility you held in your hand that you just couldn't make happen. . . .

This can be the hardest issue to face in pursuing our creativity—when it doesn't come out as we had hoped and planned and expected, when, for whatever reason that is within or out of our control, it just doesn't work out. Sometimes, there simply are no pat, comforting answers, and at least for the moment, until the next creative challenge presents itself, we are left in the dark, grieving and wondering.

The Creative Challenges of the Formal Classroom

When children are in formal schooling, more challenging creative issues surface. Children are no longer seeking and winning only their parent's approval of their creative projects. They are entering a world in which competition with peers and acceptance or rejection of their creative attempts by "authorities" are sometimes painful realities they must encounter. How your child faces these early challenges—how you help him or her face them—may be diary stories with important lessons for life. One important lesson children need to learn is that when their creative expression is blocked through one door they can summon the courage to try another. I was delighted that my son learned this when he submitted a drawing to his school's literary magazine that was not chosen for publication:

> **To Landon (age 9), April 29, 1996**
>
> . . . The mail brought **The Key** today. I looked, hopefully, for your drawing, but it wasn't there. I broke the news to you when I picked you up from school to go to Perri's dance class. You thumbed through it and kept repeating, off an on, "I can't believe they didn't pick mine." Certainly, I couldn't either, but I assured you that it was nothing personal—the items were judged blind—and that judges make mistakes. I'm not sure you believed or understood all this. You weren't devastated or anything, but you **were** disappointed and you seemed to be struggling to make sense of this. I told you about my writing career . . . and how I dealt with times when I submitted things that weren't accepted, and that I had to learn to trust in myself, and always, always, **keep** trying.
>
> . . . On the way home, you and I continued chatting . . . and you said—"why don't we have a family contest?" which through excited dialogue between you and I evolved into our own family literary magazine which we are going to call **The Family Key**. Excited and inspired you sat down as soon as we got home and drew the cover. . . .

Overcoming Blocks to Creativity

In school, artistic impulses may be managed or directed by the expectations of teachers who assign creative projects for grades, and children realize the results—the artwork, writing, acting, trumpet playing, or science projects—are often publicly presented and open to review by peers as well. This can place significant pressure on your child's creative explorations. Children wonder how they can follow an authentically imaginative impulse but also conform to the expectations of authority figures who are evaluating and judging them.

Diary writing can help to show our children *how* the creative process works, giving them the courage and confidence to face the risks involved in creating anything. One fall, my son's fourth-grade class was given an assignment to gather autumn leaves, dry and prepare them, and create a collage using the leaves as the medium. Typically, resistance to the project had caused him to wait until the very last minute, and so the pressure was on. As often happens, helping him work through his creative challenges included an opportunity for me to face my own. In this diary story, we both worked through a variety of creative blocks, including fear of failure, fear of disapproval, fear of competition, fear of self-revelation, fear of the blank page, and fear of worthlessness. Whether or not the diary story means something to him later on, it surely helped me as his parent to write it:

To Landon (age 10), November 20, 1997

"The Creative Process"

Yesterday, it was the leaf project. You have had three weeks or more. Drilled home, hit home, it's due Monday. We collected your leaves two weeks ago w/ G.T. You never washed and prepped yours; I did some for Perrin. I let you use those.

It is dark, late afternoon. I get you the paper, the glue gun, the leaves, all the assorted items I have saved, hoping you'll use them. They are not **your** leaves. They are not the **right** leaves, not the **right** materials. You are staring at the blank white paper and you have no idea, no inspiration, nowhere to begin. And you are angry, and afraid, and you lash out at me—why didn't I get you the **right** leaves?

There is nothing to be done but wait. Not react, in anger and blame, to lash back as I am so tempted to do.

Instead, I realize I know this feeling. Know it from the depths of me and every creative project I have ever been faced w/ You are in the hopeless place where nothing lives but failure.

It is the feeling I get as a writer when I don't know where to begin, blank page a death sentence rather than an opportunity.

It is the terror I feel as a psychodramatist when the protagonist starts walking w/me onto the stage, and I suddenly realize I don't have the right materials, and I have failed, completely, before I have even begun. The empty stage is a death sentence, and I will fail not only myself, but the helpless protagonist!

Or, when a client has entered my office in complete chaos, hurling and swirling in a tornado of emotions and words and I feel the horror of the empty chair, as if, facing her, I have nothing I can say, nothing I can do. I give up.

You began, angrily, but tentatively, slapping leaves here and there in the arctic desert of the paper. Maybe? A car, some kind of car takes shape. A mouse? No.

Stupid. Stupid nothing. There is nothing, nothing but a definitive endless self-pitying whine. There is an ageless, timeless period of whine.

Your father jokes w/ you audaciously. He is teasing your internal critic. He is trying to get him to laugh. Somewhere far beneath the whine is a laugh, because your father is hopelessly funny when he wants to be. He gives you twenty stupid and silly ideas that prove you are the only one who really **could** come up w/ a good idea, if . . . just if you could find one, head buried in the couch pillows.

Maybe that's where you did find your idea. Something, some urge drove you back to the paper, some spark. Silently I worked beside you in the kitchen at dinner, watching out of the corner of my eye as a leaf alien boy took shape, holding a laser gun.

"Adorable . . ." I murmur.

"What?" you say, defensively.

"Adorable . . . I mean, good idea."

"I thought you said terrible."

This is how I feel in my writer's group—will they like what I've written, or will they hate it? I inevitably prepare more for the latter.

The alien seems now to have emerged from the flying saucer taking shape on the page. And there are trees, perhaps this scene is, as so many alien sightings **are**, in a secluded and relatively uninhabited place.

Perhaps it's done? No. No, you see that something is missing, there is too much blank space around the alien.

"Yes," I say, "That's good, that's your artist's eye, judging the whole, looking at it aesthetically. I agree, it does look like something is missing."

You try a few things and give up, for now. It's done enough **for now**. The most anxious part of the creative process has been endured, and resolved. We put it aside. We have time to see what's missing.

Last night, sleepless at 2:00 a.m. I figured out what might be missing, and plan to run it by you in the morning, my idea of how to help you finish it.

And then I dream my own creative problem, obviously because I'm planning on going to Perri's classroom next week to perform a story; I offered to do this, my own creative impulse. I plan to perform a new story, a version of Cinderella: "If the slipper doesn't fit, don't wear it." It will be my first official performance outside the family, outside her pre-school. I am anxious.

In the dream, I show up in her classroom unprepared. I have forgotten my scarves, my instruments, and to finish writing the story. But it's time to go on, or almost time. I must wing it. I go to the music room in search of some instruments and decide that instead of finishing—or trying out the as yet unfinished new story, I should tell an old one and try to work the theme of friendship out of it.

The classroom is, despite the teacher's presence, in chaos, children, noisy and unfocused, doing as they please. Teacher does not seem to care, after all, it is my wish to tell the story, not necessarily hers, or theirs. But I am committed, and feel a responsibility to do it anyway, because I said I would. I feel helpless, almost hopeless w/o my scarves! I begin the Princess & the Pea, trying hard to capture the unruly children's attention, because I believe a good storyteller can and should do this. It's not working. Not only, I realize, as I perform the story, am I performing for an inattentive audience of children, now the teacher herself has stopped watching completely and has turned on the TV set! Humiliated, or trying not to be, I gather the shreds of dignity I have left, say I am ending the performance abruptly, though no one is really listening, and tell the teacher how upset I am. She implies or states, that the story was boring her, and I say,

*"Well, the least you could do in that case would be to be **polite**."*

I leave.

And this is my statement to the internal critic that lives inside all of us:

*"If you don't like what I am creating, I can live w/that. But don't beat me up in the process. You can tell me so **politely**, w/kindness, w/ gentleness. Then I won't be so afraid of you, and I won't be using or wasting my creative energy being angry at you. If you treat me decently, we could work together on a story that won't **bore** you!"*

. . . And so, this morning, I went in to wake you, help you get ready, and I said I had an idea for the empty space.

"It could be a golden aura made by crushing the big golden leaves, you know, like the shining aura around the stars? I think an alien might have a glowing aura like that around him."

You agreed.

Do you think I could try out my story on you?

All children will approach the variety of creative tasks they take on with their own unique behavioral style. As you write stories about their creative endeavors, patterns will emerge that can help you understand their style of learning as well as the predictable challenges and blocks they will tend to encounter. You can use the information you glean from these observances and stories to help you come up with more effective strategies when approaching creative tasks. The more you understand about your child's gifts, talents, struggles, and stumbling blocks, the better support you can be when your child, for whatever reason, takes on a creative assignment.

The next chapter focuses on the dance of change that parents and their children engage in throughout their lives. But first, try these Diary Door Openers.

Diary Door Openers

1. Play Zone

   Write a description of a play area you have made for your child, whether it's a room or a corner, inside or outside your home. What inspired you? Describe the shape, space, design, or objects in it. What is your child like when she or he is there? How do you feel when you are in this space? Did you have a space like this as a child, or did you long for one?

2. Body Language

   Observe and describe your infant's nonverbal process of exploration and communication. Watch him or her following a creative impulse, whether it's bubble-making, or rolling over, or making a noise to attract your attention, and write a description.

3. Creative Zest

   Observe your child engaging in a creative activity in which he or she seems happily oblivious of time or outside influences and in which she or he seems to be following an authentic, original creative impulse, whether it's building a sand castle or playing house with dolls. Describe what your child is doing and reflect on what seems to excite, motivate, and free your child to experiment.

4. Make a Mess

   The next time your child makes a mess, before reacting (unless it's dangerous), take a few moments to observe the scene as if you're standing outside looking in at the mess. Then reverse roles with your child and try to spontaneously imagine the mess making process from your child's point of view—What inspired you? How did it feel to make this mess? What are the sensations involved in the process? How does it feel to be caught? When you are done exploring from your child's point of view, you may return to your own and reflect on what you discovered.

5. "What I Want to Be When I Grow Up"

   Without judging or evaluating, write a story about what your child wants to be when she or he grows up, capturing dialogue and quotes. (Do you remember what you wanted to be when you grew up? Have you done it?)

6. Dream Power

   Write the story about how a dream wakes your child up to a new insight or perspective, including as much detail as possible. Set it within the context of current issues in your child's life.

Chapter 9

Learning the Dance
Connecting with Children
through Change

. . . this is the warp and weft
that weave you to me loosely, the gravity
that never releases us when we let go.
This is the embrace that holds as lightly as the sky.

(Alice Fogel, "Letting Go," *I Love This Dark World*, p. 59)

Parents and children take journeys toward and away from each other their whole lives. This is the dance of relationships. However necessary and normal they are, transitions can feel disruptive and threatening to intimate relationships. It's normal to fear disconnection from someone you love when you are in one place and your child is in another, either physically or emotionally. But the world beyond the diary door that you have created may anchor and sustain the relationship through journeys of adventure, journeys of discovery, journeys of conflict, journeys of physical and psychological loss, and journeys of new growth. This chapter looks at how diary writing is a path toward connecting with your child through many types of change.

Writing through Absence and Distance

Leaving your children to go on a trip can be stressful for parents, but it's sometimes necessary and unavoidable during the early childhood years. Bringing the diary with you on a trip can benefit you and your children in many ways. Writing to your children while you're separated from them can help minimize your anxiety by letting you feel close to them. In the diaries, you can tell them interesting stories about your adventure. You can write to them about what you hear they are doing while you're gone and how they seem to be coping.

Journey anxiety is certain to surface at some point in your preparations and departure. Diary writing can calm you down and help you to focus on the purpose of the trip and to clarify what you hope you and your child will gain from the separation. Writing the following entry to my daughter Perrin helped me to manage my anxiety about leaving her and my son for a weekend of professional development and play that I had planned to attend at a resort. As often happens in my decision making about trips away from my children, what seemed easy and attractive in theory when I was making the commitment seemed difficult to follow through with as the time to leave approached. Writing out my reasons for planning the trip and for what I hoped I would gain from it helped me resolve the guilt about taking time for myself. Whether or not it was rational to need my three-year-old daughter to understand why I would be leaving her for a few days, I did. By taking the time to explain it to her in the diary, I realized that taking care of myself was one of the primary ways I had learned to nurture *her*:

To Perrin (age 3), June 21, 1995

"Journey Anxiety"

I am going to be going away for the weekend, a long weekend, and the mother in me does not want to go, or does not know how to go. She has forgotten how to spend time away from you—extended time, since she left her practice one year ago this month.

I'm not sure why I'm going at all. Some hungry part of me craved it and planned it with great longing. But just as a pregnant woman's craving can suddenly and radically shift, I have lost touch w/the craving—the need—to go, and I'm left in my mother's role, dreading the departure, anticipating lonely, lonely long moments of being split off from my self.

But I know it won't really be like that. When I head to the airport, or arrive at the resort, I will shift into the woman who loves adventure, independence who misses her friends and longs for hilariously stimulating dinner conversation w/adults. Adult play.

That's what psychodrama is for me, in large part. Home of my adult play. I'm going to further my training, yes, I'm going to engage fully and completely w/ creative aspects of myself that need to be stretched or primed like an unused pump. But, I'm going for play. . . . I'm going to find my future.

*Yes, find my future. I found **you** in psychodrama four years ago. In the spring I did a psychodramatic enactment where, confronted by the pull from all of my vari-*

ous roles, I chose motherhood and a new baby—the idea of a new baby—as the most important aspects of my life.

That baby was you. When I went, after much conflicted emotion pulling me in every direction, to the summer training w/Nina and Dale four years ago, I had just, within a week or two, conceived of you. I did not yet know it. Or, did I?

The first night of the training I did a little piece on having a baby girl. I reversed roles into the baby girl, and felt the pure beauty of my little girl's body. I freed myself from any vestiges of shame and embraced my femininity in all its beauty and mystery.

This little role-reversal was a very necessary warm-up to having you and my ability to teach you to love and explore and value your body w/o shame. . . .

Ultimately, I took the trip, had a great time, and made note of it in her diary:

To Perrin (age 3), July 3, 1995

Whatever the hungry part was, she returned home fed and full, and very content. I've carried my contentment into every activity since like a tranquilizer smoothing over every potential stress. . . .

The Return of the Traveler and the Story Fire

We come close to and then go away from our children. We travel, and we return home. We are present and we are absent for varying reasons and amounts of time. Our children also travel and return home. Diary writing breaches distances, closes gaps, stretches to build bridges between our children and us when we are absent and distant from each other.

One way that diary writing helps us to build bridges from separation to intimacy and connection is that diary writing can help us to identify our feelings, recognize or establish our values, decide what's important, communicate our values to our children, and then act on them. When we feel that we have made a mistake in our thinking or behavior, storytelling allows us to reflect on our actions, and this diary writing can help us to respond and resolve the problem. Diary writing helps us to deal with our regrets by giving us an opportunity to make a commitment to change, as I did in the following entry to my son. Through his participation in Boy Scouts, he had begun to take adventures away from home that often involved overnight trips away from the family. Writing this entry to him about his canoe trip got me in touch with my concerns that, perhaps because he was the oldest, his traveling seemed to threaten our family togetherness. Through my descriptive and reflective writing in the diary, I realized how easy it is to take a family member's comings and goings for granted. Preserving family intimacy, I learned, would not mean that we had to stay together all the time, but that it would involve changing the way we handled the traveler's return:

To Landon (age 11), Oct. 7, 1999

The canoe trip was a success! Sun. night, Fran, Daddy, Perrin and I had a casual dinner in front of the TV w/dinner. Dad had brought home a movie about an Irish family and insisted that I sit down and watch it—

"I rented it for you." (He knows how hard it is for me to sit down to TV. . . .)

Anyway, I wasn't expecting you until 9 p.m. . . . So, I was surprised to hear the door open at 7 p.m. A big wide smile covered your face as you snuggled proudly into our arms. You were very glad to be home because you had a great time.

We asked you some questions and you snuggled beside me on the couch, insisting as you fought w/ your two sisters that you were the most tired and deserving of the spot on the couch nearest me. I worked you in.

*In retrospect, the next morning, as I was thinking about your return home, I regretted that we had not turned off the TV upon your return. We really should have. A homecoming is **that** important. And, though I see why I felt caught in a can't-please everyone predicament, I **do** think the importance of a homecoming for a traveller should be paramount.*

We should have turned off the TV and sat around you in a circle by a warm fire to hear the tales of your journey. This was the only right thing to do. I know this in my heart.

*Consciously, I do not think you were aware of this need, but I **do** believe in my heart that every traveller has a need to be welcomed whole heartedly home, back into the circle of family or friends. A traveler needs to be told by the attentiveness of his listeners that he was missed, that there is much to be **shared** in the stories of his journey. I believe that's how it works—believe down to my core—the traveller makes the journey for everyone in the circle, if he has the proper reception, the proper re-integration.*

We achieved this, only partially. We welcomed you physically home, made a special place on the couch. . . .

But, what if the television had been a roaring fire that we had been gathering round?

What if we had been focused on a fire when you re-entered the house?

*Then, you **really** would have had a proper homecoming. Easily, you would have found a place encircling the hearth, and the crackling of the flames would not in the least have disturbed our attention to the recap of your experiences on the canoe in the Saco River.*

*This is how I **want** to live my life—it's what I want to give my family. I know we didn't fail you Sun. night, and I suspect you actually **liked** the idea of settling into a movie, since you love movies and your mother watches them w/ you so rarely.*

But, this is a disappointment that nags me from my own family up-bringing. . . .

I want to do this differently—I want to do it right. I can't turn back time, but I can be more attentive in the future. It is cold, the heat is on now, and it is time for fires. . . .

Diary writing offers us a way to keep track of the times when we meet our goals. Because I had gotten in touch with these feelings and values through the diary entry and flagged my desire for change, just a few weeks later I had a chance to put change into action when Landon went on another Boy Scout adventure and return in this next diary entry:

To Landon (age 11), October 28, 1999

Last Sunday, I was out for a long, peaceful walk in the golden woods when you arrived home, unexpectedly, from your day of rock climbing.

*This was a trip you had gone on for the day w/ Boy Scouts. I was pleased at your enthusiasm about going even though none of your good friends would be there, and neither Dad or I could go, though Dad wanted to. How **do** you take these risks so confidently? It sounds fun, it sounds challenging, and so you do it. . . .*

When I came in, dusk was approaching, and dad had built a roaring fire in the family room. There, w/ a cup of hot chocolate, you sat on one of the little white chairs, warming your toes.

"Hi!" you said, cheerfully.

"How'd it go? Did you have fun?"

I pulled a little white chair over next to you in front of the fire, and you told me all about your experience. I sat listening, asking you questions, while Dad brought you a bowl of soup and crackers, filling you up, as well as warming you up. Franny sat beside you eating a cup of whipped cream, listening. . . .

*It wasn't until some time later, perhaps the next day, that I realized we had unconsciously, **spontaneously**, and brilliantly co-created the perfect homecoming for your journey, just as I had hoped, just as I had imagined it.*

The fire. . . .

Writing Stories Can Help You Let Go

Writing diary entries that allow you to express your feelings can influence your decision making as parents as well as help you come to terms with change and heal from loss. The diary provides a container for your stories that allows you to hold tight to what is important to you, even as you must, inevitably, let it go. Diary writing, of course, cannot prevent change, transition, or loss. But it can ease the feelings that accompany it. The diary is a comforting shoulder, a bracing, sheltering, sturdy constancy to cling to and lean on through change.

Writing in the diary gives you a chance to express and reflect on your feelings about both the everyday choices and the major decisions you make that effect your children. For instance, the decision to wean my third child began in a similar way as the first two—by introducing an occasional bottle of formula while still nursing as the primary form of nourishment. The process ended, however, quite differently. The diary writing guided me through the emotions of letting go that I had not anticipated I would feel:

To Frances (age 6 months), October 1, 1997

*. . . Slowly but surely I am weaning you. About a week and a half or two weeks ago I began introducing a bottle which you, slowly but surely have begun to accept. So w/ your two meals a day plus bottle we are doing a whole lot less nursing. And I have strongly ambivalent feelings about this rite of passage, letting go of the beautiful peace and intimacy I have enjoyed in this stage of our lives. I know in my heart that I'm saying goodbye to this stage of my life, this role forever, and it has been the single most satisfying thing I have ever done w/ my body. Pure pleasure. Especially w/ you, because of experience I was able to approach nursing you w/complete confidence. I knew exactly what I was doing. And you responded with gusto and ease and we worked so well together, Frances. And also because w/ Perrin & Land I combined a bottle from the very beginning, and I was seeing clients and not quite so fully available to them. I left them regularly for business reasons. I've never left you w/ anyone, not even Dad. Never. And you're almost six months old! I just haven't **had** to, nor have I wanted to.*

But, I am ready to wean you. I'm ready to let go and share you a little more. Let others feed you.

Ooops, I hear you, like a kitten mewing, from your room.

Letting go is a process, of course, not a decision, and not an event. It was as a result of writing the previous entry and discovering how powerfully I felt about nursing her that caused me to decide to keep nursing her for the rest of the first year and not to rush through it. Entries throughout the next six months capture the emotional process of letting go of this cherished aspect our relationship. The diary gave me a place to express both my joy and sadness about the loss of an important role:

To Frances (age 11 months), March 16, 1998

You are weaning yourself. It's almost over. I sat feeding you in the rocking chair tonight realizing this whole phase of my life is about to end forever. There will never be an experience to match it, nothing ever as fulfilling, ever. It is **the** single most satisfying and rewarding thing I have ever done. And I must say goodbye to it. We must. It feels like an ache at the center of me.

But, we're both ready. It's not like you're just rejecting me. No, we have naturally evolved together to this passage. Oh Frances, you have given me so much. I feel so sleepy and numb, like I can't begin to get close to the feelings of letting this go forever. I just enjoy you so much. Our time alone here every day.

Maybe I can't let you stop. Maybe I can reverse this process somehow. Hold on.

But we've made it a year, as I had hoped ... I don't remember grieving it w/ Perrin. I don't remember grieving that I might never nurse again. I must have known, somehow, about you. But I really feel like you are my last, for sure, this is the end. I don't want it to go. I don't want it to all go by so quickly, this whole phase of my life. **No more** babies. Impossible!

It's an ache.

When a relationship we value ends, having the chance to say a proper goodbye can help us to achieve closure so that we can move on from our grief or sadness. This is where the ideal listener role of the diary writing can be so helpful in allowing us to heal. By writing to my infant daughter as if writing letters to her future self, I could communicate with her as if she were able to listen to me as an adult, say goodbye to the nursing, and begin to move on:

To Frances (2 days before 1st birthday), April 8, 1998

...You haven't nursed in days. I suppose I have to accept that it is completely over for good. How stark and finite that sounds, and I'm not certain I can accept that I'll never nurse you or another child again. It isn't grief I feel so much, but hunger. Hunger. Insatiable hunger. And, strangely, gratification. Gratification and fulfillment to the core of myself. I nursed three children, you longest of all. I miss you. I hunger to feed you. And yet it's over.

But we went a year.

Honoring Endings and Beginnings

Every child has a unique style for dealing with loss and change. Observing and writing diary entries about your children's behavioral style can give you (and them) clues about their needs. This process can help you recognize patterns and discover how you can best support your children when they are learning new things or joining new groups. Writing while your child attends a new class, a sport, or any activity can make waiting time interesting. While observing your child, you notice whether she is confident and positive—joining right in—or whether he is cautious and needs reassurance before risk-taking. Writing to your children can be a way of resolving and responding to your own anxieties as well as of showing respect for their behavioral style and developmental needs. It can help you be more conscious of managing your expectations so that your children are free to have their own unique experience of taking a risk in a new area of their lives, rather than trying to perform in a way that will be pleasing to you.

Every child has an emotional response to starting kindergarten, and, as parents, so do we. Whether your child is eager or reluctant, the diary can help you validate the range of feelings you or your child is experiencing. Beginning formalized schooling, whether it's public, private, or home-based education, is a rite of passage that can be honored through storytelling. I didn't know what to expect when my daughter Perrin attended her kindergarten orientation, and her response, which I wrote about in the next entry, surprised me:

To Perrin (age 5), April 28, 1997

*Perhaps your transition into Kindergarten will be defined by the two-handed assertive **push** you gave me today as I walked you into your orientation classroom. For a split second I thought you were reaching out to grab me to join you, cling to me as you entered the room.*

Nope. You're ready. You're ready. I laughed to myself as I headed back to the mother's meeting in the room next door where I had left Franny—2-weeks old—sleeping.

*The next time I tried to get you to go to [pre-school] you balked. Why should you have to go back **there** when you're fully ready for Kindergarten?...*

What is it like for your child to *end* a class, group, or activity? These transitions can be just as interesting to observe. Watch for a story to tell your child about an ending of one thing that is the beginning in another. One way that children, like adults, take on new roles is through pretending, imagining, or role playing. We make the new role our own by practicing *as if* it's ours already. Through writing diary stories, I have learned that when my daughter Perrin is approaching a new role she begins making up stories that seem true, but that on closer examination are fiction she's creating to explore the role. It always takes me a while to catch on, as it did during the spring when she was getting oriented to the idea of attending kindergarten in the fall:

To Perrin (age 5), May 7, 1997

All day, the day of your graduation from [pre-school] all you could think about was going out w/ Daddy at night....

This is the season of pretend for you, and it's very hard to tell what's real and what's not with you. Kindergarten preparation seems to be blurring the lines of fantasy & reality.

For instance, at dinner two nights ago, I asked you to tell everyone about the school bus that visited the parking lot of your school:

"Oh yes. We went to Frosty's," you said.

"You did?" I asked.

"Yes!"

"Are you sure?" I asked, wondering how I had missed this event. "What kind of ice cream did you have?"

"Yes. Everyone had purple ice cream."

"Really?"

"Oh, yes."

"But I never signed a permission slip for you to go . . . they couldn't have taken you w/o a permission slip . . ." gradually I become firmer and firmer in my conviction that this trip to Frosty's was all in your imagination & need to keep up w/ your older brother who is being taken to Frosty's by Mrs. Logsdon for learning his multiplication tables. . . .

Thursday, while dropping Landon off in his classroom after a field trip to the Pilgrim Church, I asked you, in the hallway, to come w/ me into the bathroom.

"No!" you insisted, and I went in w/Franci. When I came out, I had to search for you for a minute, and finally found you at the far end of the hall near the Kindergarten classrooms. On the way to the car, I figured out what you had been doing.

"Don't hold my hand when I'm in the school," you instructed me. "Don't talk to me like I'm not a Kindergartener. Pretend you're picking me up from school." . . .

Transitional Stories—
Weighing the Balance of Life's Losses and Gains

Stories of transition put a spotlight on your child's growth and change. The growth may be cognitive, spiritual, psychological, social, or physical. These stories capture you and your child in a transitional world of moving from an old belief to a new one, bringing with it the paradox of transforming a loss to a gain. In these stories you observe your child perched on the edge of something new, sometimes clinging desperately to the old, afraid of letting go, sometimes leaping toward the new role perhaps faster than you can follow. Just as your child is making the transition, so are you. As a parent, you cling, let go, and leap in a dance of change with your child. Going through the diary door at these times can be particularly beneficial to you. Writing to your child of the changes you observe and notice in yourself can help you to clarify your own feelings, your own needs, your own resistance and fears, as well as your own strengths and hope. It can teach you about your own losses and gains and can lead you toward a path of integration and acceptance. The diary writing puts you in touch with your own best instincts. In the diary, it's as if your child can listen to your side of the story, perhaps before she or he is ready or able to in real life.

There is never an exact time, a specific moment to put your finger on and say my child is different today, or now I am different today. So much about the change and growth in you and your child is gradual and invisible. But if you pay attention to the passage of time, writing regularly to your child, the emotional dynamics of the stories you find yourself writing will blossom with the signs, the symbols, and the directions pointing you where you need to go and where you need to let your child go.

These stories often begin with a question. At some point, every parent wonders such things as, when will my child stop believing in the magical figures like Santa Claus and the Tooth Fairy? Or, when will I be ready to stop playing these roles? These are questions that you can explore through diary storytelling. If you have enjoyed playing the role of the magical figures that visit your family you may be just as conflicted as your child about when and how to introduce the "truth" about these mythical roles. Facing these questions as a parent of a first-born, I had no experience to guide me with my son when he began to question some of his magical beliefs. Through diary writing, I began to sort through some of my concerns and to understand more clearly what each of us might need:

To Landon (age 7), November 10, 1994

"Is Santa Real?"

...Tuesday, when I came home from a shopping trip, and mentioned for you not to go through my bags, you said, matter of factly:

"Mommy, I know that you and Daddy put all the presents under the tree."

*We argued it out a bit. I really want you to believe in Santa as long as you possibly can. Probably because I have a strong intuition that what you want most this Christmas is, not to be **right**, but just to have that magic a little longer.*

But I'm also glad that you are growing in all the right ways, and it's a beautiful thing to have the cognitive power to explore the real meaning of things and not just see and believe in the surface of things.

Writing to your child can help you discover when both of you are ready to make the transition out of old beliefs and find your ways into new roles—as well as when you're not. There's no single right time or way for a parent and child to deal definitively with magical beliefs. I found that my many questions about how to handle my son's growing suspicions about who it was who filled the stockings, collected the teeth, delivered the eggs, or played the mischievous St. Patrick's Day pranks at our house could not be resolved in one entry. Enchantment is pure pleasure for most children, and I wanted my son to enjoy these beliefs as long as he could. I was determined that I wouldn't lie to him to preserve his enchantment, but I was also determined to let him find meaningful answers to his questions, which I knew he would, in time, when he was really ready. He, of course, couldn't come right out and tell me when he was ready to learn the truth, but writing stories about his wondering told me everything I needed to know:

To Landon (age 8), February 29, 1996

You are playing with the idea that the tooth fairy is . . . well, me or Dad. Sitting at the breakfast room table this morning, sipping your hot chocolate, you send out little test balloon questions in the form of what-ifs . . .

"What if I lost a tooth, and there wasn't really a tooth fairy, would you give me $5 for my tooth?"

This question comes out of the blue, and I haven't even had my first cup of coffee.

"Ummmm . . . I don't know. I'd have to think about that."

I'm stalling, you see. I'm trying to figure out what it is that you are really asking me. Do you want to know the truth, and trade in your fantasies of omnipotent fairies for cold, hard cash? Are you trying to see whether I'm itching to give up the role and come back down to earth in the cold light of day? Do you want me to reassure you that the tooth fairy treasures your old teeth like gold nuggets she picks up cheap under kids' pillows? Do you want me to hang on, or let you move forward? I know we're both involved in this ambivalent process of losing the magic of the omnipotent beings who have supposedly visited our household frequently since you were born.

You get up from the table, still probing, still asking, still telling me about the pos-sibility that the tooth fairy doesn't exist, as you walk through the kitchen and go past me, you tell me Jonathan's mother gave him a $10 bill.

"Isn't it really you and Daddy who take my tooth and just throw it away and leave me money?"

Your back is to me now and you are gliding out of the room like a skater, head-ing off to the bathroom, and I start to say something, anything that might explain it all somehow, but you are gone, and going about your business, and you can't hear me now, anyway.

On the way home in the car from Joey's tonight I mention to Perrin that the Easter Bunny is coming. You speak to us both about him in an authoritative voice:

"He doesn't wear clothes you know, like he does in the movies. He's just a plain bunny who hops around."

I guess we'll get through one more magical Easter and St. Patty's day, anyway....

Swinging, Clinging, and Shifting into New Roles

Children want help with the challenges they face. How much help, what kind of help and from whom are questions for which the answers may change radically from day to day as a child grows and as a parent grows. Writing to your children about their daily activities may help you stay connected to a moving, shifting, trans-forming being. The swing of your child's ambivalent feelings causing him to want two paradoxical things at once—to cling and to separate—provides the momentum for his leap across that invisible boundary into the next stage. When your child is ready to change, actions that may nurture and support him one day may block him from growing the next. Diary stories help you recognize and acknowledge what may seem like sudden shifts in the kind of support he needs from you and the ways that you, as the parent, are being called to change your own patterns as a result of his growth. One summer afternoon, I noticed that I seemed to intuitively recognize an opportunity for my son to move forward through taking a new risk, and I got out of the way:

To Landon (age 10), June 12, 1997

... Something happened today at the Club that marks a lot of growth for you—exactly what I'm talking about.

It was another broiling day, and Grammy took us to the Club for a dinner and swim. You finished swimming—cold from the pool—and went around the corner to where they have a game of baseball going, usually. I suspected you would hang back and watch, and when I checked on you, yes, there you sat on the side of the hill watching the boys hit and catch the ball and run, and I thought, there he sits in his observer role, happy . . . I'll leave him alone.

Shortly, I went over to ask you if you wanted chicken for dinner, and I decided to just check in—did you want me to ask them if you could play? I knew you'd say no, and you did, but for once I felt like I could let you just watch if that's what made you happy, and I didn't have to worry about it. But you surprised me by starting to stand up as I walked away, and said no, you would ask them yourself.

And you must have, because when I peeked around the corner, there you were, playing first base, running happily after the ball.

You *joined the game; something you wouldn't have pursued on your own a few months ago.*

Well, lately I've been feeling the promise of our future relationship, being able to envision being ***friends*** *w/you for life. Real friends. I don't have to always be your nagging old Mom.*

It's not always easy to let our children change and support them to change when it means we must face a loss or change in ourselves. If you write through the diary door, you will inevitably find yourself looking into the mirror and encountering your resistance to your child's growth. You will see that your child needs you to change even when you don't want to. You will see that your child has a right to ask you to look at yourself and be honest with yourself, even when you think it's only your child who needs to do the changing. I'm not, and never have been, a good dancer. But this diary entry to my son about dancing lessons taught me a lot about what I needed to know to dance more gracefully with my growing son:

To Landon (age 11), November 1, 1998

When I first carried the brochure up the driveway from the mailbox reading it as I went, I felt certain that you would never be interested in a social dance class. So, I almost threw it away.

But, then I noticed the names of some of your friends mothers . . . who were local organizers and when you learned that they were going, you looked like you wouldn't resist very strenuously if I were to insist. . . .

Dad took me to Florida for my 40th birthday weekend, and the Mon. night that I returned home you and Perrin gave me a little party that Grammy BL had set up in the basement. Somehow I found myself dancing w/you; you asked me to show you how to dance, which, of course, I simply cannot do. I stumbled squarely through a kind of four-step thing which inspired you, and I showed you how to lead.

"The man leads. . . ." [I said]

"What do you mean? How do you lead? How can I lead if I don't know how to dance?" You were much more excited, really, than anxious, because you were smiling rather than doing the big whining thing that you do when you're feeling overwhelmed.

Grammy B. went w/me to Decelles where I picked out your jacket and tie. . . .

Thurs. afternoon, Daddy was home early from Florida and here when you got off the bus. We followed you into your bedroom and helped you dress. Hovered and primped and teased and badgered you a little, I guess. Then we decided, Daddy decided, we had just enough time to buy you some new shoes, so we dashed to Payless and he helped you pick a tan hush puppy. Then, we dashed back to the community center where all the boys and girls were arriving in the suits and dresses. All your buds spiffed up, smiling. I wanted to walk you in, but you would not let me and said an abrupt goodbye in the parking lot.

Then I ran into Allyn who offered you a ride home, giving me an excuse to follow you upstairs through the busy hallway and see you seated next to all your friends across from the girls. I crossed the dance floor to speak to you, to tell you about Mrs. C., and you were abrupt and irritated, rushing me away.

"All right, all right. **Now go!**"

Later, you chastised me for walking over to you in front of your friends. I realized I had crossed a boundary that you've just realized you need. I fought you on it, trying to minimize my carelessness, it was no big deal, all I did was cross the dance floor to give you a message!

But later I realized how resistant I was feeling to your need for new boundaries. After all, didn't I still have the **right, as your mother,** to cross floors of classes I paid for to give you important messages?

My conscience soon helped me to see that it wasn't about having the right. It was, of course, about respect. Respect for your new needs. Respect for new ground rules, despite my own wish to cling. I was trying to convince you and me that it was okay to cling, it was cute, in fact, for me to cling. Didn't you think I was cute when I clung?

Then, the mirror. The fights we've been having about your homework, your whining, clinging time. For hours. Begging me to sit w/ **you** to help you, show you, do for you. The screaming back and forth. **"Help me!" "Help yourself!"** The sheer, physical impossibility of me giving you the time and attention you were asking for. Your expressions of abandonment when I would give up, walk away, detach, encourage you to seek help from Mr. C.

Ugh, the mirror. It's okay for **me** to cross floors you don't want or need me to cross, but it's not okay for you to cling and whine over the homework.

So, I'm getting that we're dancing, or trying to, differently. But we each want to cling and detach in exactly opposite directions.

As the years pass, as your child grows, the diary stories will grow in their complexity and depth. There is room behind the diary door for all of these stories. In the next chapter we look at dealing with parent/child conflict through the diary door. But first, try these Diary Door Openers.

Diary Door Openers

1. Bridging Absence and Distance
   If you don't live with the child for whom you are keeping the diary, write up a description of the most recent telephone interaction you had with him or her, including as much detail and dialogue as you can remember. Reflect on what the phone call meant to you.

2. Warm up to a Journey
   As you get ready for a trip you are about to take away from your child, write to your child about what benefits you hope you and your child will gain from the experience. Include a description of how your child seems to feel about this separation and what you do or say to attempt to comfort and reassure him or her.

3. The Traveler's Return and the Story Fire
   Imagine your loved ones in a circle around you, listening, and tell a tale from your journey, something you have brought back with you from afar. Is there something intangible—a thought, insight, feeling, or inspiration—that you want to try to hold onto and integrate into your daily life at home?

4. Enchanted Role Playing
   Write an enchanting story about a magical figure like the Tooth Fairy or Santa Claus visiting your home and describe your child's response.

5. Crossing Thresholds
   If your child is facing a transition of some sort, describe the threshold she or he seems to be standing on. Describe the change or changes your child is undergoing. As your child moves forward, reflect on what your child seems to be leaving behind and what your child seems to be reaching for. Is your child's development reminding you of anything in your own life? What old behaviors, thoughts, or feelings are you being called on to leave behind or to gain in your parenting response?

Chapter 10

Conflict as Quest
Taming Each Other's Dragons

I did not know what to say to him.
I felt awkward and blundering.
I did not know how I could reach him,
where I could overtake him and go on
hand in hand with him once more.

(Antoine de Saint-Exupéry, *The Little Prince*, p. 28)

Speaking metaphorically, a storyteller observing normal family life might say that parents are often called to go on quests with their children. Like knights in shining armor, we are often called to embark on adventures that require us to perform heroic feats of endurance, wisdom, skill, patience, fortitude, and courage in the noble pursuit of raising healthy and happy children.

We choose to go on quests with our children according to our values, attitudes, and goals. But our children, following their own wishes and inclinations, choose some of our adventures for us. Just because we are called to go on a quest with a child does not mean that we are both seeking the same things from the journey. This is the nature of conflict, pure and simple—my child wants one thing, and I want another thing (either for her or myself), and it seems as if only one of us will be able to get what we're looking for.

There is room for conflict through the diary door—room for stories of clashes and struggles and for all the dark feelings that go with them. After all, what's a good story without conflict? Conflict thrives at the core of storytelling. The tension, confusion, and hostile feelings that struggles generate make stories interesting and compelling to the writer and reader alike, and writing about conflict offers great benefits to both parents and children. We can use diary writing to learn from the clashes we have with our children and the problems we see our children having within themselves or with other people. In the diary, we can write stories of conflict that lead us through confusion to clarity, through stress into peace, through unwelcome feelings into comfort, and through scary thoughts into responsive action plans for negotiated peace.

When we're in the midst of conflict with someone, we may be stuck in a black-and-white, winner-take-all mindset in which we believe that one of us will have to change, and we'd prefer it to be our opponent. He'd prefer, of course, for us to change. In the midst of all of our strong feelings, it may be impossible for us to see at first that we're both going to need to change to solve our problem. It is through this struggle—the struggle of how we find our way with each other through a wilderness of disconnection back into the light of reconnection—that conflict deepens intimacy, rather than weakens it. The conflicts that we have with our children give us *both* the opportunities to stretch and grow as human beings. We know, in our heart of hearts, that the only solution to conflict with our children will be a solution in which we both get to be winners. But how do we get there?

Diary Storytelling as a Path for Perspective

Diary storytelling offers us the perspective of distance and the power of reflection. Writing can help us see what the real nature of the conflict is and how we discovered or might pursue a solution that will respect the dignity and needs of both parent and child. Writing in the diary invites our willingness to be honest with our children and ourselves. Storytelling gives us permission to expose the darker side of our impulses and feelings, and it gives us the opportunity to admit a mistake, say we're sorry, or hang in with patience when our child's darker side (or our own) surfaces to be encountered and tamed. Diary storytelling inspires us to show our commitment to our children to deal with conflict by attempting to resolve it rather than just leaving it hanging in midair, hoping it will resolve itself magically, or, that if we ignore it, it will just go away.

Encountering Adversity

We're always *seeking* something as we go on these quests with our children, even if we're not sure what it is. We may start off, perhaps, on a path together with our child, possibly even heading in the same direction to the same destination. We may or may not know what each of us is hoping to get from the quest. Then, we inevitably encounter adversity. Something crops up in the middle of the path that seems to prevent us from continuing our quest and finding what we're seeking. We meet an obstacle that we must overcome. Somehow, we find ourselves in the center of conflict, a dark and lonely land of disagreement where opposing forces are clashing. The call to the quest tests our limits and stretches them. We begin the journey, convinced that we can go only *so far*, handle just *so much*. But the requirements of the journey take us into new territory, where we find strength beyond our expectations, secret stores of patience, and a sense of humor we hadn't known we possessed.

How do we encounter or overcome the obstacle blocking our path? How do we meet this conflict with our child or children? There is much to be learned by telling our children stories of conflict through the diary door. In the following entry, I naively embark on a quest with my son and daughter on a hike through the woods that I soon realize I'm not prepared to make. What I struggle with internally is how to manage my fear that I've made a big mistake. For the safety of all, I wonder, shouldn't I just turn around? I clash with my son when he wants to go forward as eagerly as I want to return. But sometimes, once we've set off on a quest with our children, there's no turning back:

To Landon (age 8), September 19, 1995

...After dinner, sensing that I needed a break, [Daddy] took you guys up to Rocky Narrows for a hike. You came back about an hour later and invited me for ice cream. On the way to Friendly's Dad said to me:

"You know, he has no hiking boots. He needs some boots."

So he drove into Payless Shoes and we went in and found a pair of hiking boots for you, and pair of sneakers for Perrin....

The next morning we got up early to leave for Vermont—you got to miss school Friday. You were quiet for a while in the backseat, and then said:

"Thanks for the hiking boots Dad, I really love them."

*It was a blessing that he got them for you, because that afternoon, while he went off to present his seminar, I hopped in the car w/you two and headed off to the Green Mtn. Nat. Forest Svc., to get a map for a hike. The lady said it was a two-mile hike to a waterfall. After lunch at McDonalds we drove out to the Vt. Woods and eagerly set off on our journey. A lovely, lovely warm, sunny day in the woods w/no one else around. We walked and walked uphill through the quiet woods over trees knocked down in our path, singing songs from **The Sound of Music**, you leading the way energetically and enthusiastically, and Perrin even keeping up nicely. You were intent upon finding that waterfall. When we had hiked for at least an hour w/o coming to it, it finally began to occur to me that when the woman had said it was a two-mile hike, she had meant two miles in one direction—**up**—and two miles in the other—down!*

We finally met a young man w/ a dog heading down toward us—the first human we had seen. He told us cheerfully that we were about half-way there! Only half way? I was all for turning back. I had grave doubts about Perrin and you being able to com-

plete the hike. But you were **adamant**; you no longer even cared if it meant you would miss **Power Rangers**. We had to get to the waterfall or it would be a wasted hike. I resigned myself to the need to drag you both out at the end, and kept going behind you, though I suggested we turn around every chance I got, to no avail. Perrin stayed in surprisingly good shape. Eventually the trail became steep and narrow—too steep and narrow for my comfort, and with a scary drop-off to our right I became very bitchy. I put Perrin on my back where I could keep track of her and barked orders at your back to watch your step, move away from the edge, slow down, take it easy. I pushed hard to turn around. But I didn't have the heart to absolutely insist. I felt really torn because I wanted to support you to finish what you started, but I was having a hard time pushing through my own fears of not wanting anything to happen to you.

Even you started to get kind of nervous—was my fear contagious? You realized at some point that if I were to go tumbling down the side of the ridge that Perrin would go with me, and **that** would leave **you** all alone in the woods on a tight, steep path. So you began lobbying me to put Perrin down, believing that would greatly improve your chances of company if one of us was to lose our footing and go. But on **this** matter I wouldn't budge. There was no way I was going to try to keep your sister under control on that path. So, heavy as hell on my back, fingers clawing on my neck, I held tight to her until we heard the subtle, unmistakable rush and gurgle of the waterfall at last.

To reach it, we had to slide down a steep embankment, holding onto trees and branches as we slid. Once down I forgot we'd have to get back up. You and Perrin grabbed sticks and hopped over the rocks, while I sat and worried and hoped you wouldn't get hurt. The waterfall, because of the drought, was not running very heavily, but it was beautiful, and would have been peaceful had I been enjoying it alone. I coaxed us back to the trail as soon as I could tear you two away. Somehow, slipping and sliding and grabbing trees you pulled yourself up and I pushed Perrin up ahead of me back up to the trail where I put her back on my back through the steep descent until we were out of danger back on the wider, safer path, and then the two of you virtually ran down the path racing each other the whole way. Whenever you'd charge out ahead of her she'd scream in anger and sit down, refusing to budge. Then I'd tell you to so solve it as I strode on ahead. You would promise not to pass her and coax her to her feet and run at a fast clip beside her until you can no longer resist your competitive drive, and then you charge out ahead of her, until she screams and collapses on the ground, again, refusing to move if you're not going to let her be ahead of you. . . .

This is your dance, your sibling dance of competition, confrontation, and negotiation. You **do** want to get home in time for **Power Rangers** so you stop, backtrack, *you coax her up, you promise not to beat her, she takes off, you join her at a fast clip, and . . . well, you know the dance by heart.*

What I learned from writing this diary story, from the perspective of distance, was that I was really proud of my son for leading me through my resistance to the waterfall. This entry reminds me that my children and I can sometimes handle greater challenges than I think we can. If I want my children to learn how to overcome their fears in the pursuit of a goal, I have to be willing to overcome my own. And it reminds me that following my son is sometimes the best way to lead him. Writing diary entries can help us discover what we've brought back from the quest and whether we got what we were seeking, lost something, or found something we didn't know we'd find. The question isn't whether we should do everything we can to avoid going to the dark place of conflict with our children, but what can we bring back with us into the light on our return.

When Your Child Meets Someone Else's Dragon

Writing stories expands your awareness and perspective and helps you understand your child's point of view. As a writer or storyteller through the diary door, you follow the plot of your child's daily life. Observing your child's conflicts with other people allows you to see what your children are seeking, how they are seeking it, and whether you can (or even need to) help when they meet their dragons. We all, as children, have a first encounter with a bully—a sitting-duck moment when we suddenly become target practice for somebody a little older, a little bigger, and perhaps a little more powerful than we believe ourselves to be. In this moment of vulnerability and disillusionment, we all discover for the first time that we may have to defend ourselves in a way we didn't realize would be necessary. We're faced not only with the conflict the bully is forcing on us, but also with the conflict within ourselves that makes us simultaneously long for rescue *and* believe that we have the resources to solve the conflict for ourselves. Writing about how your child handles this type of conflict may provide her with both the reassurance and the comfort she is seeking, as the following entry does for my daughter:

To Perrin (age 3), August 15, 1995

"Perrin Meets a Bully"
. . . Yesterday, here in this playground, you had your first encounter with a bully, a four-year-old boy who seemed to feel he owned the playground. I didn't see anything happen, but you came quietly over to me and sat down beside me on the picnic table w/a gloomy expression. I casually asked how you were doing, and even though you

answered, 'all right,' I knew by your subdued behavior something had scared or upset you, so I gently probed. You finally gave out that a boy had stepped on your sand-castle. As we sat talking, the boy in question showed up at our picnic table—where his family was also situated w/their snacks, and after pouring himself a big drink he asked me in a gruff voice, pointing to you:

"Is she **deaf?**"

"Why no, why?"

" 'Cause I was talking to her and she wouldn't say nothing."

"Well, no, she's not deaf, in fact she's a very nice, friendly girl, and if you talk to her nicely she's very friendly."

The boy wandered away, bored, and we went over to the sandbox to play. Later, you eagerly told your big brother about the whole experience, and he was comforting and gave you some advice, which was to ignore him. And that's exactly what you had done!

Stories of Parent/Child Conflict— When You Tame Each Other's Dragons

For obvious reasons it's not always easy to motivate yourself to write about conflict. Conflict can be painful, disturbing, disruptive, confusing, and stressful. Often, it may feel tempting to take a nap, eat a cookie, or turn on the television instead of focusing on reflection, dialogue, and solutions. You may not be motivated to write when you feel angry, betrayed, abandoned, or frustrated with your child or yourself. It can be difficult to write when you feel enraged at your helplessness and at your inability to change or control someone or ashamed by where your attempts to control lead you. Perhaps unresolved conflict leaves you feeling depressed and hopeless. All those fire-breathing dragon feelings that *feel like* they will destroy a relationship surface.

Through the diary door, however, you can contain these feelings. There, you see the possibility of approaching conflict as a quest *for* relationship. What if conflict is seen as just *that*—as a quest for relationships with our children that are fulfilling, sustaining, resilient, and honest? As parents, we are called on to find a mutually respectful way to resolve our differences with our children so that we can go on, hand in hand, once more. We can approach conflict as a search for meaning, for understanding, for greater intimacy, for personal and reciprocal growth. This is where diary storytelling can help, with its offer of a quiet room for reflection, a time-out zone where there is always access to an ideal listener. Through the diary door, you reach for the transforming power of story to restore your equanimity, perspective, and respect for your child's dignity while regaining your own.

When Your Child Meets Your Dragon

We all have a fire-breathing aspect of our behavior, and sometimes, we—the *parents*—are the dragons who need to be tamed, or humbled, or enlightened by our heroic children. This makes a compelling story, too, when we're willing to write it. It's not always easy to recognize the ways in which we find ourselves playing the bully with our children. It's not easy to evaluate the expectations we have that drive the forceful behavior, to admit when we see how misguided they are, and to let go of them willingly once we've managed to create a big fuss over them.

This is exactly what I did with my daughter on her first day of preschool when I tried to impose my expectations on her without respecting her feelings. Writing this entry gave me a chance to admit my mistake, to learn from my own bad behavior, to make amends to my daughter, and to make a commitment to myself and her that I would try to curb my impulses to bully her in the future. My second daughter may benefit the most from the message of this story when she starts preschool soon and gets to pick out her own outfit without a battle:

To Perrin (age 3), September 19, 1995

"First Day of [pre-] School"

*I woke up fifteen minutes early to be sure and get us out of the door on time, really, to no avail. There was no hurrying either of you this morning, and since I had not slept well, and since Daddy has been away so long, my nerves are raw and **I** was having a temper tantrum before any of us had had breakfast. Landon responded to my tantrum by finally getting himself dressed, but **you** would not budge.*

*Yesterday I bought you another pretty outfit for school while shopping at Decelle's w/ Grammy: Dungarees w/ sequin flowers and a long sleeve tee w/ rosettes at the v-neck. **This** is what I expected you to wear for your first day of school.*

*But you emerged from your bedroom in faded blue and pink shorts and a grey T-shirt with a soldier boy on it that Grampy had given you. With your short hair, bald spot, and jagged bangs from where you gave yourself a trim, you did not really represent yourself in a very favorable manner. I angrily insisted that you change out of that "stupid" (I **never** say stupid!) outfit. You rebelled, throwing yourself face down on your bed to cry. I left you, but returned shortly, determined to have my way and have you look nice for the first day of school. I pulled you out of your outfit and pushed you into the new one. You sobbed. Landon came in and said how pretty you looked, and you still sobbed. I left the room again, still hoping to convert you.*

Standing in the kitchen by the sink my conscience got the better of me and sent me back to you with apologies. I pulled you out of the new outfit, pushed you into the old, and said I was wrong to insist you wear what I had picked out. Fine.

*I decided that it just doesn't really matter what you wear. What matters on the first day of school is that you are wearing something that gives **you** comfort, not me—you're the one taking the big risk.*

As always, you went into the new situation with enthusiasm and confidence, and when I picked you up you gave me a big welcoming hug and I could easily see by your smile that you'd had a great time. You even drew a picture of Landon!

Encountering Resistance

Even though you are sometimes wrong, sometimes you're right, and you know you are because your thinking is based on sound principles, ideals, or values that you believe are important to teach your children. Children naturally struggle against the lessons we're trying to teach them every day about how we think they should live, how we want them to behave, what we want them to do or not do. Just as we grown-ups do, they resist learning lessons, and parents often resist teaching them because such teaching can require what feels like heroic effort to overcome their resistance. We have to learn to ride the resistance if these values conflict with what our children want to do—and the resistance we encounter can be very powerful, indeed.

Sometimes we need to tame our child's dragon, and how we do so can make an interesting and enlightening story for our children and ourselves. The diary helps us connect with the parent within who *is* a hero and who has the energy and commitment, drive and discipline to overcome the fire-breathing dragon that exists in every child when he is told to do something he doesn't want to do. The diary also helps us listen to the dragon's side of the story and find a way to overcome the resistance and guide our children with wisdom, dignity, and love.

When my son was a Cub Scout I was his den leader. Our most important annual activity was the fall food drive, where the boys collected bags of food from houses in their neighborhoods and then delivered the bags to a local food bank for the needy. As the day in the following story approached, I had anticipated the disappointment my son would feel when he realized that the food drive would conflict with something else he really wanted to do. My husband's younger brother and sister needed to be picked up at the airport, and my son was eager to see them. My advance thinking convinced me that even though welcoming our company at the airport was important, I needed my son to learn the importance of honoring a commitment previously made and delaying the fun until after the work was done. The conflict was clear—we couldn't do both. I failed to anticipate how stormy this lesson would be for both of us, and how strong my own impulses—in the face of his resistance—would be to just give up on my ideals and give in to his wishes. Writing about it in the calm after the storm helped to reassure me that I had made the right decision to follow through despite the storminess of his resistance after my husband drove out the driveway without him. Having written this story, I carry its lessons with me into many encounters with my children's resistance as a reminder that hanging in with patience pays off for both of us in the long run:

To Landon (age 8), November 24, 1996

Out the window I saw Dad's car pulling down the driveway, and I heard a dramatic wail rise up beneath the closed window [outside where he stood]. The car headed out of the driveway and, as it disappeared up the street the wailing increased, and knowing I was the cause of your despair gave me an impulse to run out of the house and chase the car up the street, to stop the wheels I had put in motion. But the car was gone. Had I done the right thing?

Stepping outside into the Nov. air, I knew I had to attempt to comfort you. Still wailing inconsolably, you lurched out of sight around the house, coatless, I caught only a flash of the blue and gold of your Cub Scout uniform. You had turned your back on me.

Chilled, defeated, I went back inside, trusting the cold air would drive you indoors in time for us to make peace before we had to leave for the Cub Scout food drive.

Wherever I went in the house I could still hear your distant sobbing as you circled the perimeter like a warrior.

Had I done the right thing, sending Daddy and Perrin off w/o you to pick up Amanda and Josh, insisting that you come w/ me to the Food Drive to drop off and help unload the food? When I realized two days ago that these events were going to directly conflict, I thought it through and made my decision. I sorted out what I saw as the values and messages and lessons involved in the conflict: Yes, it's true that Amanda & Josh's arrival is a very special occasion, and, under other circumstances, if this were just a run of the mill cub scout meeting and you wanted to miss it, I would agree. But this is our major community service project of the year. . . . I decided that **this** commitment outweighed the possibility of going to the airport to pick them up. We'd see them almost as soon as they arrived at the house. . . .

As I had predicted, you walked in the kitchen door, sobbing **still**, hurling epithets as you ran to your room. . . .

We must try to talk, I thought entering your room w/ a heart trying for patience. . . . I stepped accidentally on the cub scout shirt you had thrown onto the floor.

I begin where I began in my head—w/ reason, and I try to gently explain why it's important for us to honor this commitment. You respond by explaining from the underworld of your sanctuary [under the bed] why you . . .

(1) hate me for making the commitment;

(2) hate cub scouts

(3) are quitting cub scouts no matter what

"…Well, we need to go when the brownies are done, but I want to make sure we eat first, so we better stop by McDonald's, Wendy's, Papa Gino's, your choice.…"

"All right," you wail, "just go out of here now!" So, I leave, hoping this is a **bit** of progress, despite the sounds of your continued sobbing and raging around your room. When my timer shows five minutes left, I return to check on you. Now you are **on** your bed, but littered around the floor are remnants of your rage—a sculpture of Jesus you made out of paper has been trashed, cub scout badges that had not yet been sewn on are strewn about the floor…

"It's okay to be angry at God.…"

(Inaudible response). I sit on the bed, offering a story of when I was a kid but you tell me you don't want my story.…

"So, what did you decide on for lunch? We need to go." The timer goes off. "Come on, let's get some lunch," and I head to the kitchen for my brownies, shocked and relieved that you are actually heading, angrily, but more quietly to the car.…

You pick Wendy's. Food tames us both, and I test the possibility of a casual conversation, about Daddy.…

"You know, Daddy's going through some mixed feelings this weekend. He's happy, of course, that his Dad & his little sister & brother are coming for a visit, but his Mom is also moving up here this weekend, and he feels torn about how to split himself between the two."

You are listening w/ some interest. I'm sort of rambling, searching for my point.

"You know, when Daddy's parents were divorced when he was 19, I'm sure he was pretty angry at god and disappointed.…"

"Probably.…"

"But you know what? If Grammy BL and Grampy D. hadn't gotten divorced, do you know who wouldn't be here today?"

You think very, very hard, and get it.

"Amanda and Josh?"

"Right."

"I'm sure Daddy wishes his parents hadn't gotten divorced, but you know how much he loves Amanda and Josh, like we all do. But, my point is, sometimes we're very angry at God because we don't like facing something, and it takes a long time to see the good in it.…"

"Do you mean I'm gong to have to wait a long time to see the good in this?"

"Probably."

*And, we're there, at the Church w/ all the cub scouts running around happily in
their uniforms. We spend the next two hours w/ our dens happily working together.
Each of you boys competes to carry the biggest load. We eat all the brownies, say our
cheerful goodbyes, and you & I drive away in the truck.*

"Doesn't it feel good?"

*"I'm so tired," you say, but you're not complaining. "I'm still angry," you say rea-
sonably. . . .*

Writing out the conflict as *story* helps you relieve stress and realize that the
struggle has been worth it, particularly since it's unlikely your child will be kissing
you and thanking you for the lesson. Diary writing will also help you to give a shape
and structure for preserving the kinds of lessons both you and your child generally have to learn and learn again every day of your life.

We all feel fears that make us want to stand still when someone who loves us is
asking us to take a risk. We all have stubborn resistance to doing things that someone else thinks might be good for us when we're sure they won't be good for us at
all. Our children may not always appreciate our efforts to help them keep an open
mind about trying new things, but this is part of what parents must do. Every child
has her own patterns of resistance to risk and change. What one child seeks enthusiastically the other passionately avoids. Diary stories help us get to know our children, to understand what motivates their behavior, and they give us an
accumulated case history of information and insight to draw on over the years that
helps us parent each child in the best possible way.

My daughter Perrin has a pattern of resisting new group activities, and diary stories like this one over her lifetime have helped me learn that what she approaches
with stubborn resistance often results in great satisfaction for her. Because I have
learned that my encouragement usually results in a positive outcome, it's worth it
to me let myself get a little scorched from the encounter with her from time to time,
as I did in the following entry:

To Perrin (age 6), December 14, 1998

"Becoming an Angel"

*"No, mother. I don't want to be in the Christmas pageant. **No way**."*

*"No way. I **will** not be an angel."*

"You can't make me, you know."

*Weeks ago, after receiving the flyer from church from Mrs. Motley about the
Christmas Pagent I began asking the two of you if you wanted to be in it.*

No, neither of you did. In fact, you were adamantly opposed to it, and remained so.

At least until Mrs. Motley asked Lan if he would like to be the MC. He agreed. . . . Mrs. Motley asked me if you would be an angel—all the girls in your age group would do this. . . . I said yes.

I said yes because I believe that you want to, and will enjoy doing these kinds of things but your anxiety gets in the way. My approach is to strongly encourage you to take part in certain things, like soccer, because it's important that you learn to manage your anxiety about joining things. It will serve you now, but also later in life. I do not think it would be good for you to avoid everything because it causes you anxiety. I was naturally shy and lacked confidence, so I quite understand the struggle.

I came home from church and said:

*"The angels get to wear beautiful costumes and wings. . . . You don't **have** to be an angel—I won't **make** you be one. But you **do** have to go to rehearsal next week and try it. If you try it and hate it, you can give it up."*

*This was not well-received. You said, of course, that you had no intention of going to rehearsal and you didn't care about a costume and there was no way I could **make** you be an angel.*

I quite understood.

But I insisted, anyway, that you must go to rehearsal and try w/ the assurance that you could then freely drop your halo. . . .

By Sun. morning your resistance reached a feverish pitch. In the hour before church we fought over everything possible, including what you would or would not wear, how stupid your ribbed white tights looked w/ your black heels, how monstrously unworkable your hair was, how you refused to go to your stupid Sunday School class, but mostly how sincere were your intentions to boycott the rehearsal afterwards.

*Daddy and I were rushing because we had to teach Land's class and get there in time to be settled in w/ Frankie. I sent all of them on ahead, knowing we'd need a bit more time to settle **you**. You had lots of testing to do. As I stood in front of the mirror finishing my hair, you walked in, pulling yours at the roots:*

*"You can't **make** me go to rehearsal!"*

"Perrin, you have one simple line to say w/ all your friends. You'll have a good time."

"What's going to happen if I don't go?"

I am so frustrated, in a split second I am deciding in my mind that I might just give up. I might just tell you forget it, never mind. I am about to, but then I say:

"If you don't go to pageant rehearsal I will take the Blockbuster movie back today instead of letting you watch it later when Jackey comes."

You storm silently out of my room. It worked.

Somehow, we get your shoes buckled over acceptable tights and a headband pushed over your unacceptable hair, and I promise a story about myself as a girl on the way to the car.

From the back seat you ask—so, what's the story?

I tell you about how when I was a little girl I got few store-bought dresses, but that Grammy would try to make matching dresses for Christmas for me and my two sisters. I remembered the red felt jumper w/ the Santa decal. The story cheers you up, now you are thinking of the magical possibilities of having a mother who sews, or a grandmother who sews, and all the items you will ask Grammy to sew for you.

And suddenly, I am filled w/ the spirit of Advent that my mother's sewing represented—the secret surprises always waited for on Christmas morning from her sewing table.

*At Church you go down to your class silently. The next time I see you is at the rehearsal, standing w/ all the angels in the sanctuary w/ your script in hand. On the second try, w/ Mrs. Motley's coaching, **all** the angels read the line aloud!*

After rehearsal you come skipping over to me and Frances in the pew.

"Here," you say, handing me the script. "I don't need this. I memorized my line! 'Glory to God in the Highest, and on Earth, peace, goodwill toward men.'"

This angel had earned her wings.

The Healing Qualities of Writing about Conflict as Quest

There are many potential benefits to be gained from writing about conflict between you and your child through the diary door:

- Catharsis – Just as your child may be calmed after a tantrum, writing about the conflict can give you an opportunity to express pent-up feelings, which helps you recover your balance and perspective. Keep in mind, however, that diaries for children are not a dumping ground for your raw, unprocessed feelings, even though they may have an important place within the context of a story that is aimed at helping you and your child make sense of conflict and heal from it. Your own personal diaries are a good place for that kind of expression. When you need to have a tantrum—to just kind of kick and scream your feelings out—then you can go to your private writing or vent aloud to a supportive person. If you want to try to tell an uplifting or insightful story about the tantrum, fight, or conflict, your child may be an ideal listener through the diary door today, and an interested reader when she grows up.

- Comic Relief – Writing can help you see the humorous side of the conflict and regain your sense of humor. You may not be ready to laugh right away.

But if the story is written in a tone that respects both sides of the problem, it may give *you* the opportunity to lighten up and *your child* a chance to laugh about it later on, as my daughter did when I read her the previous story, "Becoming an Angel."

- Clarity – Diary storytelling can help you reflect on and understand the big picture and see clearly what the problem was about for each of you, perhaps leading you toward a solution or avoiding unnecessary repetition.

- Creativity – Writing about conflict as quest can help you loosen your hold on a one-dimensional view of the situation and be surprised by insights, themes, or messages you hadn't expected to find.

- Communication – Stories that include the real dialogue of your conflicts offer a lot of food for thought. Writing can help you express your thoughts, feelings, values, and behavior in a nonjudgmental, supportive way. It can also demonstrate that you try to listen to, respect, and incorporate your child's point of view in an effort to to reach a compromise or truce.

- Comfort – When our emotions are raw, we seek comfort. Your child, developmentally, may not be able to validate your views right now at all. This ability takes maturity. Writing about the conflict in the diary, you may be able to gain a sense of validation that even if your child doesn't understand you today, perhaps she will some day in the future when reading the diary. This act of future projecting may provide some comfort to you while you're waiting.

- Commitment to Change, Reconciliation, and Amends – Writing can help you to see what you're sorry for and to say it as well as to forgive your child for his or her shortcomings and mistakes.

- Closure – None of us wants a fight to go on forever but we also don't want it to be just ignored, forgotten, or left without resolution to crop up without warning later on. Writing diary stories can help us express feelings, let go of resentments, wrap up a fight, accept a truce, and then move on.

When approaching conflict as quest, you can pay attention to how the conflict was resolved and to what you and your child seemed to learn. If the conflict was solved in a mutually respectful way, it's doubtful that either one of you got completely what you wanted. Probably, you each both lost and gained. Let your story reflect this. Think about how you managed the conflict. Try to create a story that rises above a good-versus-bad power struggle into a lesson about what it means to be human, or to live according to certain values, or the struggle to live in community with people who are different from each other.

Stories of Reconciliation and Amends

The diary is a place where you can pay attention to a variety of aspects of the healing process. Saying "I'm sorry" and accepting your child's apology help tremendously. In order to end a fight or conflict, somebody usually needs to be the first person to reach out, take the risk, and wave the white flag. Isn't it nice when it's your child who goes first?

To Landon (age 8), April 23, 1995

. . . Later, trying to get you ready for bed, we battle again since you are wound up about the day and the anticipation of returning to school to be "Star of the Week." Later, from the shower, you call a genuine, cheerful apology to me:

"I'm sorry we fought, Mom."

This helps, tremendously. We read from the Mayflower book. . . .

It's especially nice when learning has led to your child's ability to help prevent a fight, as my son did:

To Landon (age 8), May 3 1995

. . . Getting your snack we clashed again, each speaking our lonely language. I said something like—

"Well, here we go into a fight," and you said immediately, and sincerely:

"I'm sorry." Our eyes met for a second. I said I'm sorry too. And it was all uphill from there. I felt so relieved that you had the ability to reach out and stop the fight. I know you're really working on this.

The Wisdom of Rereading during Times of Conflict

Conflicts with your child can make you feel as if you don't even like someone whom you loved deeply just yesterday. Because conflict cools you, at least momentarily, toward the people you love, your misbehaving child may suddenly seem like a stranger. It is just at these times of misbehavior, when your child has been caught doing something you never imagined she or he would ever do, that you need the diary stories to remind you of many things. All these wonderful stories, dialogues, and memories you have saved will warm you back up to your child. Rereading will help you to look at the bigger picture of who your child really is, with all her assets and shortcomings.

Looking back at what you have written to your child in the diaries from the beginning can help you move forward in your parenting with care and concern for the unique needs of your children. As children grow, their needs change; but *some* needs certainly remain the same. It may be easier to remember to hug and cuddle a two-year old as you go about your busy day if he is by your side or crawling up into your lap. It's easy to forget that an eleven-year-old boy likes and needs hugs, too. Rereading the diaries of early childhood can remind you of what your child needs.

When your child enters a period of misbehavior or turbulence, sitting down alone or with your partner with a cup of tea and rereading diary entries from earlier, easier times can be extremely therapeutic. Reading about your child's sense of humor, sense of wonder, successes, yearnings, and struggles can help you cope with a present problem.

Conflicts tend to remind us that we're human and imperfect parents after all, often just when we've been feeling smugly satisfied about our child's brilliance, talent, or maturity. Rereading may reconnect us with the wiser parent we can be. Rereading reminds us why we love our child. It points us in a calmer, more centered direction for helping our child by reminding us that we have solved similar conflicts in the past. If, before we started rereading, we felt as if we were in the role of the critical, judgmental parent, by the time we finish reading we will probably feel more connected to the truly nurturing parent we want to be. Rereading may help us see what appropriate limits need to be set, what feelings need to be expressed and acted upon, and what we need specifically in order to transform this conflict into a mutually satisfying quest.

In the next chapter, we look at conflict through the lens of sibling rivalry. But first, try these Diary Door Openers.

 **Diary Door Openers**

1. Walking Hand in Hand Once More
   Write a story about a time when your child reached out to you with a gesture or words to make amends for his or her part in a conflict and describe how you responded.

2. Admitting Mistakes
   Describe a conflict in story form about a time when you were in conflict with

your child and later realized or accepted that you were wrong. Tell your child what you did or said to make amends. If you haven't yet, respond in the diary with the amends and then make them in person.

3. Values Clarification
Think about a ground rule or boundary that you are enforcing in your relationship with your child that you feel is appropriate and necessary even though your child is resistant to it. Without becoming defensive, explore and explain to your child about the values and beliefs you hold that are guiding you in this and how you believe your enforcement of this ground rule or boundary will benefit your child in both the short and long term.

4. Making Amends
Tell the story of an apology or amends someone made to you when you were young that made a difference to you.

5. In Your Child's Shoes
In reviewing a recent conflict with your child (of any age), imagine yourself in your child's shoes. Speaking as if you are your child, write one thing you think she or he strongly believes that you are having a hard time hearing and acknowledging. Going back into your own point of view reread what you've written, and putting your critical parent role aside, reflect on this message and respond to it from your own point of view.

6. Comic Release
Write about a recent conflict that either you or your child was able to mutually resolve by recognizing, admitting, and laughing at the absurdity of the disagreement.

Chapter II

Brothers and Sisters Growing through Sibling Harmony and Rivalry

Trickster is one of our guardian spirits,
keeping alive the childhood of humanity.

(Stephen Nachmanovitch, *Free Play – Improvisation*
in Life and Art, p. 47)

Through the diary door, stories of how brothers and sisters live together and how they relate to each other over time may develop into entertaining and intriguing relationship histories. These diary stories reflect the reality that sibling relationships, which last a lifetime, thrive in periods of both harmony and rivalry. If you write regularly to your children, you will see stages and roles in relationships taking shape from birth as well as altering and adapting to new conditions over a lifetime. Our siblings may provide us with our most intimately satisfying or our most hostile and alienating relationships, presenting us with opportunities both for great blessings *and* supreme challenges in human relations and family dynamics. This chapter looks at diary stories that arise from issues of sibling harmony and rivalry from childhood through adulthood, through happy and harmonious as well as painful and conflicting periods, highlighting the unique opportunities that diary storytelling provides to guide us through painful periods into inner wisdom in our parenting.

Not every child, of course, has siblings. How and when siblings enter your children's lives over the years is part of the story you will tell in the diaries. Children who grow up as only children may develop siblinglike relationships with other children—friends, cousins, or neighbors. Whether or not your children have siblings when they are born, they may end up with them at some point in their lives as families blend for many reasons and in many ways over time. Step-brothers and -sisters and half-brothers and -sisters are common in families with divorce and remarriage and may change the family relationships in dramatic ways. And brothers- and sisters-in-law become siblings to a certain extent after children grow up and marry or find life partners.

The Diary as an Antidote to Sibling Rivalry

All children compete with their siblings for your attention and favor and strive to be the chosen one in your eyes. This seems to be universally one of the most stressful and confounding challenges for parents. You may have empathy for your children's rivalry based on your own experience as a sibling growing up, and you pride yourself in making sure that you treat your children fairly, going out of your way to be consistent and careful to avoid favoritism. Whatever you seem to do, however, fails to convince your children that there's enough of your love to be spread abundantly around. Normal emotions of envy, jealousy, and insecurity fuel fears that you love the other child or children more, and the task siblings take on is how to get enough of your attention to convince you that you are mistaken in the preferences they believe you show.

There is an essential irony about children's ideas of what it means to play fair. They want to believe their parents operate according to principles of fairness, doling out the family's resources evenly. But they seem to realize that it's only human if their parents do err on the side of a more generous helping to one of the children every now and then, and that's perfectly all right as long as *they* are the recipient. The irrationality of most sibling rivalry can drive parents into a frenzy of frustration.

Diary storytelling offers an opportunity to address sibling rivalry creatively. The diary door opens into a special place in which your child has your sustained attention without having to step on somebody's toes to get it. Children of every age keep their eyes on you to make sure you're watching when they are doing something new or exciting for which they want praise and encouragement. It's as if children who have siblings need to ask you the same questions over and over, hoping for a reassuring answer:

- Will my parents have enough love, attention, and resources to go around?
- Will they notice how special I am?
- Will they see the real me—*as a unique individual*?
- Is my brother or sister really more worthy and deserving of love than I am?

The diaries are a place in which parents can write the stories that contain the reassuring answers to these crucial questions. The entries that you have taken the time and made the effort to write reinforce all the words you tell them and assure your children on the deepest level that you *are* watching. Through the diary door, your child is in the spotlight and brothers and sisters are just bit players in the drama. Throughout this book, you see that the diary offers you freedom to shower your child with praise and observation that may be difficult to give during the day with other siblings around vying for attention. Diary writing is a way to give each child individual attention even while she or he is busy or sleeping—attention that makes them all feel special and chosen.

Greetings

Have you ever wondered how your sisters and brothers felt about you when you were born? Have your parents told you stories that celebrated sibling relationships in infancy, or the special roles they played in your upbringing? Children attach a lot of significance to their sibling's opinions of them, for better or for worse. Diary stories can celebrate your children meeting each other for the first time. In the following entry, I captured the enchantment my two older children experienced when their new sister was brought home:

To Frances (age 6 weeks), May 24, 1997

"That's a big smile for me, sister!" your brother croons, leaning over the seat of the car toward you.

Perrin holds your long, delicate fingers as she sits beside you.

"Can I hold her, Mom?" Landon asks, and I let him. He is in love with you; has been from the beginning, the moment of your birth.

Yes, he was there.

He turned away only as your head was crowning. He told me he was afraid they were going to pull your head off. And, he thought the umbilical cord was kind of gross. And he still doesn't like to change your diaper or wipe your nose, and he's kind of grossed out when you spit up on him, but you are the star in his sky. You please him very much. . . .

In addition to the attention children want from you, they want to feel noticed and appreciated by siblings. Diary stories can feed your child's need to feel special and can provide nourishment for years to come, as I think the following entry will for my daughter. Diary stories like this one can be powerful in their simplicity. Just one question or one statement can portray a deep and abiding affection:

To Frances (age 1), April 14, 1998

"Where's Frances?" Landon asked, sitting down to dinner w/ Perrin and me on a sunny evening.

"Sleeping," I answer. You fell asleep at 5:30 after a raucous time at Cub Scouts, running around in the yard.

"Oh, dinner is no fun without Frances!"...

Learning from Sibling Role Relationships

As you write in the diary, you may sense when siblings are going to develop a special role relationship that will have a significant impact on their development and their sense of identity. You can show your children the roles they are creating and playing for each other over time. Children naturally learn to play certain roles in the family, such as the responsible one or the protector, jokester, peacemaker, or nurturer. Some roles they play will be chosen and others may be assigned, like birth order—oldest, youngest, or middle child. Some roles they like, and some they don't. *How* your children play the roles they choose or are assigned is worth paying attention to as an aspect of each child's development.

Diary writing gives you the opportunity to reinforce the positive aspects of reciprocal roles they play with each other. For your children, stories about being wanted, valued, or protected by siblings may offer a strong foundation in their self-esteem and identity. Though I can imagine a period in her life when her brother's protectiveness may feel inappropriate and stifling, I thought that at this vulnerable period of her development, Frances might find the portrait of her protective older brother reassuring:

To Frances (age 11 months), March 27, 1998

Almost 80 [degrees] in March! ...

...After Land got home (w/ GT) we walked up to Grammy's to see [cousin] Dusty et al. Sammy loves you—won't leave you alone. He says, 'Franci, Franci!' and puts his arms out to give you a bear hug. Then he pushes you. You push back and push him out of the way. Land comes and gently scolds him: "Don't push Franci, Sam!"

*In the back yard, Sam, Huck, and Alison run down the hill. You follow, feet going faster than you can handle and you fall onto your face and cry. Landon hears you and comes running into the back yard just in time to see you, in motion again, take a second tumble. Then he scolds **me**:*

*"Mom, watch her, she keeps falling!" The rest of the afternoon he never leaves your side w/o telling me to **watch** you. He only runs off to play w/ GT when he's sure I've got you under my wing.*

Cooperation, Collaboration, and Sibling Harmony

Shared adventures and mischief can be bonding experiences for siblings—a time when they are appreciating the value of sticking together. These stories can be charming reminders of the times they have connected through shared play, as my son and daughter, who are frequent rivals, display their ability to collaborate in mischievous yet harmless play:

To Landon (age 8), May 11, 1995

. . . Today, you had your last sign language class. Perrin ran & gave you a big hug when we picked you up in the cafeteria.

After school, the two of you worked on finishing the Easter Eggs we colored last night. I'm afraid I failed to give you adequate supervision. You hid your eggs, went on a hunt, ate half of them, and apparently tossed half of them outdoors in a smashing contest. Perrin, at dinner, confessed this last point:

"Where are your eggs?" I ask.

"We smashed them outside!" [Perrin answered]

*"You **did**?"*

"Yes, we did!"

"No, we didn't, Perrin," you say.

"Oh, yes we did!"

"No," you say, getting up into her face, increasing the firmness of your tone, "No, we did not."

Guess who I believe?

It's okay, I think some sibling collusion is very healthy. You two need to be bonded w/each other against us at times—it's very natural. Your relationship is meant to survive us both. I love to see the two of you getting along & playing w/each other.

Blessings versus Curses

Writing to your children about their sibling relationships when they are getting along or being supportive of each other may later remind them of their relatedness during periods of rivalry. Diary entries serve as concrete reminders of the more affectionate and harmonious periods of their relationship and may reassure and remind you both that their relationship *is* built on a foundation of affection and goodwill.

It seems to be our human nature to take criticism more seriously than the compliments we receive, and the criticism we take from siblings can be particularly painful and can have an enduring impact on our self-concept. My approach in the diaries throughout the years of writing about sibling relationships has been to preserve as much as I can of the positive aspects of their relationships. Siblings will curse and bless each other, but because of its sting, a curse may be remembered longer than a blessing.

Through the diary door, compliments can be taken seriously and can gain lasting value as they are read and reread over time. Written down, compliments gain significance and can be taken more seriously and ingested more deeply by the child who really needs to hear them. When siblings give each other the gift of a compliment, you can give it to one or both of the siblings in a diary story, as I saved this compliment that my son gave to my daughter one peaceful afternoon during a winter vacation in Florida. As the second sibling, middle child, and biggest rival of my son, my daughter Perrin takes a regular dose of negative feedback from her older brother, who dotes on his baby sister. So, when his positive feedback does come her way spontaneously and generously, as it often does, it seems to take a while for her to let it really sink in and trust that he means it. All the more reason for me to take it through the diary door and leave it for her to "hear" again, and again:

To Perrin (age 7), February 28, 2000

> . . . *Right now, and all afternoon, you and Landon have played like best friends, and it's a joy to be around you when you're like this. Swimming, jumping, pushing, falling, screaming, laughing.*
>
> *We just got back from a long rollerblade through the neighborhood—longest trip I've seen you take on blades. I compliment you, and you seem surprised that I notice how much progress you've made. And Land says:*
>
> *"You're a natural, Perrin."*
>
> *You make him repeat it three times before you hear him! . . .*

Sometimes, in a single day—or entry—there are surprises, and your children, who were at each others throats the day before as you pulled your hair out by its roots, bless each other when you least expect it, as my son and daughter did:

To Perrin (age 8), September 20, 1999

...*"Mom, I know I have pretended before, but this time I really **am** sick and you don't believe me!"*

Okay, I know. This I did, and felt, many times when I was your age. Some times I just needed a day at home w/ my Mom.

Most of the morning you spent playing w/ Lan's lego in the basement, while I tried to show Frances, legitimately sick Frances, some extra attention.

When you came upstairs you were craft hungry. But, busy, I directed you to the computer. You brought out a notebook where you write. Recently, you had written a poem in it: "I see, hear and feel w/ my Body."

"If you type it for me I'll get it done quicker."

I made you a matte out of fiber board and we typed and taped your poem onto it. Then we got out the poster paints and made you an artist's palette so you could paint a background for your poem. I left it propped on the dining room table to dry.

Later that afternoon, it was time to bake, as you had requested.

Brownies. I gave you the bowl and chocolate and the recipe, and ran up & borrowed a stick of butter from Mom, & then you were on your own.

On your own for the first time!

Reading the recipe yourself, you measured your sugar, your flour, your vanilla. . . .

Busy starting dinner, I glanced over at you, perched on your barstool at the butcher block, stirring, you suddenly said:

"Oh, I feel so sad. . . . Land is going to be growing up and leaving us so soon!"

"What?" I'm startled by your sincerity, the maturity of your unexpected sentiment.

"Land's going to grow up and leave for college. . . ."

*"Perrin, are you saying this because you're pretending to be me while you bake—or is this how **you** really feel?"*

Softly, you answer,

"That's how I really feel. Why is this how you feel too?"

*As always, you have knocked me out of my mindless preoccupation, and I realize this is one of those afternoons when I should **pay attention** to you, because you will say and do magical things. . . .*

At dinner I show Dad & Lan your poem poster. Dad reads it aloud.

"Wow Perrin, that's really good. That's a great poem," Lan says. "You ought to put it in the Idea Box at school and read it at school meeting. I mean it. I've seen fifth graders who couldn't write a poem that good."

*Then, I get to feel really proud of **both** you and your brother. . . .*

The role relationships your children play with each other may alter naturally over time and along with your child's personal growth and development. Rereading certain diary entries may later remind them that their relationship with each other develops and evolves in stages, some more conflicted than others. Even though the roles they play with each other seem to be reciprocal and satisfying at the moment captured in the next entry, I seem to be anticipating potential future conflicts for my younger daughter:

To Frances (age almost 2), March 28, 1999

. . . Did I tell you your name for Landon, whose name is too much of a challenge for you right now?

"Boy."

You say "Where Boy Go?" when he gets out of the car.

"Hi Boy!"

"Boy on Bus" etc. He likes this very much, the idea of you making up a name just for him. But his feelings are hurt regularly if you fail to hug him every time he demands one, or if, like today, you fail to demonstrate proper enthusiasm to see him after you have been separated from him by an overnight w/ his cousin Joey.

(Boy gets jealous so easily, Frances. This will be a challenge for you, won't it? But you do know how to use your charm on him!) . . .

Jealousy, Envy, and Sibling Rivalry

There is no escaping the normal feelings of jealousy and envy when it comes to siblings. These are not rational feelings to be talked through, reasoned with, or given in to. We want life to be fair according to our own standards of what that means. We see what someone else is getting, and we want it, too. Whatever it is we are longing for seems to call out to us like a magic cookie promising to make our lives feel perfectly complete. We may feel convinced that we deserve this thing we want more than our rival who possesses it. For a moment, we feel lost. We don't know how to manage the feelings surging up from some dark and stormy place within that makes us feel we can't bear to see someone else enjoying something we crave but lack. We can't bear the injustice of it, and we make our feelings known forcefully to those people we feel might be responsible for our deprivation.

Jealousy and envy are normal, human emotions, and we may struggle our whole lives to keep them in check. Sometimes, just venting our emotions helps us focus on the comfort of enjoying what we do have rather than on resentment and longing for the magic cookie. We could all probably benefit from a guardian angel who watches over us while we swing off on our emotional binges, looking out for us until we're emotionally spent and ready to return once more with acceptance of our lot or a reasonable plan to change it. My son has played the guardian angel for his younger sister on more than one stormy occasion, like the one that follows in this entry:

To Perrin (age 7), September 20, 1999

Even though you had a birthday party—the second in two days to attend, you were insanely jealous when you learned that Landon would be going to the movies that night w/ Dad and Ross.

This was Friday afternoon, after school. K.'s party was at 5:00. You didn't care. You started to rant and rave. How could we be letting Landon go to the movies w/o you?

But, I didn't see it as unfair. I didn't consider you deprived. It was Fri. night and Land had no plans. It seemed reasonable to me that I help him make some. I know you don't agree w/ my philosophy that everything does not have to seem **equal**. In my mind, you had plans, he did not.

You thought, however, that you could decide that you didn't like your plan and just change it.

So, you picked up the phone—I watched you dial not believing that you would really **do** it—and you called Mrs. G., and while I listened, assuming you were faking it, told her that you would not be coming to the party because you realized you had other plans.

When I realized you had actually **made** the call I was furious! And sent you to your room.

Embarrassed, I called Lois to apologize, and she perfectly understood what I was dealing w/, since she has a 2nd grade daughter herself.

In the midst of this madness, Landon tried his best to comfort you, reason w/ you, manage your envy. You see, neither one of you ever enjoys your treat if the other is resentful of it. Landon felt two things—

(1) he wanted you to let go of your resentment so that he could fully embrace his pleasure, and

(2) he was really trying to understand what you were going through.

So, while you were packing a duffel bag for an extended absence from home, he came to me in the kitchen and asked,

"Did you ask her if everything was all right at school today?"

This was actually quite insightful of him. Because he saw himself in the way you were acting—you were mirroring him. Land and I have danced this dance many times, and often, for him, there is a deeper disappointment going on that he hasn't shared that he is acting out, instead of talking out.

That did not, however, seem to be the case here. So, even though dad got home and tried to help, there was no talking you out of leaving, bag strapped on your back, apple in hand. You left.

But your brother followed you, sneaking behind as you headed up Course Brook. He said you knew he was there because you kept stopping and looking behind you.

The clock struck 5:00—time for the party, so I sent Dad out in the car looking for you.

After he left, you & Land came wandering in.

"I ran out of cookies," you said.

Dad pulled in, and you ran cheerfully off to the party.

Siblings as Scapegoats

When something we're involved in goes wrong, we all have an impulse from time to time to find someone to shoulder the blame. It can be hard to admit we're wrong when we've made a mistake and we fear the consequences. It's tempting to find a scapegoat, and when we're young, unsuspecting siblings are readily available to fill the role. Even when we blame someone else, as we inevitably do, we may learn that the price of the imagined consequences isn't nearly as high as the cost of a guilty conscience. There are ways to redeem ourselves by learning to admit our error and make amends, as my daughter does in the following entry:

To Perrin (age 8), March 21, 2000

"Your Birthday Party"

. . . Sat. morning I baked and decorated your "tower" cake in green and blue and pink stripes. You seemed to like it. Maelyn arrived early. Franny set the party table and I tried, amidst all the bustle and chaos to practice my story in the living room.

I had set up the goodie bags on the dining room table next to the large vase full of yellow glads dad brought me for St. Patty's Day. You Fran and Mae were fussing with the goody bags, trying to nab your own favorites. Then you came running to me—

"Mom, Frances knocked over the flowers!"

I went in to find the vase had spilled water over the table and was streaming down onto the carpet.

I chased you all out of the room, and cleaned it up myself. Then I went back to my rehearsal. Again you came looking for me. Mae was behind you and you silently motioned her away.

"Mom," you said quietly and seriously, looking straight into my waist.

"Yes?"

"Frances didn't knock over the vase. I did."

"Oh? Oh, I see. Well, thanks for telling me," I said, giving you a hug. "Will you guys stay off the table now?"

You agreed, and very soon your friends arrived, and the party began.

Siblings as Tricksters

Even if we don't like having tricks played on us ourselves, we may enjoy playing them on others. Playing the trickster endows us with magical qualities that can help us resolve our disruptive feelings when we find that words won't express the depths of what we're really feeling. When all else fails, playing a harmless trick may offer us a magical solution to getting what we want when we want it whether anyone else likes it or not—even if it's just for one, sweet, satisfying moment or two.

A few days before I wrote this entry to my daughter, I had written another one about an argument we had when she was upset because I had bought her brother a new, thermal sleeping bag for a winter camping trip. She was going to a slumber party and didn't understand why this didn't justify her need for a new bag. Perhaps I had kidded myself when I assumed she had accepted the fact that I wasn't going to get her a new bag. The story reminds me that the issue wasn't about whether she got a new bag; it was about what a lot of sibling rivalry is about—her fear that I loved him more:

To Perrin (age 7), October 1, 1999

. . . Last night, as Landon sat at the table after soccer soaking his cold feet from a wet soccer field, and crunching his cereal, you decided it was time to do your homework.

"Can I have a bowl to soak my feet in?" [you asked]

No, I'm afraid not!

"Can I have a bowl of cereal w/ my homework?"

You never eat cereal. Ever. But, fine.

*You take out your corrected homework from last week, and I must say I'm **very** impressed. Your teacher has given you accolades at a job well done. Hooray. You spread your homework across the table, and Landon manages to find some corrected homework to collect on his fair share of praise.*

Meanwhile, it's time for bed. Lan decides to read to Fran inside his new thermal sleeping bag spread on the living room floor, as is their recent custom. I would like to read you Harry Potter, but you have left him at school.

Landon spreads the bag across the center of the blue rug as we are all getting ready for reading. At some point we're all ready and head to the living room, but the rug is empty—there is no blue sleeping bag in sight.

"Mom, have you seen the bag?" [Landon asked]

"No."

"Perrin, where'd you put it?"

"What, I didn't touch it, I swear!"

"Franny? Did you take the bag and put it somewhere?"

"Yes!"

"Where?" She leads Landon on what turns out to be a wild goose chase to the family room. She has not seen the bag, really.

"Perrin, are you **sure** you didn't take the bag?" I am trying to not be too accusatory, just in case there is another reasonable explanation, which, alas, there isn't.

"No!" You're sitting in the black swivel armchair casually munching your dry Captain Crunch. "No! (indignantly) I didn't take it!"

Now, we reluctantly begin to doubt ourselves. Perhaps we didn't really see it there, spread out across the middle of the floor, empty, waiting to be cuddled in. We go off, yet again, searching, while you watch from the black swivel chair.

But I stop, just around the corner in the hall where you can't see me, but where I can hear **you**, still munching. I am remembering the argument we had after school on Friday when you were getting ready for Abby's party, but deciding not to go, since there was no sleeping bag in the house, that would accommodate your needs for this party. I showed you four among all the possibilities we own. None of them, apparently, would be warm enough.

"Warm enough? You're not sleeping outside!"

"But it's not summer anymore!"

"Perrin, you'll be sleeping in a heated house."

Wishful thinking, I guess, to imagine the sleeping bag drama would end there, just because you chose, finally, backed into a corner, the Lion King bag that Mae had given you. I heard movement from your chair, some shifting. I peaked around the corner. There you sat, still in your chair, hand in your cereal bowl. But there **behind** your chair, from this angle I could clearly see the lump of blue bag on the floor behind the chair.

Had you moved it so that it could be seen? Or had the swivel of the chair shifted it into a more revealing position?

I walked over to the bag. You seemed surprised that I would discover it there. I called to Landon.

"Perrin," I said, picking the bag up and spreading it across the middle of the floor, "are you sure you don't know how this got here?"

"No, I had no idea. . . ."

But I looked down at the floor behind the chair where the sleeping bag had hidden itself, and saw three golden kernels of Captain Crunch cereal.

In my mind, anyway, the mystery had been solved.

Family History and the Evolution of Sibling Relationships

Watching your children grow up with their siblings may remind you about the roles you have played, or still play, with your own siblings or those people with whom you developed sibling relationships. Your children are interested in your family history, your upbringing, and your relationship to your own siblings today. Writing about your relationships with your siblings may be a source of family history your children will appreciate having preserved. Knowledge of their family history will add meaning to their sense of family identity.

In the following entry, I write about a transitional period during which my family of origin was experiencing rapid change and expansion. My parents raised five children, and then through the marriage of each of their children acquired five more. These marriages introduced new sibling relationships and influenced the roles we had grown up playing with each other. Suddenly, we each began having children. No longer just brothers and sisters, now we were aunts and uncles and grandparents, all learning to play a variety of new roles with each other. Written from the summer cabin where the family often gathered, this entry documents a honeymoon period of harmonious sibling bonding in our rapidly changing role relationships:

To Perrin (age 4 months), July 19, 1992

. . . We arrived here [at Laurel Lake] from Grammy's yesterday, Sat. morning with Dusty & Billie & Bobby & Pam and Hanna. We rushed here so the guys could participate in the annual canoe race leaving from the beach. Bobby and cousin Jeff P. won in their category, and Daddy & Uncle Dusty came in 3rd in theirs—and all of them got trophies. We girls sat on the beach most of the day. Today I may try water skiing! Uncle Dusty and I swam to the Boys' camp, which was great but I feel like I lack the stamina I had in my pre-children days, and wonder if I will ever swim across the lake and back again. Yes, I know I shall. Maybe some day with you. . . .

This is the first summer since the summer before Daddy and I got married, (six summers that would be) that my family has not had a wedding to plan and participate in.

In 1987, Daddy and I got married . . . on June 27. That summer, after our Honeymoon in the White Mountains, we spent only one night here before I moved to Fl. with Dad.

[interruption, entry continued on August 4, 1992]

I was interrupted that beautiful morning by Aunti Pam and Hanna who came out to join me. . . .

Next summer, '89 [I inadvertently skipped over the summer of 1988] was when Aunti Karen married Uncle Tom and I was a Bride's Maid. They planned the wedding in about three weeks, and they had a really lovely wedding at the Fitzwilliam Inn. Landon was a very adorable and wild 1-yr. old. Karen's wedding cake broke, during delivery, I think. Jo-Jo, Mom, Great Grammy B. and I all dressed in aunt Marion's room in Donn's cabin. . . .

Next summer Uncle Bobby married Pam at the end of June, and I came w/ Landon—Daddy had to stay in Fl. and work, but he joined us shortly after. Uncle Bob had a gorgeous wedding by the pool at the M.'s house; a beautiful sunny day. Landon was completely wild and out of control. I never even sat down. He never stopped for a second, and made quite a hit on the dance floor. . . .

Then, next year, Billie & Dusty married at her house on the Vineyard, July 27, 1991. I was already pregnant with you!

The finale of this trip, from which we returned home today, was an incredibly beautiful weekend at Billie's house with all the family for the weekend.

. . . We all got along so great—everyone had a blast. I covered you up well and walked out to "The Point" where the Atlantic meets the Great Pond. You were silent, walking w/ me, totally engaged in watching the birds, feeling the breeze, listening to the surf . . . and then, rocked by the rhythm of the surf and my stride through the sand you would sleep. . . .

When the Story Shifts—from Harmony to Rivalry

After the honeymoon period of our new, expanded family with its period of bonding and blending old rituals with new roles, conflicts began to surface that rocked the boat. Everyone suffered, and everyone struggled to keep the boat from going under completely as roles and alliances shifted and confusion and chaos reigned. The toughest challenge of managing grown-up family members who are having conflicts is to keep the children off the battlefield without keeping them in the dark. Children pick up on your obvious and subtle cues when you are troubled by something, and they may imagine the worst if they don't get an explanation. Or, they may imagine they are responsible for upsetting you if you fail to clarify that the stress you're under has nothing to do with them.

During this chaotic period of grown-up sibling rivalry in my family of origin, I faced the same challenges in communicating to my children in the diary writing as I did in daily life. How could I tell my children the truth about unexpected conflicts that were permeating our closest relationships with aunts, uncles, cousins, and grandparents in age-appropriate, honest, and fair ways that respected the complexity of the people and the conflicts? How could I explain an abrupt shift in our previously secure lives? Of course, in the midst of crisis, I didn't begin writing with the *answers* to these questions. But, as I continued to open the diary door, I found my own inner wisdom to these questions *in the process*—even through the process of making "mistakes."

Reaching for Inner Wisdom during Times of Family Crisis

In piecing together the diary stories of this period of family conflict, I seem to have written mostly to my two daughters in very different ways, consciously and subconsciously, telling the story. Together these diary entries, excerpted in the following sections, tell a deeper level of the story of this period of their lives than I was able to explain to them in real life as it was happening.

One of the most important things I learned by writing in the diaries during this turbulent time of conflict was that in the diary you don't have to pretend during a dark time that everything is okay. As I have learned in my many years of practicing psychotherapy, there is a destructive power of *untold* stories—stories that are held onto as family secrets. When families try to hide living, breathing secrets in closets they end up with skeletons hanging in them.

And so, inevitably, you may write painful entries during times of family crisis or conflict—perhaps intentionally *or* unintentionally. There is room behind the diary door for your pain. Allowing yourself to be human and real is an important message to communicate to your children about how they can learn to handle their own feelings. Your children also need to know that feelings aren't good or bad, right or wrong, but that they are a natural expression of their integrity as human beings, signals that point them in the direction of finding ways to satisfy their emotional needs. Your children will learn to trust and value their own feelings when they watch you tending appropriately to your own. A family is a place in which everyone's feelings matter and are taken seriously as part of the dialogue about getting along together and learning to resolve conflicts. Just as you work on establishing and maintaining this emotional safety in your home and family, so do you establish it in the diaries by being honest and open about a range of emotions in the stories.

As the following three entries in my daughter Frances' diary show, feelings can shift abruptly and radically from day to day, particularly when unexpected conflicts and crises surface in the family. The diary has a remarkable capacity for mirroring our mental and emotional states—both conscious and subconscious—and is in this way able to tell a story on a deeper level, perhaps deeper than we intend. Even though I did not know it at the time, this next entry, which ends by anticipating a happy and harmonious family holiday season, actually precedes a series of painful entries that unexpectedly follow:

To Frances (age 7 months), November 14, 1997

The morning of your first snow.

A white frosting over layers of brown leaves, sleet now tapping at the windows. You looked out, surprised, before showering w/me and napping. I will write, then take us for a wintry walk.

Last night, I walked alone in the dark, lit by a full moon, up to Grammy's. Clouds moved in slowly over the stars. Landon woke us at 7:00 to the excitement of a first snow, took you to the bedroom window to show you.

Daddy home this week (so life is blissful). The season of fires and hot chocolate w/ whipped cream. The happiest, warmest days of life as the holidays approach.

Sometimes the feelings sneak up and surprise the writer and reader alike, as they do in the next entry in my daughter Frances' diary, immediately following the one above. It's always disruptive when dearly held illusions are shattered. When I first reread the following entry some time after it was written, I was shocked and disturbed to discover that I had inadvertently, perhaps subconsciously, written an entry intended for my personal diary into my daughter's diary instead. The sudden shift in audience, mood, and tone startled me, as I saw my cheerful expectations wither with the emotional challenges that were suddenly and unexpectedly on me in a period conflict with my family of origin. Sometimes it's the imagery we describe in the diary stories that speaks most strikingly of our feelings—feelings we may not even, on a conscious level, be aware that we are experiencing in the moment:

To Frances (age 7 months), November 20, 1997

Everyone is letting their doorstep jackolanterns rot under the unexpected snow.

The crab apple tree, stunning in its skeletal symmetry, studded with golden crab apples that refuse to rot, cling to the bare branches, shining globes of light.

And me. I see, walking up the snow-encrusted front lawn, pushing my sleeping child [Frances] through the snow to the door, that my role, right or wrong, good or *bad, w/ the men right now is to be a buffer. I am the buffer. I am used this way, like it or not. Mostly not. But what else? Let their rivalry destroy each other—is that what I would prefer? I **am** the buffer. I choose to buffer. Do I really know what a buffer is, how it works, how it's supposed to work? I think, perhaps, if I better understood how a buffer is meant to work, then I could play the role less painfully, more effectively. After all, isn't the buffer supposed to survive intact? What is a shock absorber? How does it work? What keeps it from wearing out? . . .*

This is what I need to figure out.

Writing the diary entries *did*, in fact, help me to "figure it out," to find some peace and understanding about the role and the process, as the following excerpt from the next misplaced entry in Frances' diary shows:

To Frances (age 7 months), November 21, 1997

Water. Water.
Water is the buffer. The still waters.
"He leadeth us beside the still waters, He restoreth our souls."
*Water, of course. Buoancy. [Buoyancy] Purity. Elemental water. The water **within me**. The water, the stream, that connect[s] us all, the ebb and flow of tides. I am water, the buffer. I am still water in turbulent times.*

These painfully revealing, misplaced entries continue for a few more days, then stop as abruptly as they began. When I first discovered my error, I seriously considered tearing the pages out and placing them in my own diary. But, I now realize that these entries *were* my way of being honest and real about my feelings with my baby daughter in a time of confusion and pain. Even though I continue to reconsider this question, I can't seem to convince myself that they don't belong where I originally put them. They tell a story about my feelings and experience (*my* side of the story) that I think will be of value and of interest to Frances *as a young woman* with whom I can discuss them some day. So, for now, there they stay, and I doubtless will revisit the question of where they belong many times before there is a risk of her coming across them on her own.

Learning to Fight Fair

Your children are able to sense when something is amiss in the family whether a conflict is actually spoken about or not. They also will overhear much of what you say when you think they're not listening. They may not understand *what* is going wrong, but they are connected to you, they tune into you, they trust you, and they know when something is wrong whether or not you tell them directly. Your children want your emotional honesty so that they can trust you and learn to trust their own feelings. If you model how to communicate openly and honestly about your feelings, they will learn how to build and sustain intimacy in their own personal relationships. They want age-appropriate explanations of problems, crises, and conflicts. If there is a divorce going on in the family or an illness, you may want to write an explanation about how this event seems to be influencing their young lives if it seems relevant. Children want reassurance that even if you're not in control of everything, you're doing everything you can to solve problems.

Intuitively, I seemed to know that stories about this conflicted time to my older daughter, Perrin, who, at age five, was much more aware of the impact of the changes in the family, needed a more conscious, intentional approach. The next entry echoes things I had tried to tell her in person. But it also attempts to include in the saved version of her childhood history the struggle through a dark period of family life over which she had a lot to lose with very little control of the process:

To Perrin (age 5), February 8, 1998

Dusty [cousin] was at the library yesterday with his brothers and sister, and Grammy too had gone down to help. I brought you, Franci, and Hannah [another cousin] to watch the Gerwick puppets. What a delightful show!

We had not seen Dusty in a long time, I'm afraid. I want to try to explain why, because even though you aren't directly asking I know in your heart you're wondering, and feeling.

You know . . . we all struggle for peace these days with our brothers. Brother hate is going around! I guess what I'm trying to say is that it's normal to fight w/ our sisters and brothers, and, guess what—

We never really grow out of it, Babe. I don't know exactly why we don't grow out of it, but that's life. Our fights might get less physical— . . . but we just learn better how to use our words for fighting.

Picture you and Landon sent to your rooms to cool off behind closed doors. Separated. Taking a breather. Safe with your anger in your own rooms. Maybe occasionally opening your door and throwing a boot or a toy out in the hall toward the other door. Or slamming your stuff around your room to show how **angry** you are.

Well, picture me and Daddy in one room at the end of the hall, and Uncle Dusty and Aunt Billie in the other. Picture Grammy and Grampy occasionally wandering between the two rooms to check on us and see if we're ready to come out yet and make peace.

*Nope. Don't you know that feeling—I'm still too ANGRY TO MAKE UP. I **hate** him. I never want to speak w/him again. He's always driving me crazy. . . .*

Well, that's where we are. Safe behind our closed doors of our houses. Every so often throwing our stuff around. Too angry to speak.

We're in Time Out, sweetie. That's why we aren't seeing them and spending time with them. A couple of times we have—I've picked Dusty up and dropped him off. But it's so hard to be fighting w/people I love, Perrin, that we really need this time out, even though I know it's hurting you and Dusty. I miss my nephews so, so much.

Some day you may want to know what the fight was all about. I hope it will seem silly and be mostly forgotten, even though I feel so hurt and troubled by it right now. . . .

I believe in the things I'm fighting for, Perrin. You should know that. This is one of those times in life that we are called on to fight for beliefs, values, needs that are very important to us. I guess that's one of the differences—as a grown up, I try not to fight over the small stuff.

You can trust Perrin, that I am working for peace even while I am standing up for what I believe in.

Modeling Ways of Coping With Conflict

Children will encounter conflict in many relationships their whole lives. If you bring conflicts out into the open—even ones that are not currently resolved—this may help your children learn coping skills for resolving conflicts within themselves and with other people.

Just as you have experienced with your own siblings, sometimes your children will get along ideally and other times their rivalry will drive you mad. Stories behind the diary door about struggles in relationships, theirs or your own, will help you and your children cope with the periods of conflict that are necessary and beneficial in all intimate relationships. When tools for conflict resolution are taught and modeled by parents and other significant caregivers, bonds between siblings can be strengthened and deepened in the process. Perhaps there is a story from your own sibling rivalries that will help your children cope with their own. Conflicts in families are not always solved quickly or completely or to our satisfaction. But these are not casual relationships we can just walk away from for relief. Family relationships endure, and there is always the possibility for new understanding, acceptance, and hope for the future. This story was a healing story for me to experience and write for my daughter through the diary door. It offered me more insight and a chance to try to explain to her a period of our lives that, when she grows up, may still not be quite understood, or may be long forgotten:

To Perrin (age 5), February 22, 1998

*. . . You and Dusty [cousin] have not seen each other in a few weeks, and each of you were shy and hesitant to approach the other, as if you were no longer sure where your relationships stood. But, I had left for Florida determined to heal as much as I could w/Billie and my brother (in time) and I left Billie a Valentine pin wrapped in a pretty box at Grammy's which she thanked me for as I approached their car w/greetings. Dusty walked sullenly toward the house w/o approaching either of us, and a gust of sadness blew over me at what we grown ups have inadvertently done to your friendship. I know that you feel something is wrong, and you have no idea how to describe it. You feel the tension, and we cannot protect you from it, we can only try in our humanness to resolve it, in time, a moment and a day at a time. I need you to know, Perrin, that we **will** resolve this, I'm determined. I'm sorry that things have come to this—you know it's no one's fault. Conflict is a part of life, a necessary and normal part of life, and all you can do when there is conflict is work through your feelings w/supportive people and stretch yourself—growth that it requires of you. Grow bigger, trust God, but mostly trust in how the Holy Spirit works for God, and shows you the path toward connection and healing. Shows what you must give up in order to gain. Shows what you must do, because love is not just feeling, love is an action. And you don't just patly forgive people—you pray for understanding, you pray for an open heart, you pray for the courage to admit your own shortcomings, the courage to say: 'I'm sorry for this,' or 'I was wrong about that,' or what you are doing is hurting me, please stop . . . or whatever . . . you can trust me, Perrin. Trust me because I have always worked for connection.*

I went over and greeted little Meg, who smiled at me, and I held her while you stayed outside to ride your bike. Dusty went right to his mother and asked if his bike was there, and she dug it out of the new basement. I suspected this might present a little problem for you . . . and it did. You came in suddenly, kicked off your black boots and collapsed sadly beside me where I held Meg on the couch.

"Mom," you whispered, "I want my training wheels off . . . and I can't even ice skate!" Dusty had none, and Dusty has also mastered skating.

Well, Billie came in and offered to take the training wheels off your bike w/a wrench, which she did. Then I put on my jacket and went out to help you, expecting a long and stressful afternoon of anxiety, trial and error.

By this time Dusty was happily playing w/Joey and Landon who were stealing and riding his bike. I took you to the field, brown from winter and it was cold, but not too cold to be comfortable w/o mittens and a hat. You got on. . . .

I gave you a push and let go, and even though you crashed and leaped from your bike, I could see in the three seconds you stayed up that this was going to be an effortless, joyful job.

And it was. Within minutes you were cruising, at least in straight lines atop the field and on the pavement, your heart lighter by the moment. Our fun was contagious. I went inside briefly to check on Frances and you and Dusty came in looking for me. Dusty asked me to do for him what I had done for you.

The launching is the part you both lack, so we worked on that some. Then I launched you both at the top of the yard and you each rode successfully all the way to the bottom of the field a couple of times. Then you decided to get Grammy's mail for her, and I walked the bikes up the field feeling so happy and so hopeful, and so satisfied that I had been able to be part of this achievement w/you and that we were making another rite of passage despite the family conflict in having you two learn to ride your bikes together at Grammy's.

And I felt, this is all we need to keep doing. . . .

In the next chapter, we learn about the value of paying attention to family history across the generations through the diary door. But first, try these Diary Door Openers.

Diary Door Openers

1. Greetings

    Whether it's before or while waiting for the birth, write the story of siblings meeting for the first time, including time, setting, cast of characters, and the actions that brought them together. If one of the children is old enough to talk don't forget to use quotes. Show and tell about the positive aspects of how they yearn for connection with each other.

2. Blessings

    Capture a word, an action, or a gesture that shows one of your children blessing the other with positive feedback or a compliment. (This can be written in either of the children's diaries.)

3. Likes and Dislikes

    Go to one of the sibling's diaries and make a list of five things your children fight with each other about. Make a list of five things they agree on. Describe and reflect upon five minutes of harmony between them.

4. Then and Now

    Describe the evolution of your relationship(s) with your sibling(s) from child-
    hood and reflect on the stages your relationships have gone through over the
    years.

5. Role Playing

    Describe a role that you observe one of the siblings playing in relationship to
    the other, such as nurturer or tattletale or sidekick. Describe what you see as
    the positive and negative aspects of this role relationship. Reflect on what you
    think and feel as you observe it. Is there anything you would like to support
    your child to change about the way she or he plays this role? Do you have a
    plan for how to do so?

6. Observe and describe a conflict that your children are able to solve on their
    own. Reflect on what seems to have made this possible.

Chapter 12

Amidst and Across the Generations
Saving Family Stories

Grandma, come back, I forgot
How much lard for these rolls. . . .
I'll tell you I don't remember any kind of bread
Your wavy loaves of flesh
Stink through my sleep
The stars on your silk robes. . . .

(Carolyn Forché, "The Morning Baking," *Gathering the Tribes*, p. 3)

We all fantasize about what it would be like to meet and feel connected to the ancestors who came before us whom we've never met, as well as to the descendants who will come after us whom we will never meet. Have you ever imagined what one of your great-great-grandmothers or great-great-uncles was really like? Perhaps you are fortunate to have a photo of her, or a watch that belonged to him, or a favorite story passed on through the oral history of your family. You might have a glimpse into her personality through her letters or diaries, or her minutely detailed household account book. Chances are, you find the perspective and details of life from a different time and place interesting and fascinating to consider. Have you ever been told you have your Aunt so-and-so's sense of humor or your great-grandfather's temper? There may be some comfort and some challenge in these kinds of comparisons that imply the deep connections and ties that are passed on through families for generations, for better or for worse.

Just as we are curious about our ancestors, our children and our children's children will want to know about the intimate and interesting details of *our* daily lives. Through our storytelling, they will have an opportunity to meet *us* in the diaries.

Whether our progenitors discover our writing in a trunk in the attic, an old suitcase in the garage, or in a mildewed cardboard box in the basement we can trust that they will read our words with curiosity, pleasure, and appreciation. As they hold hand-written diaries in their own hands, they will enjoy the fascinating stories of times gone by. We keep these diaries for connections with our own children and to all the grandchildren who will come after them as well.

As we keep the diaries, we may find ourselves evaluating how much or how little we know of our own family history. We may come from families that proudly possess extensive genealogical histories with photographs and other prized heirlooms that have been cherished, protected, and passed on to successive generations over centuries. In this case, the diaries we keep for our children may be included in a rich archive of multigenerational family history.

Or, we may come from families that know little of their history for a variety of reasons, and we long for information and material that would give us clues to our cultural identity and traditions, our ethnicity, and the places and the people from whom we have descended. We may begin or join a genealogical search for our roots in an effort to satisfy our craving for connection. But whether or not we search our family history, the diaries we keep now will provide historical information and a sense of the past for future generations.

The diaries shape and contain a family history that is woven into the web of daily life. Stories of family history in the diaries are not necessarily organized or planned family histories, but they will become worthy sources for family genealogists in the future. If you write to your children in the diaries about the people with whom they spend time, the loved ones they celebrate with, the friends and relatives they ask questions about, you will be creating a portrait of significant relationships in your child's family history. You will be giving them hints, allusions, facts and feelings, sights, sounds, flavors, and moving or still-life portraits of the people to whom they feel connected and who fulfill the role of family for them.

Creating Portraits of Family Members through "Snapshots"

Sometimes we are able to piece together family history from a shoebox full of unsorted, unlabeled snapshots of ancestors. Diaries collect stories like a photo album collects snapshots, and our descendants may build family history from these written snapshots—diary entries that provide sketches or portraits of family members like grandparents, aunts, uncles, cousins, or old family friends who serve as family. In fact, one satisfying quality that diaries always possess but that photographs may lack is that entries are usually dated.

You can profile family members (from the present or the past) in the diaries by writing a portrait of a particular person, like a grandmother. Include details and description that convey her personality, characteristics, or adventures you think your child will be interested in knowing or remembering about her. If this grandmother is still living, you can capture your child's relationship with her over time by letting your stories accumulate as a series of written snapshots that show how she plays the role or captures her in a pose that evokes aspects of her personality. These verbal pictures combine to make a realistic and effective portrait drawn through the diary door. For instance, many entries and stories throughout the diaries contain references to my mother. A talent that she shared with her children she also extended to her grandchildren—she loves to sew. One could not read the children's diaries without recognizing that sewing is one of the primary ways she shows love to her family members. Stories of her sewing are embedded in entries that are directly relevant to the children's lives, such as this one about a trip I took with my daughter to the fabric store that my mother had taken me to as a girl:

To Perrin (age 3), June 8, 1995

...Do you know how many times I've walked into that store w/ my mother to buy patterns & fabric? You **loved** the place, loved looking at patterns and hugging the big reams of fabric. You finally agreed on a gingham gingerbread man fabric for the sun dress which I **hope** I can make. I had to keep fighting off the compulsion to give up on the process and walk empty handed out of the store because of my negative self-defeating thoughts: what's the use? I can't sew! Karen, Joanna and Mom can sew **anything**, but....

Somehow I talked myself through the old tapes successfully enough to emerge from the store w/ fabric, pattern, thread and two adorable gingerbread buttons, and for the millionth time I'm going to try and have my mother teach me to sew!

Just promise me, if I get the dress made that you'll wear it!

Remember, diaries for your children are not solely memoir, biography, or autobiography based on giving shape to a life *already lived*, but they embody some of the elements of all three. One unique characteristic of diary writing is the quality of *immediacy*. The compelling nature of the diaries is that most of the action is taking place in the present tense in the present moment, *as it is happening*. Watching life unfolding as it is being lived is the central concern of diary writing, not historical research or recollection of the past. The diaries will be more interesting to your children if you try to relate the family history that you want to include to aspects that are relevant to your child's life *today*. Again, contained in this next story, there is a story about my mother's sewing, and this time it is a reference to a special tradition of sewing my son Halloween costumes from her home far away:

To Landon (age 5), November 5, 1993

A couple of nights ago, with you in bed with me, you say, in conversation:
"I'm a lucky boy because I have such a big family."

You were thinking of all your relatives up North and how much you miss them, particularly Grammy B. [maternal grandmother] (who, now, by the way, has a new dog!)

Halloween was very nice: you wore the new Black Ninja costume that Grammy B. made for you. . . .

. . . Joey wore your old Spiderman costume this year, and I was proud of you for sharing it w/ him—he appreciated it very much. I suppose Baby Dustin may wear it soon. I feel very glad that my Mom is able to do these costumes long distance for you. It seems to mean a lot to you. . . .

Another family tradition based on my mother's sewing is mentioned briefly in this entry to my older daughter. Each and every grandchild has, sitting in his or her bedroom, a hand-sewn gift of a stuffed and dressed, long-eared bunny from Grandmother B., usually given on Christmas or a birthday:

To Perrin (age 4), March 20, 1995

It has been a delightful weekend for you, w/ Grammy BL [paternal grandmother] arriving Friday afternoon, bearing birthday presents of the lion king puppets, raincoat, backpack, etc.

Sat. we spent the afternoon w/ the cousins—(Ben, Joe, Mae) at the park in S— where I picked some lovely pussy willows. Sat. night you had dinner at Grammy B.'s Aunt Billie babysat for you & Maelyn.

Sunday, Maelyn came & spent the early afternoon w/ you here playing dolls in your room (which I fixed up for your birthday w/ new bedding & curtains).

Everyone *came to your party Sun. afternoon! I made lasagna . . . and two wonderful kitty cat cakes—one chocolate, one lemon. (But you never even blew out your candles!)*

Just after opening your gifts, at the very beginning of the party, you curled sleepily up like a cat yourself in Daddy's lap & fell asleep in the midst of all your company. Mae, Hanna and Dusty played happily w/ the doll house Dad & I gave you. Grammy B. gave you the bunny she made for you . . .

Your Family of Origin and Family History

Your children will change your relationship with your family of origin, for better, for worse, or somewhere in between. Whatever *your* relationship is and has been with the people who raised you, your children will develop their own unique relationships with your mother, father, sisters, and brothers based on the experiences your children have with your relatives over time. Grandparents and other extended family members, such as your own or your partner's siblings, can be major players in the drama behind the diary door, both in their presence and in their absence.

Even if you are estranged from or comfortably distant with members of your family of origin your children will want to feel connected to your living relatives and your ancestry. Children are curious about their family history, and they want to meet and understand the people they came from. Some families celebrate their history, living out their ancestral heritage in appreciation and celebration. For others, ancestry may be a source of shame, conflict, confusion, or bewilderment. If you are fruitfully connected to your family of origin, there is much to tell your children behind the diary door. And, if you're in conflict with or disengaged from all or part of your family of origin, there is also much to tell.

Family history is not something you package neatly or one-dimensionally through the diary door. Through storytelling, you embrace the complexity of family history. You shape what you know against what you don't know. You sort what you want to tell with what you don't want to tell, staying mindful of what your children may *need* to know for their own health and happiness. For instance, children can greatly benefit from awareness of inherited health problems and may benefit from information about diseases they may be susceptible to that might be prevented with knowledge. They need information about shame-based problems and family illnesses, such as alcoholism, which may repeat themselves in future generations when they are not addressed openly in the family with education and healing and when they are kept hidden in a shroud of secrecy and shame.

But how do you as a parent address these thorny issues? You write as honestly as you can, providing age-appropriate information, but with the awareness that some of what you write may not be read until your child is older and has a more mature understanding of the information you are offering. Despite the fact that their diaries are left around the house on various end tables or shelves, my children continue to show very little interest in reading the diaries on their own, preferring the ritual of having them read aloud by me. So, I'm always in a position to choose whether I read a particular entry to them now. Some entries have been written to them to find at a later date, when they might have a better understanding of what I'm trying to explain. But I haven't ever written anything that I wouldn't be willing to try to explain and discuss with them now if they were to come across it on their own.

Though honesty is a vital quality through the diary door, it's important to avoid planting secrets like land mines in the diary, hoping that if you leave them there you won't ever have to discuss them with your children in person. You don't write anything you wouldn't be willing to talk about honestly and openly with your child some day at the right moment. Also, you don't write anything that would be confusing or disturbing or overwhelming that you won't first have had a chance to discuss with them at the right time before you hand the diaries over to them to keep. If your children do tend to peruse the diaries without you, it's better only to write things that would be easily digested if they viewed the entries on their own without you.

You may find, however, as I have, that you can go ahead and write information you want your children to have in the future while it's on your mind now, knowing that it will live through the diary door for you both to remember and discuss in more detail later on. Never write anything that your child would be afraid to ask you about face to face, because whatever your child's questions are, you will want to be able to offer an honest and supportive answer.

When addressing family secrets or distressing issues in family history through the diary door, you need to write with sensitivity and with a willingness to explore some of the family strengths and secrets, virtues and vices. Every family has skeletons in the closet. You choose when to take the skeletons out of the closet in the right time in a thoughtful and considerate way. Through storytelling, you put the flesh back on the bones of the skeletons so your children can meet them in the safety, the comfort, and the wisdom of your presence. And, why not? Your children will meet them someday whether or not *you* take the skeletons out of the closet for them. Just as *you* did.

You write about family history to give your children pleasure and to save your children pain. You write about family history so that uplifting rites and rituals will be passed on and will bring meaning and comfort, intimacy and joy to your children and to *their* children. If dysfunctional family problems have been handed down through generations in your family, you write so that history does not have to repeat itself and so that family problems can be exposed, understood, and healed. You write about family history to leave your children a legacy of honesty, healing, and hope. You write the story to *change* the story. You write to embrace the gifts your ancestors have left you and your children and to summon the courage to face challenges. This means that sometimes in the diaries you might include an honest but painful aspect or portrait of an ancestor that exposes an uncomfortable truth about family dynamics. I wrote this entry to my older daughter as an attempt to explain some of the emotional challenges we have inherited from various people in our family history. This entry was part of a larger discussion we were having about how people express love in different ways and how some, like her maternal great-grandmother, might have been inhibited from expressing loving feelings openly by the circumstances of their lives:

To Perrin (age 3), April 14, 1995

. . . *I've grown to believe that there really wasn't enough love to go around in Grammy B.'s family, at least from her own Mom who grew up not having enough herself. [Great-] Grammy B., Grammy B.'s Mom, was born out of wedlock, and never knew her Dad. Her mother, Annie J., was sickly and [Great-] Gram B. had to leave school at a very young age to go to work and help support her Mom. I believe she was very embittered by this. I believe she never got enough love, enough opportunity to learn how to express her love beyond the narrow constraints of an un-worked muscle.*

Families Create Sacred Places as Legacies

We all inherit tangible and intangible things from family members, and these things may include favorite places. When these legacies have meaning to you and your children writing about them is a way to capture family history and to explain the emotional significance of places where the family tends to gather.

I don't know whether my maternal grandparents, Clarence and Marguerite, hoped their grandchildren would be enjoying their spot at Laurel Lake more than fifty years after they discovered it for vacations for their young family. But we do, and now, so do their great-grandchildren. Will *my* great-grandchildren visit the spot, I wonder? Who knows? But this entry to my daughter recollects my own childhood memories of the place while incorporating the current pleasures of time spent there with my children and their cousins at our own family-owned cabin:

To Perrin (age 3), July 3, 1995

As children, we usually had two, too short, blissfully happy weeks here at Laurel Lake w/ Mom, staying in our big tent on Uncle Donn's grassy hill, each year. Our cousins were my age, and we were painfully envious of them because they had their very own cottage, right in the grove, a few fast steps to the beach and docks. They stayed the whole summer and had lots of friends who welcomed us, during our visits, into their gang. Our consolation was that we camped right next to Donn's coke room, the major attraction, right after the beach. We never passed his store on the way up the hill from the beach each afternoon without an ice cream treat from the store.

The beach was a blast. Almost everyone who hung out there, practically, was a relative, and there were always plenty of people to play with. Mostly we loved the freedom of the beach, since it was the opposite of the very ordered, controlled, highly supervised beach we were condemned to at home. Where we had to endure our lessons. Laurel Lake had no restrictions on eating, drinking or floating on rafts. Laurel Lake had no buoys for boundaries, and we could stretch ourselves as swimmers as far as we liked.

As we were waking this morning, in our very own cabin, I was thinking how lucky we all are to have expanded our resources here. As Dad and I, w/you in the middle, slowly came to consciousness on the futon in the middle of the living room, Hanna and Dusty [cousins] hopped onto our bed & we all had a very cheerful, affectionate romp before breakfast. I was thinking how wonderful, for all you kids to have each other as best friends around, always available for play, pure blissful play. As we lingered over the morning, the Dads joked over the very late poker game, and you and Hanna swapped clothes in the back bedroom. You coveted her Pocahontas T shirt and Purple Shorts; she donned your yellow skirt w/ pink flowers and your turquoise hat. Her feet are a bit smaller than yours, but you insisted on wearing her flip flops.

Now it's a brutally delightful hot sunny day, and the beach is packed. You sit on [Aunt] Billie's lap and cuddle while I write. Landon floats in the rubber boat on the water. This is the weekend, almost fifteen years ago that [Aunt] Virginia and I were nursing Aunt Marion in her cabin as she lay dying. And Great Grammy B.'s birthday was July 5.

The Stories That Pieces of Furniture Pass on

Family history may be contained in special pieces of furniture as well as in special places. Furniture that our ancestors have used as part of their daily lives can invoke powerful emotions for those of us who possess these heirlooms, particularly if we know the piece's history or we're familiar with it from our own childhood. In addition to the item itself, our children may value details of how the furniture was used if we write about it in the diaries. This entry to my youngest child explores the significance of childhood furniture being stored in the attic, as well as the emotions involved in closing a chapter of child rearing. Writing it allowed me to give voice to feelings that surprised me in their intensity when I expressed them through the diary door:

To Frances (almost 3), March 6, 2000

... But the big deal yesterday was the surprise Dad & I had waiting for you after your nap.

You strolled out into the dining room and saw it on the front lawn out the picture window—your big girl bed!

While you were napping on my bed dad and I took down your crib (shedding a few tears as we lifted it into the attic) and cleaned your room....

This bed was Perri's bed for her second birthday when we lived in Palm Harbor. We called it her Barnie Bed because she had Barnie sheets and comforter.

Now it's yours.

So, we set it up and you went happily off to sleep there last night. You did not seem to miss your crib. I let you climb in the stairs of the attic w/ me to say good-bye to it. We also took out the white wicker rocker in which I nursed you—the rocker Dad & Grammy BL gave me for my birthday the month before Landon was born! Just writing this makes my stomach flip and my breasts sting and my eyes fill. Three babies nursed in that chair. And three times it has been stored in the attic. Now what?

Must I put away these baby things for good? How does one pack away such memories, so much joy? What does one do w/ the ache, the ache of memory, the pull of the heart toward the past, the sweetness of those lovely, lovely days of infancy, of nursing, of the sweet aloneness in the world w/ one's baby, in the quiet house, when all is still except for the sounds of the baby, innocent, beautiful, loving, just nursing. Nothing else in the world matters in those moments of a still afternoon. And they are moments that feel like they will last forever. And then, My God, one is taking the nursing chair to the attic, w/ one's youth gone, one's own innocence gone, knowing there will be no more **new** babies, no more mysteries to unfold w/ such charm, delight, extreme and utter bliss.... Oh, God. I **hate** to say goobye to it Franny. It's so hard.

How did all go by, so fast? W/ Landon twelve?

And you, so much fun now, so amusing. But not the sweet baby at my breast.

Is this selfish of me? To have taken so much from what you did to survive? Is this selfish of me to have felt so fulfilled. So much longing fulfilled.

How can I **not** ever do this again?

Maybe one of you children will want the wicker rocker. Maybe one of you will use it. I'll save it in hopes of that. We shall see....

When Special Visitors Arrive

When a loved one makes a particular effort to show your child that she is special in her eyes, a diary story will serve as a lasting reminder of this special attention. Grandparents may sometimes face the challenge of sharing their love among many grandchildren, and the diaries are a place for individual stories that demonstrate a grandparent's special attention for each of their grandchildren. As a girl raised in the age of large families, I was one of many, many grandchildren on both sides of the family, where grandchildren tended to feel loved en masse, rather than individually, because when we were together we were always such a large group. There is a single photograph, however, of me sitting on my paternal grandmother's lap in a frilly dress taken during my fifth birthday party in the back yard. It reminds me of the feeling I tried to capture in this entry for my older daughter on her fourth birthday—that special feeling sparked by a special effort made on her behalf:

To Perrin (age 4), March 10, 1996

Grammy BL [paternal grandmother] flew in during a March snow storm last Wed night for your birthday....The snow had finally all melted. The crocuses were up. Everything was beginning to thaw, but the snow fell again, around four inches or so, anyway.

Grammy said it was beautiful; she hadn't seen fresh snow in years.

You woke up at 2:00 am when she arrived and gave her a sleepy, sleepy kiss. You had stayed up late, wide awake, dying for her to come.

*Friday, more and more snow, until we had a foot and a half **again**. Landon got to miss school. You both stayed home fighting for Grammy's attention all day.*

Friday at noon Grammy and Daddy went shopping and Grammy bought your bike at Toys R us....

Significant Events

Children sometimes carry vivid memories from childhood about the health challenges of loved ones like grandparents. Even though from our adult perspective we may have information or judgment that reassures us that all will go well, children may not share that trust. They may feel threatened by the awareness that their seemingly omnipotent grandparent or loved one is suddenly vulnerable. Whether it's a major or minor health problem or surgery, children sometimes fear losing a loved one. The diary entry may offer them information to combine with their memories of these anxious times. I knew my daughter would remember her grandmother's surgery later on. Writing the following entry was one way I tried to keep her connected with her grandmother during her grandmother's arterial surgery while I sat and waited in the waiting room:

To Perrin (age 6), May 10, 1998

Grammy BL is in surgery. We are waiting to hear from the doctor that she is in the recovery room. We are here w/ Grampy Mike.

Daddy and I left home at 5:00 a.m. after Grammy B. came down to stay w/ you kids, who were all still asleep.

We expect Grammy to be just fine, in fact, tons better once she has her carranded [carotid] arteries cleared up! But you have been worried over the past day or two, wondering if she is going to "get killed," which she certainly is not. You and Landon each handle your feelings about her surgery differently, and each of you are expressing a real and normal response. Landon is full of optimism and confidence that she'll come through fine, because she is "strong."

Your view—afraid of losing her—is a side of what we're all feeling too. Of course it's a possibility: she could have a stroke at any moment. You are very intuitive—you tend to connect w/ the emotional depth of the situation....

Her grandmother survived the surgery just fine.

Name Changes as Reference Points

The evolution of family names is an important link in the chain of family history. As we discuss in Chapter Two, the diaries are an appropriate place to write about the history of a family name and an important place to make note of any changes to the name. For example, the following entry documents for future generations, as well as for my children, the change we made to our surname, the date, and the reasons we changed it:

To Frances (age 2), October 15, 1999

Since before you were born, we planned to change the spelling of our last name from D. to DuMar. Grammy BL did this when she was still using DuMar, before she married Grampy Mike ...

Why?

Well, because we think the "French" spelling is much easier to pronounce, and we don't like being called "dummer" as many people do, ever since we were introduced at our wedding reception as "Mr. & Mrs. Frank Dumber!"

So, I registered Perrin & Landon in school as DuMar, and began the paperwork w/ the court to have it changed legally, but when we were ready w/ the paperwork to go to court & finalize it, Dad got too busy and we put it off. Once put off, we let it slide off the agenda into the background of our lives.

Then you were born, and we had to put Dummar on your birth certificate.

Well, in September, the school started badgering me for legal documentation of the name change, since they had to provide it to the state. Our procrastination time was up.

So, we went to court. Twice last week we tried to go, but Thurs and Friday you were sick w/ colds.

Tuesday was the day....

... So, now we're all legal—

DuMar

*We had a cake w/ candles that night w/ dinner to celebrate our new name—this pleased you **very** much....*

Family Legends and Heroes

Through the diary door, you can write family stories or legends about grandparents or other relatives who may not be around to tell them later. If you need a refresher, perhaps the source for the story or legend is still available to tell it to you again. Maybe you have access to written documents or other family history remnants. If you don't have all the details, you can imagine them in a way that feels realistic or authentic to the story considering the facts and information you have. Of course, you aim for the facts. But if you choose to speculate, you can say so.

The story in the next entry about my father is based on the original story that was told to me as a girl immediately after my parents returned from the trip where it took place. My children appreciated the version I told them aloud so much that I knew they would appreciate its being saved as a written story for many years to come. Before writing it, I checked on some facts with both my parents by encouraging them to tell me the story once again, which they did. Then, I made a copy for the diary of the document that accompanies it—a signed testimonial from Her Majesty the Queen of England that hangs in my mother's bedroom attesting to my father's act of bravery:

To Landon (age 10), December 1997

"The Hero of Horseshoe Beach"

*... one year, in 1968 to be exact, during their annual autumn trip to Bermuda, Shirley and Dusty [grandparents] had a great adventure, and, thankfully, lived to tell about it. And yes, Grampy **will** tell this story if you beg him, and I strongly encourage you to do so to make sure that you get his version which will be far superior to my own.*

It was a sunny day, Nov. 6, 1968, when Shirley and Dusty hopped aboard their motor bike after a hot game of tennis with friends, and headed for a swim and sunbathing to Horseshoe Beach, a secluded beach....

There were only a few scattered beachgoers that day; no one was in the water swimming, and it was easy to see why: the angry waves were breaking at heights of 10-12 feet, the result of a storm brewing off the coast. Shirley ventured to wade but was knocked over and quickly retreated. Dusty pulled out his paper and was reading comfortably in the sun, undisturbed by the noise of his children who were safely at home. . . .

Suddenly, there was a distant but urgent cry for help . . . .

Dusty, an excellent swimmer all his life, leaped to his feet to survey the situation. Trained as a swimmer in lifesaving many years ago, he looked around for any equipment that might assist in a rescue: a boat, perhaps? No! A phone! No! A lifeguard? NO! The drowning man's cries were becoming more urgent. What could they do? There were no signs of help available.

One can only imagine the thoughts that ran through Dusty and Shirley's heads, as Dusty instinctively grabbed his oversized beach towel, and waded into the rushing surf, beating his way through the waves. (You'll have to ask him, I can only speculate.) Another man from the beach joined Dusty on the trek out to reach the man. It looked futile—how could they reach him in time against the power of this surf and the rip tide, and dragging a heavy, wet beach towel no less? But Dusty knew there was no choice. He had to try. He swam harder and faster than he had ever swam before. His own life must have been flashing before his eyes. He might never see his wife, his children, his parents, his brothers and sisters, his Harvard students ever again. The surf pounded him; his shoulders ached. The man's cries grew more desperate. He couldn't give up. . . .

Somehow, he got close enough to the man to throw him the beach towel, shout a few encouraging words that he didn't really mean—the trip back seemed hopelessly difficult and long . . . The man seemed to be moving along behind him back toward the distant shore. Still no sign of help. The other swimmer may or may not have made it out as far as Dusty; Shirley thinks not.

. . . Shirley, standing helplessly watching from shore, fearing her husband might never return with her. . . . But, slowly but surely he seemed to be making it back. How would they ever keep their strength to endure those twelve foot breakers? She's not sure time ever moved so agonizingly slowly. It came to a dead stop. She prayed prayers she had forgotten she had known.

And there they were, thrown against the sandy beach by the force of the waves, too exhausted to move. They were alive. . . .

In writing about legendary figures in family history, it's also important in certain contexts to communicate their shortcomings as well. If you're choosing to write about heroic family figures because you want to give your children real-life role models, their humanness combined with heroism is what will make them seem real to your child. Because it's a sure thing that no one—despite his heroic accomplishments—in your family history is perfect. Children (as well as adults) often need help overcoming a tendency to think in black and white, all-or-nothing terms. With the diary stories, you can help them to see family heroes and legends as real people.

You may be surprised at how *simple* the story can be—any screw up, gaffe, or *faux pas* of a family member that you can tell from a caring perspective will entertain your child. Children love stories about the grown-ups they love goofing up or making mischief. Your children will appreciate the message that their grandparents or other ancestors had a sense of adventure and mischief and sometimes had to learn painful lessons the hard way.

The Comings and Goings of Family Members

Anytime there is a birth or a death of a family member, there is a change to the child's social world. Births and deaths of relatives and family friends are momentous events for children. Recording them for your child will place their own lifetime within the context of another person's lifetime. Writing the following entry to my daughter Perrin about the birth of a new cousin also inspired me to reflect on what this addition to my brother's family might stir in my own. Until I reread this entry some years later, I had forgotten how powerful an experience it was for me. My sister-in-law, Billie, and I actually fulfilled the wish we made together that day when our daughters Frances and Margaret were born a few months apart a year later:

To Perrin (age 4), March 23, 1996

You awoke early Thurs. morning to find Dusty and Huck here to await the birth of their new baby brother or sister. Landon soon went off to school, then you also. After lunch, I took you guys over to T.J. Maxx . . . and as soon as we returned home I had a message from Uncle Dusty that the boys had a new brother, Samuel!

. . . All was well w/ Sam. I dropped you at Grammy's so I could bring the boys in to see their mother and brother at Brigham & Women's [hospital].

This was really a very touching and special role for me, to be there in the intimacy and joy of this meeting, and to see Samuel so soon after his birth, with Billie sitting up in bed, hair still styled from the day before, looking queenly and very joyful. Dusty kept climbing up on the bassinet holding the sleeping and contented bundled Sam. . . .

. . . The boys leaped and jumped over their mother and stared in awe of their new brother.

I, of course, kept imagining what it would be like for me to be the one in the room having my third. Billie said Dusty [her husband] had already agreed to go gung ho on the fourth . . . and so I said to Billie maybe we'd have the next one together. . . .

There are births and additions to the family, and there are deaths and losses as well. You may find that writing about a family member's death is difficult to manage while dealing with the stress and preoccupation at the time of the event. Sometimes it's during periods of quiet reflection or on anniversaries of major events that you feel inspired to write to your child about it. There was no way, during the tumultuous period of transition my family was experiencing around the time of my husband's grandmother's death, for me to write about her death to my son. But I knew that my son's great-grandmother was important to him and that he might like to have an entry about her death in his diary later on. So, a year later, on the anniversary of her death, I found myself spontaneously attending to the entry I had left out. I wrote about taking him, the afternoon of her death, out to a special dock on a serene pond near our home that we often visited on our bikes:

To Landon (age 8), April 13, 1995

. . . I wanted to tell you of Nana's passing in a beautiful, serene setting, so that if you remembered, some day, being told, you would remember the salty air of the bay and the sound of the gulls and the blue of the water as we walked out onto the fishing pier in Palm Harbor.

You weren't particularly shook up, just thoughtful and distracted by the need to throw rocks and find little treasures to pocket. You really had lost Nana when she had her stroke over a year ago and lost her words and never seemed to make much sense to you any more. She had begun to tire easily, and in the nursing home she could never pamper and spoil you with treats and princely pampering the way she once had. She couldn't shop for toys that she knew would delight you, and she couldn't really handle or understand money, so she rarely gave treats of money. Which isn't to say that you responded to Nana less because she could give you less, but she couldn't really communicate her love for you any more in ways that you could understand or accept. I don't think you could get over her no longer being able to call you by name.

But you loved Nana dearly when she was really "alive" to you, because she was filled w/ joy at the sight of you and she would dance and sing w/ you in her arms.

In the next and final chapter, we look at issues that evolve in the diary writing process when you have been keeping them over a long period of time, including how and when you decide the diaries are finished and ready to be passed on to your children. But first, try these Diary Door Openers.

Diary Door Openers

1. Portrait of a Loved One
   Write a portrait—a description of looks, personality, roles, life-style, behaviors and stories—of a relative or loved one who was alive when you were growing up but who died before your child was born. Reflect on what the relationship you had with this person meant to you.

2. Grandparent's Adventure
   If they are living, ask your child's grandparents for adventure tales that your child might like to have preserved. Write them down in their own words or to the best of your memory. If you are a grandparent who is keeping the diaries, write down your adventure stories for your grandchildren and look for ways to make these adventures seem relevant to their lives today through interesting details, comparisons, contrasts, or themes.

3. Family Homes
   Describe a home your family grew up in that your child has never seen and compare and contrast the description with the home your child lives in now.

4. Legacies and Heirlooms
   Describe an heirloom or legacy that is still in the family that you treasure and reflect on why. Don't forget to include as much of the history of this legacy as you know.

5. Family Places and Gatherings
   Describe a place where members of your family have gathered and continue to gather for more than one generation. Reflect on what it means to you to share this place with your child. Has this place or the people who go there changed over the years? If so, how? If no place like this exists in your life, describe a place like this that you would like to find or create and share with your child.

6. Mischief Makers
   Write a mischief story about when your child's grandparent got in trouble as a child, or write one about yourself. Reflect on what he, she, or you learned.

Chapter 13

Surveying the Stack of Diaries
Making Peace with the Past,
Present, and Future

> While the novel and autobiography may be thought of
> as artistic wholes, the diary is always in process,
> always in some sense a fragment. That is not to say
> that diaries do not have distinct shapes, but that their
> shapes derive from their existence in time passing.

(Margo Culley, *A Day at a Time*, p. 19)

Growing from a Single Diary to a Stack

Beneath my cluttered desk, I sort through the pile of diaries I have been keeping for my three children since before each was born. Picking out the diaries I've written for my oldest child, my son, I make a tall stack of the oddly assorted notebooks whose covers are already fading from handling and age. This baby to whom I wrote in the very first diary—*the baby who wasn't even born yet*—is now thirteen. But through the diary door as I reread the stories I have saved for him, time is suspended. We live in the present moment and his future waits through an open door.

Looking back over the more than thirteen years of writing diaries for him, I realize that the stack of diaries I visualized in the dream I wrote about in the introduction to this book has materialized. Now, in fact, there are *three* tall stacks of diaries—one for each child. I cannot yet share from personal experience the process of actually finishing the diaries. But I can look back over what I have done and think about what I still hope to accomplish in the diary writing, as well as imagine what it might be like to hand the diaries over to my children in a few short years.

This chapter explores issues that may surface after you have been writing the diaries for some time. For instance, this chapter looks at how we can use diary writing to make peace with ourselves as diarists, and it shows us how embracing moments of grace can inspire us to keep writing through the years. It includes strategies for how we can begin writing again even after a long silence or gap in the diaries. It shows how diary writing can help us encounter "the future" when it becomes the present much sooner than we had expected. And, finally, this chapter explores how we know when the diaries are finished and ready to be passed on to our children.

In writing this final chapter, I was surprised to discover that an entry, "Future Shock" (To Landon, January 16, 2000) includes a dream with a symbol of a flower, as does a diary entry included in the Introduction. This discovery reminded me of the power that diary writing possesses—as do other types of literature—to educate, enlighten, and uplift us, and to transform our understanding through the mysterious beauty and truth of enduring symbols.

As I continue to write diaries for my children, I find that diary writing is a lot like gardening. When you plant stories in the diary you can never be quite sure how they will grow, whether they will survive, or how they will be harvested. Any one who grows things, a gardener or a diarist, learns to make peace with the process—with both the abundant harvests, as well as the periods of drought. Diary writing for your children can help you make peace with yourself as a parent—with what you have hoped to do, with what you have done, and with what you have left undone.

Stories of Absolution and Moments of Grace

As we grow in the parenting role and as we write through the diary door, we begin to know our true selves better and better with each passing day. We grow to recognize, admit, and take responsibility for changing our shortcomings. There are stories to write about the thirst for change and for a need to be relieved of guilt, shame or disappointment regarding some aspect of parenting where we have fallen short of meeting our own standards. There may be times when we feel that we owe our children an apology but they may not even be aware that we've done something wrong. If we apologize to them, they would probably forgive us willingly. But is this what we are really looking for? Is it what we need? Children regularly benefit from reminders that we love them even though they are not perfect. So do parents. My son is never as critical of me as I am of myself, as is seen in this next entry, where the diary writing involves my search for inner peace at the end of a challenging parenting day:

To Landon (age 10), July 16, 1997

*On summer hours we don't read regularly in the evening, but we did last night, at my suggestion, just you and me on the living room couch. **You** read to me from **"Dear Mr. Henshaw,"** a book you read last year w/ Mrs. Logsdon, and liked so much you want to share it w/ me.*

*Like sunshine and stillness after the storm, this quiet half-hour before bed after a day full of **your** boredom and my irritable frustration, saved only by running into Mrs. C who took you off to Cole's baseball game.*

I tuck you in, the most important ritual of the day, and you say you love me. One of those nights I don't quite feel I deserve it! I should be better at handling you being at home w/ your sister for a week!

We may write in the diaries about feeling guilty or remorseful, but the diaries are not a junk heap where we carelessly toss our guilt toward our children as a way of trying to say, "I'm sorry." However, the diaries may sometimes be used like a *compost heap*, where we bring our mistakes or shortcomings for recycling, using them as fertilizer to grow fresh insights and develop new assets in our parenting, such as:

- To gain awareness by giving us a chance to speak to our children as ideal listeners so that we have a sounding board for learning important lessons about parenting and making the most of the time we have with them.
- To receive emotional support through providing ourselves with reminders and encouragement to follow through on our commitments to change.
- To connect with the objective part of ourselves that helps us to accept our human limitations and forgive ourselves for not being perfect.

The following entry to my son begins with the regret and remorse that comes from making a mistake and the admission that my parenting has fallen short of my own ideals. The quiet, centering sanctuary available through the diary door invites reflection that leads me to clarify what it is I want to change and how I want to improve as a parent. And, it also leads me to an inner wisdom and awareness that brings a sense of *balance* to the self-criticism by helping me recognize the ways that my parenting *does* fulfill my ideals, as it does in the following entry. The entry begins with my complaining at myself for what I did wrong, helps me state what I want to do differently and why, and then spontaneously leads me to a recognition of the ways I'm already doing it:

To Landon (age 8), October 25, 1995

"Doubts and Misgivings"

I wish I could slow down, relax and pay better attention to you at those busy, pre-occupied times when I feel frenzied and fragmented and try to jerk everything under my control because I think I'll feel better if I can just rush through and be done.

I'm rambling, I know, but it's because I'm so stirred up w/impatience w/myself tonight, in reviewing the past few days, and the way I've been w/you guys a lot: uptight, rushed, impatient.

*Tonight I had to show the house to a couple right at dinnertime. I didn't **have** to, but I am very anxious to have it rented. You two were starving because you had been playing nicely in the yard. The couple arrived as I was trying to put the food on your plates, and so I rushed them through the tour of the house, trying to be a sales-woman, trying to get it over w/so we could eat in peace.*

As I sat chatting w/them in the living room you and Perrin were eating, and you kept interrupting me as I spoke to them, and I wouldn't listen, I just insisted that you eat your dinner and wait 'til I was done. I assumed you needed something from me that was unrelated. As they were leaving, I finally let you speak, and it turns out you were trying to help me rent the house! You had a lot to add to what I'd shared about the town and schools, but I said goodbye to them and realized I should have listened to you.

*I hate it when I get like this, I truly do. These are mistakes I don't want to make. True, you often do interrupt me when I'm on the phone & such, w/unrelated stuff in an imperious, badgering way. But I want to be more attentive **in general**. I really want to pay more attention **to you!"***

I guess I'm really starting to feel the stress of the move and all there is to do.

I spent the whole morning preparing for the Cub scout meeting with all of you boys this afternoon. . . .

You were sweet when I picked you up. You changed at Grammy's and looked gor-geous. All seven of you [Cub Scouts] were there, and I really liked the guys. You felt very important when you said goodbye to Perrin at Grammy's:

"Goodbye Perrin. We're going to the Cub scout meeting at the library."

*I'm so glad I'm doing this, because I love spending this time w/you, and because even though you don't say so, I know it matters a lot to you that I'm the **Leader**. . . .*

We write about our courage to change ourselves when change is called for. As growing parents, and as diarists, we learn to pay attention to what is really impor-tant by making ourselves conscious of our shortcomings and gifts and of our wants and needs. Then we are ready to embrace the signs and symbols of good things to come that are sent our way. Stories of when we experience grace capture golden moments when something unexpected and beautiful happens and brings particular meaning to an otherwise mundane or ordinary experience. These are moments of symbolic beauty or harmony that give hope, peace, and guidance for attitudinal change in the future.

Holidays can be exceptionally meaningful, rewarding, and joyous occasions of family celebration. They can also be chaotic and satisfying or chaotic *and* depleting experiences. For many people, certain holidays can be painful and disastrously stressful experiences for a variety of reasons, particularly when the holidays fail to live up to our expectations of what we think they should be or what we think we should be feeling.

Whether or not we can give and get all that we would like on holidays, we can be open to experiencing moments of grace when they appear like unexpected gifts. We can celebrate them in the diary, as I did one Thanksgiving in an entry to my daughter:

To Frances (age 1), November 26, 1998

Thanksgiving Day. "Under the Rainbow"

*. . . Grey and rainy and cool, we watched it pour through the afternoon until, about a half hour before dusk, it suddenly became bright. Perrin ran up to get me from the TV room, insisting I come down and see the rainbow hanging in the backyard. There it was, a magical **double** rainbow that arced right up from the mud, rocks, and bare trees behind the house. Dad, Lan, and Perrin ran out over the wet ground to stand under the rainbow that seemed to spill its color right onto their heads, and standing in a lump there together, they looked to me like the pot of gold. Our gold, Fran. Our pot of gold. . . .*

Listening to Silences and Recovering from Gaps

One task for the reader of any diary is to identify the "silences"
of the text. What the diarist did not, could not, or would
not write sometimes shrieks from the page.

(Margo Culley, *A Day at a Time*, p. 22)

When you've been writing long enough to begin to see what you are doing and to see what you have done, inevitably you must also look at what you have left undone. There comes the time when you feel that your diary writing has fallen short of your expectations—you fear that you haven't written enough of the stories that there are to tell. Suddenly you are more conscious of all the stories you have left out—all the stories you *haven't* written, or can't write, or don't want to write.

You think about all the stories you feel you could have told or should have told, and yet you haven't written them. There are no perfect diarists, of course, and no perfect diaries, as I'm sure my children will some day discover. In the following entry, after ten years of writing diaries for my children, I am aware of ways I fear the diaries will fall short of what I hoped to accomplish, and I admit my fears to my youngest child:

To Frances (1 month before birth), March 10, 1997

> . . . I imagine that at some point the three of you will compare your journals, how much I write at certain times, things I left out, books you prefer . . . I'm certain I'll fall short for each of you many times. But, in many ways, each of the journals I keep for each of you belong to all of you, because our lives, happily!—are completely intertwined and it's often that I tell a story in one of the your journals that involves all of you. . . .

Silences are a normal part of the rhythm of the diary. There are many reasons you will find to stop writing for certain periods of time. If you make yourself feel like a slave to the process, that feeling will rob the fun from the writing. Occasionally, you will find yourself avoiding topics that you would like to write about but feel you *can't*, or that you don't want to write about but feel you *should*. Perhaps something compelling is influencing your child's development that you resist opening up as a topic in the diary.

It makes sense to be thoughtful about your choices of what to include in your child's diary, so don't try to rush or pressure yourself into or out of writing about a certain topic. You can get at the root of the silence by asking yourself questions or by exploring the issue in your own diary or with a close friend. You can keep writing about the things that you *do* feel motivated to write about. After all, you have plenty of time to break silences and taboos when you're ready as long as you have kept the diary writing process alive for you and your child.

Your child may not let you neglect the diary for long once she or he is old enough to be aware of and value the diary and the process. Over the years, my children have occasionally given me prompts that remind me just how much they value the diaries (and just how much they expect me to include!), as my son does in the following entry:

To Landon (age 9), August, 1996

> . . . My goodness . . . how to catch up on a whole month of summer when I've been neglecting your journal—Perri's too—like this?
> You don't let me neglect it for long, however.

One day last week Dusty, you & Perrin were out in the yard just before lunch, and you found a little brown toad which you immediately captured in a bucket and attempted to domesticate him. Very soon you found another and another and another until you had four. What fun the three of you had making a grassy home for these friends whom you soon named according to their personalities.

"Mom, you have to be sure and write about this in our journals!" You shouted to me in my garden. I was delighted that you asked me too, and so, I know when truly wonderful events happen for you, because you ask me to record them.

Once you have been writing long enough you may notice varying sizes of gaps in dates. The amount of time that can fly by unrecorded in the diary so quickly may shock and disappoint you. Days lost are stories lost—stories of early childhood that will never come again. Dealing with that concern in this entry, I reconnect with my baby daughter after a gap by starting with a report on the day's weather, as I often do in the first paragraph of the diaries. I also use the diary writing technique of making a list to summarize what she has accomplished in her developing language during the gap:

To Frances (age 1), October 15, 1998

The first bright sky we have had in a week! Golden and bronze, Land and Perrin going coatless out the front door to the bus stop....

It's impossible to apologize for neglecting your journal the way I feel I have. But I do remember my quiet writing time screeching to a halt when Land was between 1 and 3, really. But to miss these days, with all your wonderful shenanigans is tragic, and so, I am determined to try harder.

Your vocabulary to date:

Horsey	*Eye*
Abby (first word)	*Nose*
Peugot	*Ear*
Momma	*B Butt (Belly button)*
Daddy	*Mine!*
Bye-Bye	*Peas (Please)....*
Waz at?	

Some silences are stress gaps that pinpoint and surround stressful periods of personal and familial change. These gaps do not represent "laziness," but rather a preoccupation with external events that occur in your life whether they are chosen or happen without your control. Coping with changes and transitions within the family uses up enormous amounts of parental energy. It's part of the rhythm of the diary that these gaps occur, as a result of a variety of disruptions and transitions, such as during a move, the birth of a sibling, an illness or death of a family member or friend, a divorce, or a change of job. All of these kinds of events may demand extra energy for coping that you ordinarily used to use for writing. Trying to cope with the emotional needs of everyone in the family can rob you of your serenity, concentration, and time. Even though there is always the potential for comfort, insight, inner wisdom, and healing through the diary door, the fact is that sometimes we lack the inner drive to go there just when we may need it most. But just because there are gaps, don't give up on the diaries, even though it may seem overwhelming to try to fill in the lost time. There is still plenty of time to write to your growing child.

Strategies for Recovering from Stress Gaps

You can use the following strategies to recover from stress gaps anytime:

- **Let Go of Guilt.** Give yourself permission to take a break until things calm down and keep the diaries handy for when you are able to center yourself and re-establish a routine. The guilt comes from a sense that you are missing an opportunity to write about things that are here today and gone tomorrow. Be aware of the *wish* to write that is underneath the *shoulds*. *Shoulds* create procrastination and avoidance, but *wishes* provide desire and inspiration.

- **Make a Quiet, Comfortable Space and Time.** Choose a day in the near future when you know you will have some free or flexible time. Pick a quiet part of a day to plan to curl up on a comfortable couch with the diary, a cup of tea, and some relaxing time to reflect and write. As the day draws near, keep your commitment by saying "no" to things that will interfere with giving yourself and your future reader this time.

- **Summarize.** Don't pressure yourself into thinking that you have to fill in all the blank days, weeks, or months. It's okay to summarize the important events to the best of your memory, or not try to fill in the missing time period at all. Just make a brief explanation for the gap. After all, there are plenty of things to pay attention to and write about *today*.

- **Make Lists.** If you do want to summarize a missed time period, using lists can be a great way to get caught up and be inspired to continue. You can make some headings and brainstorm the lists under the headings until you've caught up on past events.

- **Jump In.** To re-enter the stream of writing, just pick up the pen and jump in from right where you're standing. After all, if you want to take a swim you do not have to climb to the top of the mountain to enter at the beginning of the stream. You enter at the place where the water is already running beside you. Close a gap in the diary by choosing a story of an important event that occurred during the gap that you have not yet recorded. Take a few moments to reflect on the sights, sounds, and smells of this occasion. Think about what tense you want to tell the story in. Writing in the present tense about a past event can add a sense of immediacy. Writing in the past tense gives a sense of reflection. *Begin writing.*

Picking up my daughter's diary one day when she was two, I made the disturbing discovery that I had not made a single entry in her diary for many months. The gap distressed me because two is such an adorable age, but I understood why it was there. The chain of events that had brought two major moves and job changes into my household in the space of less than one year, including a relocation from Florida to New England in the middle of winter, had drained all my energy, free time, and focus. It seemed impossible to catch up on everything I had missed in the diaries during these stressful months, but I felt I had to do something to revive my inspiration and motivation to write. I chose to write the story of when my daughter, my son, and I were baptized together as an important reconnecting point, a story I wanted told in her diary even though it had happened three months earlier. Then, three days before her third birthday, I began writing again:

To Perrin (age 2), March 12, 1995

It was warm and sunny and joyful the morning of our baptisms [in December 1994]. I had been afraid that I wouldn't be able to get you to dress up. But Fri. night, when Grammy & Grampy Mike showed you the dress w/ white lace they had brought you to wear, you had it on, dancing around the house before any of us could blink. You wore the Easter Hat I had bought for you last year, as well as white tights and shoes w/ a bow, and next to Landon, in his black suit, you looked adorable. Your friend Amelia w/ her Mom, Jan, and brother Thomas, were there, as well as my friends Byron and Phyllis, and a number of people from the church (also Greg). Grammy and Grampy served as Godparents. . . . The Priest, Father Hall, spoke to us as a family as we sat in the front pew just before performing the rite of Holy Baptism. He said *something to you & Landon, leaning over & looking grave, about how someday you might get caught in a problem you would find hard to deal w/, etc. and after he moved away you put your arms around my neck and said earnestly that you wanted to go home:*

"I don't want to get caught, Mommy!"

Soon, we were standing in the altar as the priest read the Baptismal service . . . You were fidgety and moving around quite a bit. Just as the priest was reading the question:

"And do you renounce evil . . . ?"

You accidentally knocked over the burning altar candle which then fell against my shoulder, dripping wax all down the shoulder and arm of my beige suit, and bouncing off me it swung against the priest before it could be settled back down.

After the service I joked w/ the priest that I had been baptized by fire and water!

You seemed to enjoy having your head wet by the pouring of the water. Whenever you have since been in a sanctuary you've asked me if the priest was going to pour water on you. . . .

The diaries are patient and forgiving, always waiting, ready to listen to the story that will help you break the silence and fill the blank pages once again.

Future Projections

Who knows what sort of lives our children will someday lead? It's fun for them to imagine being cut loose from parents, living on their own, left to their own devices. Perhaps it will be fun after they actually have left home and taken the diaries with them to come across passages that contain plans they made from another time and another perspective. My daughter likes to project into the future, imagining the home she will make for herself some day. This entry captures some of those wishes for her to review and reconsider from another perspective later on:

To Perrin (age 6), January 17, 1999

. . . One day last week as we were hanging around the house together in the late afternoon, you began talking about what your life is going to be like when you get sprung from this joint.

"Maelyn [cousin] and I are going to live right next to each other w/ our husbands."

"We're going to go out at night together and leave the boys home."

"The Boys" meaning, your husbands.

As you chattered on you fleshed out this picture of next-door neighbor cousins w/ a bond of friendship and fun that seemed to far surpass any bond of marital togetherness.

Future Shock

For parents, there is such a thing as future shock. Ready or not, here it comes—the next unpredictable phase of parenting growth. One moment you are reading the positive pregnancy test strip, the next moment your child is toddling, then talking, then meeting his kindergarten teacher. You may feel as if you're scrambling to keep up with all the changes your child is going through, and too many times you may end up feeling like a bumbling idiot rather than a mature, intelligent parent. There's simply no way to feel consistently prepared to face the next, unknown, unanticipated challenge your child's growth and development brings to your relationship and the demands this challenge makes for your own personal growth. Perhaps this may be particularly true when it involves the integration of a whole new technology. Just as our parents faced the influence of television, so do we now face the influence of the Internet on our children. As children who grew up with color television as a ubiquitous appliance in our homes, we now may evaluate television's influence on our upbringing as we face issues and challenges in raising our children. We may wonder whether our parents let us watch too much television, or not enough? Did they let us watch too much of the wrong shows and not enough of the right ones? Did they make the right decision by buying, or not buying, a television, or in letting us have our own in our bedroom? Did they encourage us to develop healthy viewing habits, or did they allow us to completely indulge our own wishes and impulses? Did television impact our growing up in positive or negative ways? How did television shape the adults we have become?

Just as our parents faced the questions about television in the twentieth century, we will find ourselves struggling with all of these questions and more in the twenty-first century regarding our child's use of the computer and the Internet. We don't really get any down time in which to prepare to answer all of these questions brilliantly before we begin raising children. But we ask ourselves the questions and we struggle to come up with the right answers. Diary writing helps us clarify our concerns, reflect on our values and beliefs, and communicate them to our children. I wrote the following entry to my son as I began to be asked and to ask myself the questions the Internet began posing in our lives:

To Landon (age 12), February 9, 2000

... Meanwhile, I attended a panel discussion last Thurs. night at the Middle school on the Internet. Came home and re-set all the parental controls and changed my password (which I had freely let you have!)

I'm sure I didn't handle it very well or thoughtfully. But I am struggling to keep up w/ parenting issues in this unknown territory. It's scary that you kids know so much and we so little!

We spent the weekend, on and off, w/ you, me and Daddy negotiating principles and discussing your use of the internet. A couple of weeks ago we had to impose some time limits because your use was out of control. Now you have three twenty-minute sessions per day that you can use when responsibilities are met (this includes video games).

It's going pretty well. You set the kitchen timer most of the time before you go on.

Well, we had some tense, frustrated and angry moments working out the boundaries w/ you, discussing our concerns. Daddy kept confronting me about my tone and my approach. He was right. But I'm not **there** yet. I'm not settled. I'm scrambling to get a handle on all these internet issues, possibilities, benefits and hazards. I'm scrambling! I'm afraid I've given you too much freedom w/o fully knowing what limits to set to keep you safe and healthy. We have only just begun to approach a discussion of the ethical issues of the internet!

Is it, for instance, ethical to have more than one screen name? These altar egos start out, perhaps, innocently enough. But have you really thought through the implications of pretending to be someone else?

Well, as we got on the computer and went through the parental controls together we learned a lot, and I hope that you got the message that Dad and I are in charge of the computer and your access to the internet, and that, w/o trying to invade your privacy, we're going to stay closely involved w/ your internet activity. I'm certain we will often fail, but we're going to **try** to stay a few steps ahead of you.

You voluntarily deleted your second screen name before I had a chance to get there. So, I think some of what we had to say had an impact.

Mon., I sat down at the computer to write during my writing time, and found myself writing a column ... on parenting issues on the internet. I e-mailed it off a couple of hours later, and I believe they're going to run it.

This is the way I get a handle on issues—I write about them.

I feel much less panicked and reactive now. Much more able to communicate from my thoughtful, nurturing self, rather than my controlling, rigid self.

But I do feel ferociously protective at times. I know there is a light and dark side of this.

I feel so responsible for doing my best parenting—facing up to the challenges of figuring out, setting, and following through on the right boundaries and limits w/ you.

I owe myself this.

I owe you this.

You are my son. Every day it is my job to be aware of my impact on you, your impact on others, your impact on yourself, and the world's impact on you.

I come from a family history of accepting denial of reality as an acceptable means of coping w/ challenges and problems in life. . . .

Deny the obvious

Deny the problem

Deny the feelings

Deny the facts.

Hope for the best.

Before you were born, I made a commitment to facing life on life's terms, and I stand by it.

I've told you about some of the family "secrets" and, as you grow, I'll tell you all of them.

As a parent, I have to face the darker possibilities of the Internet and the free and limitless world it offers.

We will approach it together. With enthusiasm and caution. We will continue to make mistakes, and learn from them.

Whether or not we are ready for the changes our children will go through, we must be willing to explore the feelings the change brings when it arrives. As children head toward puberty, there are all the questions and concerns about budding romances that we must begin to explore. I wrote this entry to my son to celebrate his first interest in dating a girl and ended up exploring my own feelings, harvesting helpful insights to guide me in dealing with these developments in the future:

To Landon (age 12), January 16, 2000

. . . So, a happy weekend was ushered in.

Seems like it was a busy couple of days organizing all the plans. For weeks you've been trying to get C. and you to the movies, and she can only go if you go in a group. I suggest you invite Kevin overnight, and you do, but his parents don't want him to go w/ girls alone yet (C. is bringing A. so, I suggest Scott, and that gets arranged . . . then, it turns out later Kevin will meet you all at the theatre w/ his father, Dad will take you. You & Scott come home [and] you include Ross . . . so I make pizza for you. . . .

Dad takes your crowd . . . you are bouncing on your toes w/ a happiness I have seen you reserve only for special events w/ Joey.

The evening is a great success, I think. You all go out for ice cream after the movie. . . .

"C. is a really nice girl!" Dad says. . . .

I think Dad felt very proud and took great pleasure in sharing this momentous event w/ you—your first real boy/girl event. . . .

I fell asleep as soon as Dad got home, and woke early for my trip down to psychodrama in New Haven, waking from a vivid dream which might very well have some relevance to our relationship.

It was winter, as it is now, and when I went into the back yard, I saw that all the flowers in the garden where the lilac tree is were in bloom. Bushy, bright white bunches of mums were in full blossom where the peonies grow.

*They were quite beautiful, but they worried me, and I felt like I should **do** something, but, of course, there was nothing I could do. There were white blossoms through the gate and down the side of the house, and I was showing them to Dad and some guests, like family, and worrying—why were the flowers blooming early in the middle of winter? How could I make them last? Would they bloom again? Was there something I needed to do to try to make them last? They were so light, so bright, so big and beautiful. . . .*

Just enjoy them, perhaps. Relax and enjoy them. Yes, they may be blooming out of season, before they are "supposed" to, but nature has its own mysteries, cycles, and timing.

As I woke, and began chatting w/ Dad about the night before, I said that I thought that this had been a peak experience for you.

Yes, it was a joyful, peak experience for you. And I watched, with pleasure to see your innocent happiness in full bloom, and yes, was surprised by your interest in girls emerging so suddenly, so intently this fall.

But I think I can relax, enjoy it, watch you blossom. "Let" you blossom. Realize that you will blossom when you're ready, in your own timing not mine.

How Do You Know When the Diaries Are Done?

After you've been raising your children and writing in the diaries over the years, you may wonder when does the process end? When do you stop writing and hand the diaries on to your children? Perhaps a good time to turn the diaries over to your children is when they leave home. Except that this leave-taking is much more likely to be a process rather than an actual event that you can pinpoint and say, okay, now my child has left home and is gone for good.

The inner wisdom you have cultivated through the diary door will offer you all the guidance you need in making this decision. Just as you have been led to solutions in a variety of parenting questions and concerns over the years through the diary door, you will find your answer to when the diary writing is done and how to pass the diaries on to your child through your story writing.

Different types of diaries offer different types of closure. For instance, travel diaries end when the trip is over. Healing diaries end when the problem has been healed. Some diaries end when the blank pages of a particular notebook are filled. Garden diaries may end when the season changes. Published diaries end when the editor chooses to end them. But lifelong diarists like May Sarton never stop writing until they die in old age.

So, when do diaries for children end? When is childhood over? Is it over at a particular age, such as when a child becomes an adolescent at age thirteen? Adolescence is a period of dependence on parents for a variety of things in our culture and may still be thought of as a part of childhood. Is childhood over when a child turns eighteen or twenty-one? Who knows? Each child and parent is unique. We don't stop being parents even though our children grow up and leave home, we just transition to another new stage of our parenting role. There are no definitive markers for the end of childhood in our culture. We can only invent them with ritual, or discover them through listening to the stories that show our children acting consistently more adult like and fulfilling the responsibilities that go along with the role.

Even though your child's leave-taking will be gradual, a planned ritual that rises out of the wisdom of the diary storytelling may help you to mark this occasion with honor and purpose. A ritual offers both child and parents an opportunity to harvest the richly ambivalent feelings that are likely to accompany this transitional time.

I do not know when the diaries for my children will end. The entries included in this book speak to and capture my son—my oldest child—before conception, during infancy, early childhood, through preschool years to elementary school years to middle-school years, and moving from his preteens into adolescence. The stories are getting more, rather than less interesting and complex, and I have no desire or need to stop now. When to end the diaries is a story I have yet to experience, write, and answer.

But I imagine a ritual that we create together will mark the end of the process for each of my children. Something, perhaps, like the one in the dream where I "knew I was dying" and stacked the diaries up together and tied them with a ribbon. They will someday be given to each child to take with them as they make homes of their own, and do as they please with them.

Leaving the Diaries

At some point you will turn the diaries over to your children unfinished, incomplete, imperfect as they may be. You will wonder if you have said all you wanted to say, said it well enough, and said it in a style you admire that your children will appreciate. You've misspelled words, been sloppy or sentimental, committed yourself to beliefs you no longer hold, exposed your shortcomings intentionally and, worse yet, unintentionally. You will be aware of all the ways you fear that the diaries, like your parenting, don't measure up to what you wanted your children to have from you.

All you have in the diaries are the stories you have paid attention to. Have you paid attention to the *right* ones? Enough of the right ones? You've bared your soul to your children, to *their* children too, perhaps—future generations who will judge you according to the standards and wisdom of *their* generation and not of the one that raised you. You wonder if the quality of your parenting will stand the test of time. You wonder if you've been crazy to be so vulnerable as to preserve it in the diaries.

Yet, you've done your best. At times, you've been excellent—the diaries reveal this. And yet, they also capture you in your weaker moments, the way you sometimes feel trapped in unflattering photos.

You will see that the diaries, unfinished, imperfect as they are, must be left to the future beyond your control. And you must accept that. Because writing diaries for your children is an act of love, and every act of love is a risk. So, at some point you leave them at the mysterious and uncertain doorway into the future, hoping they will nurture your loved ones in the ways they have nurtured you.

Diary Door Openers

1. Shortcomings

    Write about one of your shortcomings (i.e., impatience or irritability, etc.) and how it manifests itself in your parenting. Reflect on your thirst for change and respond with a plan for how you might work on changing this aspect of your parenting.

2. Moments of Grace

    Describe a moment you had with your children when you felt in harmony with them and with the universe, when you felt uplifted and at peace with yourself and the world.

3. Recovering from Stress Gaps

    Go over the strategies for recovering from stress gaps that are listed on page 208 and use them as motivation to return to the diary writing today.

4. Future Projection

    Write about what you hear your child imagining life will be like when she or he leaves home.

4. Final Entry

    If you recognize that it is time to turn the diaries over to your child, write a final entry to your child that allows you to reflect on what the diary writing process has meant to you. How does it feel to be turning them over at this time? How do you hope your child will receive them? What is the final thing you want to say in the diaries to your child?

Bibliography

American Heritage Dictionary of the English Language, Fourth Edition, The. Boston: Houghton-Mifflin, 2000.

Baum, L. Frank. *The Wizard of Oz*. London: Cathay Books, 1983.

Clemens, Samuel. *The Adventures of Tom Sawyer*. NY: Magnum Books, 1967.

Culley, Margo, *A Day at a Time – The Diary Literature of American Women from 1764 to the Present*. New York: The Feminist Press, 1985.

Fogel, Alice B. *I Love This Dark World*. Cambridge: Zoland Books, 1996.

Forché, Carolyn. *Gathering the Tribes*. New Haven, CT: Yale University Press, 1976.

Gilchrist, Ellen. *Falling through Space – The Journals of Ellen Gilchrist*. Boston: Little, Brown & Co., 1987.

Mallon, Thomas. *A Book of One's Own – People and Their Diaries*. New York: Ticknor & Fields, 1984.

Mellon, Nancy. *Storytelling and the Art of Imagination*. Rockport, MA: Element, 1992.

Moreno, J. L. *Words of the Father*. New York: Beacon House, 1971.

Nachmanovitch, Stephen. *Free Play – Improvisation in Life and Art*. New York: Jeremy P. Tarcher/Putnam, 1990.

Saint-Exupéry, Antoine de. *The Little Prince*. Orlando, FL: Harcourt, Brace & World, 1971.

Salas, Jo. *Improvising Real Life – Personal Story in Playback Theater*, 2nd ed. DuBuque, IA: Kendall/Hunt Publishing Co., 1996.

Wilder, Thornton. *Our Town*. NY: HarperPerennial, 1998.

Index

critical English teacher, 27, 31
critical parent voice, 31-32
criticism, 32, 43
Culley, Margo, 201, 205
cycle of creativity, 121

darker side, 146
date, *see* only rule
Day at A Time, A, 201, 205
death, 49, 63, 121, 124, 198-199, 208
decision making, 71, 102, 130, 134, 215
delivery, 19, 56-57, 61, 71-72, 176
descendants, 185-186
describe, 24, 28, 37, 44, 51-52, 59, 61, 75-76, 91, 112, 127, 143, 160, 178, 182-184, 200, 217
descriptive writing, 24, 28, 37, 50, 54, 61-62, 65, 94, 103, 127, 143, 187, 200
dialogue, 29, 45-46, 50, 94, 100, 123, 127, 143, 150, 158, 177 *see also* quoting your child
diarist, defined, 12-14
Diary Door Openers, 23-24, 36-37, 51, 61, 75, 90-91, 112, 126-127, 143, 160, 183, 200, 217
Disaster Stories, 81
disconnection, 129, 146
distance, 26, 33, 80, 82, 93, 129, 143, 146, 149, 188
divorce, 33, 164, 180, 208
dragons, 43, 145, 149-152
dreams, 1, 4, 66, 97, 113, 115-119, 125, 127, 201-202, 214, 215

editing, considerations of, 31, 177-179
emotional development, 47
emotional process of letting go, 134-136 *see also* letting go

emotional safety, 114, 177
emotions, *see* feelings
enchantment, 16, 24, 64, 108, 139, 143, 165
endings, honoring your child's, 136
Everyday Advice, 68

Falling through Space, 27-28
family conflict, 177-183, 189
family crisis, 177-186
family history, 4, 26, 33, 37, 39, 51, 96, 175, 182-183, 185-187, 189-192, 195-198, 213
family identity, 175
family illnesses, 189
family legends, 77, 196
family of origin, 175, 177-178, 189
family secrets, 177, 190, 213
family stories, 2, 26, 185-187, 196
family traditions, 188
father's voice, 5
Feature Story, 46
feedback, 67, 69, 168, 183
feelings, 19, 24, 27-28, 40, 42, 44, 47, 49, 52, 61, 72, 75-76, 78-83, 88-89, 98, 103-104, 106-107, 109, 113, 124, 131, 138, 143, 146, 150-161, 177-184, 186, 191-192, 194-195, 203, 205-206, 208, 211, 213, 215
feelings, ambivalent, 140-141
feelings, and sibling rivalry, 170-176
feelings, as a motivation to write, 3, 30, 33, 38
feelings, as part of decision making, 133-136
feelings, as part of the creative process, 124
feelings, in dreams, 118-120,
feelings, positive expression of, 67-70
fiction, 42-44, 119, 137

Firsts, 21-22, 34-37, 42, 59-62, 70, 78, 81-83, 88-91, 93-102, 104-107, 109-112, 115, 149, 151-152, 165, 169, 178, 183, 213-214
five senses, 44
Fogel, Alice, 129
Forché, Carolyn, 185
forgiveness, 158, 182, 202-203
four aspects of diary writing, 28-29
Free Play - Improvisation in Life and Art, 163
future child, 19, 29
future projection, 13, 158, 210-211, 217
future shock, 202, 211
future tense, 44

gaps in the diaries, 202, 205, 207-208, 217
Gathering the Tribes, 185
genealogical history, 186
genealogical search, 186
generations, 4, 39, 69, 96, 107, 183, 185-187, 189-191, 193, 195, 197, 199, 200, 216
Gilchrist, Ellen, 27
goals, 43, 102, 116, 133, 149
godparents, 5, 26, 210
grace, 202, 204-205, 217
grammar, 27, 31
grandchildren, 5, 26-27, 37, 186-187, 191, 194, 200
grandparents, 5, 26, 43, 53, 56, 76, 99, 175, 177, 185, 186, 189, 191, 194, 196, 198, 200
greetings, 165, 183
grown children, 1-2, 9, 13, 21, 210, 217
guilt, 25, 33, 78, 130, 202-203, 208

happy endings, 55
harmony, 163, 167, 176, 183, 205, 217
healing, 5, 41, 55, 104, 157, 159, 181-182, 189-190, 208, 215

Healing Qualities of Writing About Conflict as Quest, 157-159

heirlooms, 29, 200, 186, 192

heroes, heroines, 23, 43, 88, 152, 196-198

heroic parent, 10, 145

heroic quest, 53, 145

holidays, 178, 205

hope, how children inspire, 69

hope, stories that inspire, 205

hoped for results, 13, 24, 30, 37, 46, 52, 97, 130, 201, 217

how to begin, *see* beginning the diaries

How Do You Know When the Diaries Are Done? 214-216

How to Make Time to Write during a Busy Day, 31

humility, 41, 68

humor, 9, 78, 80, 87, 91, 147, 157, 160, 185

"I'm Running Away" Stories, 88-89, 91

I Love This Dark World, 129

ideal listener, 19, 135, 150, 157

ideal parent, 15, 86

illness, 106, 180, 189, 208

imagination, using your, 1, 8, 12-14, 21, 24, 31, 40-41, 44-45, 55, 86, 89, 112, 113, 115, 120, 127, 137, 143, 161, 177, 196, 201, 206, 210, 215, 217

immediacy, 44, 187, 209

Improvising Real Life, 53

initiation rites, 107, 109, 112

inner resources, 3, 43

inner wisdom, 3, 6, 15, 58, 78, 163, 177, 203, 208, 215

insecurity, 114, 164

insight, 8-9, 39-40, 104, 127, 143, 155, 181, 208

inspiration, 14, 23, 30, 64, 124, 143, 208-209

internal critic, 31, 125-126

Internet, 211-213

intimacy, 14, 57, 78, 100, 131-132, 134, 146, 150, 180, 190, 198

intuition, 3, 15, 28, 40, 139

jealousy, 164, 170

journal writing, 12-13, 29

journal writing versus diary writing, 13

journaling, 12-13

journey anxiety, 130

judgment, 3, 32, 43, 109, 111, 123, 125, 127, 216

language milestones, 100, 207

leave-taking, 214-216

leaving the diaries, 214-216

legacy, 5, 7, 190-191, 200

"Letting Go," 129

letting go, 42, 59, 129, 134-135, 138, 171, 207-208

literary devices, 40

Little Prince, The 145

living history, 7, 39, 189

loss, 3-4, 30, 38, 50, 107, 120, 129, 134-136, 138, 141

losses and gains, 138

magical beliefs, 138-139

making time to write, 30-31, 209-209

Mallon, Thomas, 25

maturity, 68, 158, 160, 169

Mellon, Nancy, 39

memoir, 13-14, 187

memories, 1, 3, 7-8, 24, 27, 51, 54, 62, 85, 96, 159, 191, 193-194

Memory Sculpture, 65, 75

mess, making a, 80, 82, 87, 114, 120, 127

metaphor, 10, 145

milestones, 88, 90, 93-103, 104-105, 107, 109, 111-112, 207

mirror, 35, 51, 86, 95, 141-142, 156

misbehavior, 82, 159-160

miscarriage, 37

mischief, 5, 75, 77, 79, 81-89, 91, 167, 198, 200

Mischief Stories, 5, 82-83, 85-86

mishaps, 75, 77-81, 83, 85, 87, 89, 91

mistakes, as a learning process 3-5, 15-16, 31, 113-114, 119, 131, 146-147, 151, 158, 160, 172, 177, 203-204, 213

Modeling Ways of Coping with Conflict, 181-183

Moreno, J. L., 113

"Morning Baking, The" 185

mother's voice, 5

motivation, 1, 23, 30, 32, 50, 63, 209, 217

mythical roles, 138

Nachmanovitch, Stephen, 163

names, 33-35, 37, 95, 101, 141, 170, 195-196, 199, 212-213

name changes, 195-196

narrator, 43, 64, 89

nature's classroom, 76, 121

Now We Are Six, 93

nurturing creativity, 113

observations, 28-29, 40, 42, 49, 54, 72, 76, 95, 98, 165

observe, 6, 28, 33, 41, 52, 61, 64, 69, 76, 114, 127, 136, 138, 184

obstacles, 44, 55, 114

only rule, 29

ordinary day, 63, 75

Our Town, 63-64, 95

pain, 55, 106, 177, 179, 190

parallel process, 15, 48

parent/child conflict, 143, 150-160

past tense, 209

patience, 85-86, 145-147, 153

permission, 14, 31, 113, 115, 137, 146, 208

About the Author

Kelly DuMar, M.Ed., L.M.H.C., is a creative arts therapist, workshop facilitator, and writer with her master's degree in education from Harvard University. She has taught *Through the Diary Door* personal growth and diary/journal writing workshops for the past seventeen years, and she has been keeping her own diaries for her three children for thirteen years.

Kelly has a long history of working with individuals and families developing self-esteem and creative problem-solving skills. She is a Certified Psychodramatist, a Fellow in the American Society for Group Psychotherapy & Psychodrama (ASGPP), a co-founder of the New England Chapter of ASGPP, a Member of the National Association for Poetry Therapy, and a Licensed Mental Health Counselor. Kelly regularly writes parenting columns for newspapers. She lives with her husband and children in the Boston area.